THE COLOUR LIBRARY BOOK OF

CHINESE COOKING

酥車輪蘇卅月餅

夾肉小燒餅椰絲雪

菊花酥燒餅蚵卵

夾肉小燒餅椰絲雪

燒餅咖哩餃鮮肉醸

THE COLOUR LIBRARY BOOK OF

CHINESE COOKING

NIM CHEE LEE

COLOUR LIBRARY BOOKS

CLB 1940
This edition published 1987 by Colour Library Books Ltd,
86 Epsom Road, Guildford, Surrey.
© Marshall Cavendish 1987
Prepared by Marshall Cavendish Books Ltd,
58 Old Compton St, London W1V5PA

Printed by Jarrold Printing, Norwich

ISBN 0 86283 531 3

CONTENTS

INTRODUCTION

Chinese food is one of the most popular cuisines in this country. Everyone loves going out for a Chinese meal, sharing and enjoying together all the tasty and various dishes.

However, when it comes to actually cooking Chinese food, many people think it is simply beyond them, believing the ingredients hard to find, the dishes themselves fiddly and time-consuming to make and the techniques impossible to master. Yet there is no more mystery to Chinese cooking than to any other cuisine. With the help of this book, by taking recipes in simple step-by-step stages, you will be surprised how quickly you too can learn to master this exciting cuisine and share with your family and friends some of the world's most delicious food.

Preparing Food
The Chinese spend some time preparing food before cooking – marinating meat, slicing vegetables and soaking dried food. Since cooking is so quick, it is worth getting into the habit of preparing all the ingredients in advance and laying them out by the cooker, so that no time is lost when it comes to actually cooking. No special equipment is needed for preparing food, although traditionally a cleaver is used for most jobs, from quartering a chicken to crushing garlic. However, if you do not own one of these, a heavy knife works just as well.

Vegetables are almost always cut into small pieces, often sliced diagonally or cut into thin strips. This allows them to cook quickly while retaining their crunchiness, and helps them to absorb the flavour of the other ingredients and seasonings. Cutting vegetables into small pieces also makes eating with chopsticks a lot more simple.

Meat is also cut up before it is cooked – especially for stir-fried dishes. Usually it is cut into thin matchsticks, about 3 mm/⅛ inch thick, but can also be cut into rectangular slices, about 6 mm/¼ inch thick and 2.5 cm/1 inch wide. Meat is also frequently marinated, often in a mixture of soy sauce, rice wine and oil. This helps to tenderise the meat and adds flavour. When marinating, always use a non-metallic container, preferably a glass or earthenware one, since metal can react with the marinade, giving an unpleasant taste to the food.

Garlic and ginger can be prepared in various ways, but on the whole they are either thinly sliced, cut into fine threads or very finely chopped. Garlic can be crushed with a garlic press if liked – this is also a quick and easy method for making ginger juice.

Cooking Techniques
In China, fuel was – and in parts, still is – expensive and even scarce. Consequently cooking had to be quick and very efficient and most Chinese cooking techniques pivot on this important principle. Furthermore, the emphasis on crispness and texture in Chinese dishes means that food rarely needs cooking for long periods. Texture is as

important as taste to the Chinese, so vegetables, particularly green ones, carrots and shoots, are normally just 'flash' cooked and meat is thinly sliced and marinated to ensure minimum cooking.

Stir-frying is, to the Chinese, the perfect method of cooking, and the wok the perfect piece of cooking equipment. Food, which has been thinly sliced, is cooked in the hot oil over a high heat. Normally the meat is added first – as the meat cooks, it is pushed up the sides of the wok and the prepared vegetables are added. None of the ingredients take long to cook and often a stir-fried meal can be cooked and ready in under 5 minutes.

If possible, always use a wok when stir-frying. Heat the empty wok over a high heat until smoke rises. This prevents food sticking. Gently add the oil, swirling it halfway up the sides to coat. Then add the ingredients in the order of the recipe, remembering to stir and turn the food over with the metal scoop to ensure the food cooks and browns evenly.

Deep-frying is also very popular in Chinese cookery, particularly when food is cooked twice – first steamed or stir-fried and then deep-fried. Traditionally a wok is used for deep-frying. However, for most people, it is probably more convenient to use a deep-fat fryer. The oil should be heated to 180°C/350°F or until a cube of bread browns in about 60 seconds. The food should then be carefully lowered into the fat, either using a wire basket, a metal slotted spoon or, for dumplings or fritters, metal tongs. Make sure to turn food over halfway through cooking, so that it browns evenly.

Steaming is another extremely efficient way of cooking. While one dish is being simmered in a saucepan, two or three others can be arranged in steamers and stacked over the top of the pan, so that they cook gently in the steam. Steaming means that food loses none of its fine flavour or colour and it also ensures that delicate food retains its shape. Consequently, steaming is a very popular method for cooking fish.

Bamboo baskets are the most common type of steamers used in Chinese cooking. These are inexpensive and widely available from Chinese supermarkets. However an aluminium steamer or even a colander will work just as well. Either way, the food should fit comfortably in a single layer inside the steamer. The steamer itself should fit neatly over the top of the saucepan.

To steam food, unless you are steaming food over another dish, pour 5 cm/2 inches of water into a saucepan and bring to the boil. Arrange the food in the steamer and place this over the saucepan. Cover with a lid and steam as instructed in the recipe. If you are steaming food over a high heat or for a long period, always make sure the saucepan does not boil dry. If necessary, top up with a little extra boiling water every now and again.

Chinese Meals

Rice is regarded as the main course of a Chinese meal (except in the northern wheat-producing regions of China). Savoury dishes are seen as the flavourings to or accompaniments for rice – quite the reverse of the Western idea that meat or fish forms the main dish of a meal.

One of the most notable aspects of a Chinese meal is that there is no set order of courses. The soup may be served first, if wished, but it is usual practice for people to help themselves to more during the meal. The food is eaten from bowls, rather than plates, and during the meal people will help themselves to a little of one dish at a time, along with the rice. Chopsticks are traditionally used for picking up the food. These were invented by the civilized Chinese centuries before Europeans first thought of using the fork.

If you are serving a dish which has to be picked up in the fingers (spareribs for instance), finger bowls of water for washing may be needed. These look attractive with flowers, or slices of lemon, floating in them. You may need extra napkins for drying your fingers afterwards. In China, steamed towels may be brought to you in a restaurant, but these are difficult to organize in a Western home.

In Chinese restaurants, food is always kept warm at the table on a small warmer. If you don't have one of these available, you can improvise by placing two night-lights in a shallow dish and standing a wire cake rack on the top to support dishes of food.

In Chinese homes, the meal is usually eaten fast – and silently. After the meal China tea – without milk, sugar or lemon of course – is served, when the company will relax and chat. The tea is drunk in small handleless cups and the correct way to hold these is with the thumb underneath the ring at the bottom and the index finger on the rim, so that you do not burn your fingers.

Menu Planning

Once you become proficient at Chinese cooking, you will want to plan your own full-scale Chinese meals.

The general practice in China is to serve one savoury dish per person, in addition to the rice dish. If wished, a soup, an appetizer or perhaps a noodle dish can also be included in the meal.

When choosing the savoury dishes, you should aim to include a good balance of texture, colour, flavour and aroma – the important elements of Chinese cooking. It is also important to choose an interesting range of meat, poultry, fish, shellfish and vegetable dishes, and to make sure that they have been cooked by different culinary techniques. If you follow these basic guidelines, you will find menu planning fun and rewarding. For further ideas, look at the menu suggestions given on pages 384 and 385.

Chinese Ingredients

The authentic nature of this book naturally means that many of the recipes call for Chinese ingredients. Some of the vegetables listed may at first be unfamiliar to you, but an illustrated key on pages 392 and 393 will help you to identify just what you are looking for! The glossary on pages 386 to 391 will help you to get to know other Chinese ingredients featured. Where possible, better-known European substitutes are suggested, but bear in mind that if you use these substitutes, the taste of the dish will be different, and less authentic.

It is worth making special sorties into those areas of the many big cities where the Chinese communities live, and searching through the shops for special ingredients. Do not be afraid to ask for assistance; the Chinese are particularly friendly people and will be only too willing to help. So, do not be put off by a recipe because of the alien nature of the ingredients; remember that these ingredients are common everyday ones to the Chinese, and that you will find the great majority of them in almost any Chinese supermarket or store.

FISH AND SHELLFISH

Fish is eaten throughout China – along the coastline there is an abundance of sea fish and shellfish, while inland there is an equally plentiful supply of river fish.

China's native fish, such as yellow fish, garoupa and milkfish, are difficult to find in the West, but many Chinese dishes also feature the more familiar types of fish – haddock, mackerel, halibut and trout to mention a few. The recipes selected for this chapter concentrate on the more widely available species of fish.

Where shellfish is concerned, many of the varieties that are plentiful in China are commonly seen in the West. Some of China's most famous and memorable dishes feature crab, lobster, scallops and King prawns and for a special meal or celebration party, Sautéed Prawns (p. 13), Baked Creamy Clams (p. 15) or Prawn Salad (p. 21) would all make stunning and delicious first courses. Do note, however, that most Chinese prawn recipes call for raw prawns. These are becoming increasingly available from fishmongers and fish counters at large supermarkets and can also be bought, frozen, from Chinese supermarkets. They are, however, quite pricey and where the appearance of the prawns is not important, monkfish, which has been cut into small chunks and which has a similar taste and texture to prawns, can be used instead.

Prawn and Spinach Broth

INGREDIENTS (SERVES 4)

225 g/8 oz raw King prawns
1 tspn grated fresh root
  ginger
450 g/1 lb spinach
6 tblspns vegetable oil
125 ml/4 fl oz clear soup
  stock (see p. 261)
2 tblspns plain flour, blended
  with a little cold water
125 ml/4 fl oz milk
½ tspn white pepper

SEASONING
1 tspn salt
1 tspn sugar
1 tblspn double cream

METHOD

1 Shell and de-vein the prawns (see Step 1, p. 55) and rinse in cold water. Pat dry on absorbent paper, then cut in half lengthways with a sharp knife or cleaver (see small picture 1, right). Place the grated ginger in a bowl, stir in the prawns and marinate for 10 minutes.
2 Wash the spinach thoroughly. Drain and chop finely.
3 Heat the oil in a wok, add the spinach and stir-fry for 3 minutes. Stir in the seasoning and then immediately add the soup stock and flour mixture.
4 Cook until boiling, then stir in the prawns and milk. Reduce the heat and simmer for a further minute.
5 Sprinkle with white pepper just before serving.

Sautéed Prawns

INGREDIENTS (SERVES 6)

600 g/1¼ lbs raw King
  prawns
4 tblspns corn oil

SEASONING
1 tblspn light soy sauce
½ tspn white pepper
1 tblspn spring onion, finely
  chopped
1 tblspn grated fresh root
  ginger
2 tspns rice wine or dry
  sherry
1 tspn salt

METHOD

1 Remove the feelers and intestinal cord or spine on the prawns with a pair of scissors (see Step 1, p. 59). Dry thoroughly on absorbent paper.
2 Mix the seasoning ingredients, add the prawns and marinate for 30 minutes.
3 Heat the oil in a wok and add the prawns. Stir-fry over a high heat for 2 minutes.
4 Remove the prawns with a slotted spoon and serve immediately.

NOTE
The prawns can be served with or without their shells. If serving with their shells, provide napkins and finger bowls for your guests.

奶油焗蚌

Baked Creamy Clams

INGREDIENTS
(SERVES 6-8)
900 g/2 lbs large clams
50 g/2 oz plain flour
4 tblspns single cream
3 spring onions, finely
    chopped
1 small carrot, grated
1 celery stick, finely chopped
2 tblspns clear soup stock
    (see p. 261)
2 tblspns grated Parmesan
    cheese
baby corn-on-the-cobs and
    red cherries, to garnish

SEASONING
2 garlic cloves, finely
    chopped
½ tspn salt
1 tspn white pepper
1 tspn sugar

METHOD

1   Clean and rinse the clams in cold water and then
place in a large pan and cover with boiling water.
Leave for 3-4 minutes, shaking the pan occasionally,
until the clams have opened. Drain thoroughly,
discarding any that have not opened.
2   Discard one half of the shell and gently loosen the
flesh in the other half with a sharp knife. Remove any
grit or loose seaweed and arrange the clams in their
half shells in a roasting tin.
3   Blend the flour with the cream and place in a pan
with the spring onions, carrot, celery, and stock. Add
the seasoning and slowly heat, stirring, until the
mixture is thick and creamy.
4   Spoon the mixture into the shells and sprinkle the
cheese over the top.
5   Bake at 220°C/425°F/Gas Mark 7 for 10 minutes.
6   Arrange the clams on a large plate and garnish
with the baby corns and cherries.

Fried Squid Balls

INGREDIENTS (SERVES 4)

20 squid balls (see NOTES)
1 tspn black sesame seeds
    (see NOTES)
75 g/3 oz plain flour
100 g/4 oz fresh white
    breadcrumbs
2 egg yolks, beaten
corn oil, for deep frying
2 tomatoes sliced, to garnish

METHOD

1   Wash the squid balls in cold water and pat dry on absorbent paper.
2   Dry-fry the sesame seeds in a hot pan for a few seconds and set aside.
3   Mix the flour with a little water to make a thick paste and spread the breadcrumbs over a sheet of greaseproof paper.
4   Roll the squid balls, first in the egg yolks, then in the flour paste and finally in the breadcrumbs.
5   Heat the oil and deep fry the fish balls for about a minute or until they are golden brown, turning them occasionally.
6   Remove the balls with a slotted spoon and drain on absorbent paper. Roll in the toasted sesame seeds and serve, garnished with slices of tomato.

NOTES

1   Black sesame seeds have a nutty flavour. They are available from Chinese supermarkets, or alternatively use white sesame seeds, which can be bought from most supermarkets.
2   Squid balls are usually available in Chinese supermarkets, sold in sealed polythene packets from the cool containers. Should they be unobtainable, use fish balls instead.
3   Squid and fish balls are delicious served with a dipping sauce: make one by mixing 3 tblspns Worcestershire sauce, 1 tblspn vinegar, 1 tblspn sugar, 1 tblspn corn oil and 1-2 tspns sesame oil. Heat until just boiling and then turn into serving bowl.

Seafood Kebabs

INGREDIENTS (SERVES 4)

225 g/8 oz fresh squid
1 green pepper
2 carrots
10 raw King prawns, shelled
    and de-veined (see p. 55)
10 fish balls

SEASONING
2-3 sheets laver, sliced (see
    NOTE p. 85)
2 spring onions, finely
    chopped
3 slices of fresh root ginger
1 tblspn sugar
50 ml/2 fl oz clear soup stock
    (see p. 261)
2 tblspns corn oil

METHOD

1   Place the seasoning ingredients in a saucepan, bring to the boil and simmer gently for 5 minutes.
2   Meanwhile, pull away the head and entrails from the squid. Feel inside the body and remove the transparent cartilage. Peel off and discard the mottled skin from the body and rinse the squid under running water. Cut into large pieces.
3   Cut the pepper into large chunks, discarding any seeds and core and cut the carrots into small rectangles.
4   Thread the squid, pepper, carrots, prawns and fish balls onto 10–12 bamboo skewers and arrange on a grill pan.
5   Brush the kebabs with a little of the sauce and then set under a medium-hot grill for 5-6 minutes, brushing and turning the kebabs every two minutes.

NOTE
Seafood kebabs can be served with a sweet chilli sauce or mustard.

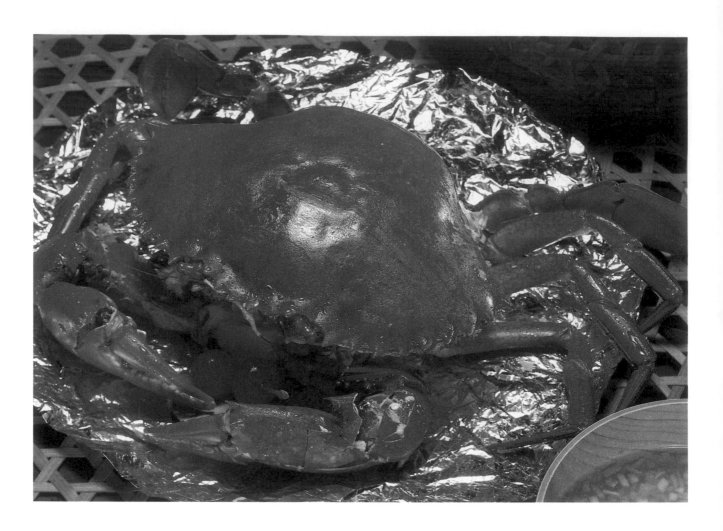

Steamed Crab

INGREDIENTS (SERVES 6)

2 large cooked crabs
Maraschino cherries, to
  garnish

SEASONING A

4½ tblspns ginger juice (see
  NOTE 3, p. 39)
2 spring onions, cut into
  large sections
1 tblspn dry sherry

SEASONING B

3 tblspns vinegar
1 tspn rice wine or dry sherry
1 tblspn finely grated fresh
  root ginger

METHOD

1 Clean the crab (see NOTE). Cut the bodies in half, and crack the claws with a hammer.
2 Put the crab shells, body and claws in a heatproof dish. Blend seasoning **A** in a bowl and pour over.
3 Place the dish in a steamer. Pour 5 cm/2 inches water into a large saucepan and bring to the boil. Set the steamer over the saucepan, cover with a tight-fitting lid and steam over a high heat for 5 minutes.
4 Remove any pieces of spring onion, and put the crab bodies back in the shells. Garnish with Maraschino cherries.
5 Blend seasoning **B** in a bowl and serve with the crab as a dipping sauce. Use skewers to pick out the crab meat at the table.

NOTE

To clean the crab, lay each one on its back with the tail flap towards you and remove the tail flap. Prise the body away from the shell, using a long sharp knife and set aside. Remove the gills (dead men's fingers) and the stomach and discard. The remaining contents of the crab, and the body itself are edible.

简易海鲜锅饼

Seafood Pancakes

INGREDIENTS
(SERVES 2-4)

3 small dried scallops (see NOTE)
25 g/1 oz dried baby shrimps
3 Chinese mushrooms
100 g/4 oz cooked peeled prawns
100 g/4 oz plain flour
½ tspn salt
½ tspn white pepper
2 eggs
2 tblspns milk
3 tblspns corn oil

SEASONING
4 tblspns tomato sauce
½ tspn salt
1 tspn sugar
1 tblspn water

METHOD

1 Place the dried scallops and dried shrimps in two bowls, cover with warm water and soak for 1 hour and 30 minutes respectively. Soak the Chinese mushrooms in warm water for 30 minutes. Shred the scallops and finely chop the shrimps. Remove and discard the stalks from the mushrooms and chop finely. Roughly chop the prawns.

2 Sift the flour, salt and pepper into a bowl, add the eggs and then gradually beat in the milk and enough water to make a loose batter. Add the scallops, shrimps, mushrooms and prawns and stir to mix.

3 Heat a little of the oil in a small frying pan, add 2-3 tblspns of batter and fry for 30-60 seconds until golden. Flip over and fry the other side. Cook the remainder of the batter in the same way.

4 Place the seasoning ingredients in a small pan, heat gently and serve with the pancakes.

NOTE
Dried scallops are great delicacy in China. Round and golden, they add a delicious sweet flavour to a dish. They can be found in most Chinese supermarkets.

Prawn Salad

INGREDIENTS (SERVES 6)

700 g/1½ lbs raw King
　prawns
4 sticks of celery

DRESSING
150 ml/¼ pint of mayonnaise
3 tblspns yoghurt
½ small onion, grated
1 tspn sugar
½ tspn salt

METHOD

1　Scald the prawns in boiling water for 5 minutes.
Drain well and soak in ice-cold water for 2 minutes.
Drain again. Remove the shells and de-vein (see Step
1, p. 55) and place in the refrigerator for 1 hour.
2　Wash the celery and cut into pieces. Soak in cold
water for 5 minutes.
3　Blend the mayonnaise with the yoghurt. Add the
remaining dressing ingredients and beat for 1 minute.
4　Stir the celery into the prawns, turn onto a serving
plate and pipe the dressing over or serve separately.

NOTE
If liked, cooked King prawns or Dublin Bay prawns
could be used in this recipe. If so, it is not necessary to
scald, or cook them, but do remove the shells and
de-vein.

Soup of Egg

INGREDIENTS (SERVES 2)

2 eggs
4 spring onions, finely
   chopped
600 ml/1 pint water

SEASONING
½ tspn salt
½ tspn white pepper
4-5 drops of sesame oil

METHOD

1   Beat the eggs thoroughly. Add the seasoning.
2   Bring the water to the boil and remove from heat.
Pour in the eggs and stir with chopsticks or a fork.
3   Add the spring onions and serve at once.

NOTE
This simple soup makes a light, delicate
accompaniment to a spicy fish dish. Double all
ingredients to serve four.

Baby Squid with Ginger Sauce

INGREDIENTS (SERVES 4)

350 g/12 oz small squid
3 tblspns corn oil
1 tblspn grated fresh root
   ginger
shreds of fresh root ginger, to
   garnish

SEASONING
1 tblspn light soy sauce
1 tblspn rice wine or dry
   sherry
½ tblspn sugar
½ tspn white pepper

METHOD

1   Cut open the squid with a cleaver or sharp knife
and remove the entrails and cartilage. Rinse
thoroughly in cold water.
2   Heat the oil in a frying pan or wok, add the grated
ginger and stir-fry for 1 minute. Add the squid and
stir-fry for 3 minutes.
3   Stir in the seasoning and cook, stirring for 5
minutes until the pan is almost dry.
4   Garnish with the root ginger shreds and serve.

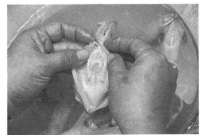

Stir-Fried Spicy Squid

INGREDIENTS (SERVES 6)

100 g/4 oz dried squid
350 g/12 oz fresh squid
3-4 tblspns corn oil
10 dried chillis
½ tblspn grated fresh root
   ginger
green chilli, to garnish

SEASONING

1 tspn salt
1 tblspn light soy sauce
2 tspns cornflour
2 tspns sesame oil
1 tblspn rice wine or dry
   sherry
½ tspn sugar

METHOD

1 Soak the dried squid in cold water for 24 hours.
Drain, remove spine and cut into 2.5 cm/1 inch pieces.
2 Pull away the head and entrails from the fresh
squid. Feel inside the body and remove the
transparent cartilage. Peel off and discard the mottled
skin from the body and rinse the squid under running
water. Cut into large pieces, scoring criss-cross
patterns on one side.
3 Heat the oil in the wok and when hot, add the
chillis. Stir-fry for 5 seconds and then add the ginger
and fry for 2 seconds.
4 Stir in the dried squid, fry for 5 seconds until they
curl up and then add the fresh squid and the
seasoning ingredients. Cook, stirring, for 1 minute and
then turn onto a serving plate
5 Garnish with chilli curls and serve.

簡易塩焗蝦

Salted Prawns

INGREDIENTS (SERVES 6)

450 g/1 lb raw King prawns
3 tspns cornflour
corn oil, for deep frying
lettuce leaves, to garnish

SEASONING
½ tblspn finely chopped
   garlic
1 tspn salt
1 tspn white pepper

METHOD

1 Trim the prawns feelers with a pair of scissors and remove intestinal vein (see Step 1, p. 59). Wash the prawns in cold water, pat dry with absorbent paper and dust with the cornflour.
2 Heat the oil and when hot, deep-fry the prawns for 1 minute. Remove with a slotted spoon.
3 Heat an extra 1 tblspn of the oil in a wok or frying pan, add the cooked prawns and the seasoning ingredients and stir-fry for a further minute.
4 Drain on absorbent paper and serve on a bed of lettuce.

糖醋魚排

Sweet and Sour Fish

INGREDIENTS (SERVES 4)

700 g/1½ lbs cod or halibut
  cutlets
3 tblspns plain flour
10 tblspns corn oil
2 tblspns chopped onion or
  spring onion
2 tblspns water
3 tblspns white vinegar
2 tspns cornflour
shredded Chinese leaves, to
  garnish

SEASONING
3 tblspns sugar
1 tspn salt
1 tblspn ginger wine

METHOD

1   Lightly coat the fish with the flour.
2   Heat 4 tblspns of the oil in a wok or frying pan.
When the oil is very hot, add the fish and fry until both
sides are browned. Remove.
3   Add the remaining oil to the pan and stir-fry the
chopped onion over medium heat for 10 seconds.
4   Add the seasoning ingredients together with the
water, and bring to the boil. Return the fish to the pan.
Stir gently.
5   Blend the vinegar and cornflour together and stir
into the pan. Heat until just boiling, stirring all the
time, then garnish with shredded Chinese leaves and
serve.

Stewed Fish with Brown Sauce

INGREDIENTS (SERVES 4)

1 large or 2 small red
snappers or grey mullets,
about 700 g/1½ lbs in
weight
2 tblspns plain flour
4 spring onions
2 red chillis
7.5 cm/3 inch piece fresh
root ginger
9 tblspns corn oil

SEASONING A
4 tblspns ginger wine
4 tspns salt

SEASONING B
3 tblspns light soy sauce
1 tblspn rice wine or dry
sherry
1 tblspn sugar
1 tspn salt
½ tspn white pepper

METHOD

1 Clean and scale the fish. Wash in cold water and
pat dry with absorbent paper. Score the fish deeply on
both sides.
2 Mix seasoning **A** and spread over the fish. Leave
to marinate for 10 minutes, then dust evenly with the
flour.
3 Cut the spring onions and chillis into lengthway-
strips and shred the ginger.
4 Heat 4 tblspns of the oil in a wok, add the fish and
fry for 4 minutes, turning once.
5 In a separate pan, heat the remaining oil and fry
the chillis and ginger for 5 seconds. Add the spring
onions and seasoning **B**. Stir thoroughly.
6 Add the fish, cover and cook for 5 minutes. Drain
and serve.

Sautéed Fish Slices

INGREDIENTS (SERVES 4)

50 g/2 oz wood ear
mushrooms
(see NOTES)
700 g/1½ lbs cod or haddock
steaks
3 spring onions
6 tblspns corn oil
2.5 cm/1 inch piece fresh
root ginger, thinly sliced
1 tblspn light soy sauce
parsley sprig, to garnish

SEASONING A
1 tblspn ginger wine
½ tspn white pepper
1 tspn sugar
2 tspns sesame oil
1½ tblspns cornflour

SEASONING B
2 tspns rice wine or dry
sherry
1 tspn salt

METHOD

1 Soak the mushrooms for 30 minutes in warm
water. Drain and cut into 2.5 cm/1 inch pieces.
2 Cut the fish steaks in half, skin and then cut into 5
× 2.5 cm/2 × 1 inch slices.
3 Mix seasoning **A** to a smooth paste and marinate
the fish slices for 20 minutes.
4 Cut the spring onions into large pieces.
5 Heat the oil in the wok, add the spring onions and
stir-fry for 30 seconds. Remove with a slotted spoon
and discard the onions. Add the ginger, fry for 30
seconds and then remove and discard as well (see
NOTES).
6 Add the mushrooms, fry for 20 seconds and stir in
the fish slices. Add seasoning **B** and stir well. Cook for
1-2 minutes turning the fish once. Sprinkle with the
soy sauce.
7 Turn onto a serving plate and garnish with parsley.

NOTES
1 Wood ear mushrooms are commonly used in
Chinese cooking. They are available from any Chinese
supermarket but must be soaked before using.
2 The spring onions and ginger are there to give
flavour to the oil and thus the fish. Discard them after
frying.

豉香炒蚵

Stir-Fried Clams with Black Beans

INGREDIENTS (SERVES 4)

600 g/1¼ lbs shelled clams
1 tblspn salt
5 tblspns corn oil
2 spring onions

SEASONING A
4 tblspns black beans
    (see NOTE)
3 garlic cloves, crushed
1 tblspn finely grated fresh
    root ginger
1 red chilli, thinly sliced
    sliced
1 tblspn light soy sauce
½ tblspn sugar
1 tspn salt

SEASONING B
1 tblspn rice wine or dry
    sherry
½ tspn white pepper
2 tspns sesame oil

METHOD

1 Place the clams in cold water with the salt and soak for 10 minutes. Drain.
2 Rinse the clams in boiling water and then soak again for 3 minutes. Drain thoroughly and pat dry with absorbent paper.
3 Heat the oil in the wok, add seasoning **A** and stir-fry for 30 seconds.
4 Stir in the clams and continue to fry for 3 minutes.
5 Slice the spring onions diagonally and add to wok with seasoning **B**. Cook stirring for 30 seconds and then serve.

NOTE
There are two kinds of black beans available, the canned fermentd black beans which come in a sauce, and the dried beans. Dried black beans can be kept for 6 months if kept in a dry place. They should be soaked for 2-3 hours before using. If dried beans are unavailable, use canned ones, but rinse thoroughly before use.

炸蚵酥

Golden Fried Clams

INGREDIENTS (SERVES 4)

600 g/1¼ lbs shelled clams
1 tblspn salt
200 g/ 7 oz sweet potato flour
    (see NOTE)
corn oil, for deep frying
parsley or fennel sprigs, to
    garnish

SEASONING
1 tspn salt
1 small egg white
½ tspn sugar
1 tspn light soy sauce

METHOD

1 Place the clams in cold water with the salt and soak for 10 minutes. Drain.
2 Rinse the clams in boiling water and then soak again for 3 minutes. Drain thoroughly and pat dry on absorbent paper. Place in a bowl and add the seasoning ingredients, the potato flour and a little extra salt, making sure to coat each clam thoroughly.
3 Heat the oil in a deep-fat fryer and fry the clams until golden.
4 Remove with slotted spoon and serve decorated with fennel sprigs or parsley.

NOTE
Sweet potato flour is available in most Chinese supermarkets, however, ordinary potato flour can be used instead.

Celery with Mustard Paste

INGREDIENTS (SERVES 4)

1 large head of celery

SEASONING
1 tblspn English mustard
   paste
½ tspn salt
1 tblspn soy sauce

METHOD

1   Separate the celery into individual stalks, and wash thoroughly. Cut the stalks into sticks about 10 cm/4 inches long.
2   Blanch the celery in boiling water for 30 seconds. Remove with a slotted spoon. Soak the celery in a bowl of ice water until cool, then remove with a slotted spoon. Wrap in a clean tea towel or double thickness of muslin and place in the refrigerator for 1 hour.
3   Blend the seasoning ingredients together, and serve as a dipping sauce with the celery sticks.

NOTE
This is a very light, pleasant salad which goes well with "Steamed Cod" or any delicately flavoured fish dish.

Steamed Cod

INGREDIENTS (SERVES 4)

700 g/1½ lbs cod cutlets
3 tblspns corn oil
2 tblspns finely grated fresh
   root ginger
2 spring onions, finely sliced

SEASONING
3 tblspns soy sauce
2 tblspns rice wine or dry
   sherry
2 tblspns water

METHOD

1   Place the cod cutlets on a plate and place in a steamer. Pour 5 cm/2 inches water into a large saucepan and bring to the boil. Set the steamer over the saucepan, cover with a tight-fitting lid and steam for 4 minutes. Remove from the heat and set aside for a further 5 minutes before removing the lid. Pour off the liquid.
2   Heat the oil in a wok or frying pan and add the ginger, spring onions and seasoning ingredients. Bring to the boil and cook for 5 minutes.
3   Arrange the cod on a serving dish, top with the sauce and serve.

Steamed Cabbage with Dried Shrimps

INGREDIENTS (SERVES 4)

3 tblspns dried shelled
  shrimps
1 white cabbage
600 ml/1 pint clear soup
  stock (see p. 261)

SEASONING
1 tspn salt
1 tspn sugar
1 tspn white pepper
1 tblspn sesame oil

METHOD

1 Soak the dried shrimps in warm water for 30 minutes. Drain. Cut the cabbage into even-sized wedges and arrange in a large deep bowl.
2 Mix the shrimps with the seasoning ingredients and place in the dish with the cabbage. Add the soup stock.
3 Place the bowl in a steamer and steam, covered, over a high heat for 30 minutes or until the soup is very hot. Check occasionally to make sure the saucepan does not boil dry.
4 Serve immediately.

Stuffed Cabbage Rolls

INGREDIENTS (SERVES 4)

8 Chinese black mushrooms
1 large carrot
10 cm/4 inch piece bamboo
  shoot
1 white cabbage
7.5 cm/3 inch square piece
  spiced bean curd
1 tblspn malt vinegar
1 tblspn light soy sauce

SEASONING
1 tblspn sesame oil
2 tblspns light soy sauce
1 tspn salt
½ tspn white pepper

METHOD

1 Remove the stalks from the Chinese mushrooms, place in a bowl and cover with warm water. Soak for 30 minutes, drain and roughly chop. Place in a steamer, cover and steam for 10 minutes.
2 Blanch the carrot and bamboo shoot in boiling water for 2 minutes and then cut into small cubes.
3 Make 4 deep cuts around the cabbage root with a cleaver or sharp knife, then boil the cabbage for 5 minutes.
4 Gently separate 12 outer leaves. (You may have to return the cabbage to the boiling water to loosen the inner leaves.)
5 Cube the bean curd and mix with the mushrooms, carrot and bamboo shoot. Stir in the vinegar and soy sauce.
6 Place a spoonful of mixture at the bottom of each cabbage leaf. Fold in the sides and roll up. Arrange in one or two layers in a steamer and steam for 10 minutes.
7 Mix together all the seasoning ingredients and serve with the cabbage rolls.

NOTE
This makes a delicious vegetable accompaniment to a fish course. Peeled prawns could also be added to the mushroom mixture if liked.

Fried Prawn Rolls

INGREDIENTS (SERVES 4)

20 raw King prawns
100 g/4 oz cornflour
10 salted duck egg yolks,
    optional (see NOTE)
5 tblspns ground pork fat
1 egg, beaten
175 g/6 oz golden
    breadcrumbs
corn oil, for deep frying
parsley sprigs, to garnish

SEASONING
1 tblspn sesame oil
1 tspn salt
½ tspn white pepper

METHOD

1 Shell and de-vein the prawns (see Step 1, p. 55).
Split each one open, but do not separate. Dust in the
cornflour and then flatten them slightly by patting
with a rolling pin.
2 Divide each of the duck egg yolks, if using, in half
and flatten slightly with the back of a knife.
3 Mix the pork fat with the seasoning ingredients
and spread a little of the mixture over the inside of the
prawns. Place a portion of yolk on top and roll up.
4 Dip the prawns in the beaten egg and then roll in
the breadcrumbs.
5 Heat the oil in a deep-fat fryer and fry the prawns
for about 4 minutes or until golden. Remove with a
slotted spoon, drain on absorbent paper and serve,
garnished with a little parsley.

NOTE
Salted duck eggs can be bought from Chinese
supermarkets.

Quick Fried Prawns with Asparagus

INGREDIENTS (SERVES 4)

20 raw King prawns
4 tblspns corn oil
350 g/12 oz can of asparagus,
    drained

SEASONING A
2 tspns cornflour
½ egg white, lightly beaten
1 tblspn rice wine or dry
    sherry
1 tspn salt

SEASONING B
2 tblspns finely grated fresh
    root ginger
1 tblspn light soy sauce
2 tspns rice wine or dry
    sherry
1 tblspn white vinegar

METHOD

1 Shell the prawns and remove the thin 'vein' or
intestinal cord that runs down the spine (see Step 1,
p. 55).
2 Butterfly the prawns by cutting each one down the
centre, but do not separate them. Flatten slightly with
the back of a knife.
3 Blend seasoning **A** in a bowl and add the prawns.
Stir gently and leave to marinate for 20 minutes.
4 Heat 3 tblspns of the oil in a wok, add the prawns
and fry for 2 minutes. Remove with a slotted spoon.
5 Heat the remaining oil. Add the asparagus and
stir-fry for 30 seconds. Push the asparagus to one side
of the wok and place the prawns in the centre. Stir-fry
for 5 seconds and then add seasoning **B**. Stir to mix
and serve.

Squid in Oyster Sauce

INGREDIENTS (SERVES 4)

3 large dried squid (see
  NOTES)
2 tblspns corn oil
5 cm/2 inch piece fresh root
  ginger, grated
1 tspn rice wine or dry sherry
½ cucumber, shredded
6 slices abalone, optional
  (see NOTES)

SEASONING

3 tblspns oyster sauce
½ tspn salt
½ tspn sugar
1 tspn ginger juice (see
  NOTES)
3 tblspns clear soup stock
  (see p. 261)
½ tspn white pepper

METHOD

1 Rinse the squid thoroughly. Cut in half lengthways and then, using a sharp knife, slice into thin strips.
2 Place squid strips in a bowl, cover with boiling water and scald for 1 minute. Drain and plunge into cold water for a few seconds. Drain and dry on absorbent paper.
3 Heat the oil in a wok and add the ginger and rice wine. Stir-fry for a few seconds and then add the squid. Stir-fry for 1 minute.
4 Mix all seasoning ingredients and stir into squid mixture. Stir well.
5 Turn onto a serving plate and garnish with the shredded cucumber and abalone.

NOTES

1 Dried squid needs to be soaked for 24 hours before using. Place in a basin of cold water, add 1 tblspn salt and leave in a cool place.
2 Abalone should be scalded in boiling water for 5 minutes before using.
3 Ginger juice is simply the juice from fresh root ginger. Either press a little sliced fresh ginger through a garlic press, or use finely grated ginger instead.

Paper-Wrapped Fish

INGREDIENTS (SERVES 4)

700 g/1½ lbs plaice or
    whiting fillets
50 g/2 oz butter
1 tblspn cornflour
corn oil, for deep frying

SEASONING
1 tspn salt
½ tspn finely chopped fresh
    root ginger
3 tspns cornflour

METHOD

1 Rinse the fish in cold water. Remove the skin.
2 Cut each of the fillets into 2.5 cm/1 inch diagonal slices. Place in a bowl and toss with the seasoning ingredients. Set aside for 20 minutes.
3 Cut out some 9 cm/3½ inch square cellophane pieces, sufficient to wrap each of the fish slices.
4 Place a fish slice at the corner of each square, dot the fish with the butter and roll up, tucking the sides in as you go. Blend the cornflour with a little water, and use to seal the final edges.
5 Heat the oil and deep-fry the fish parcels for 6-8 minutes. Remove and serve in their paper wrappers.

Pan-Fried Tuna

INGREDIENTS (SERVES 2)

2 tuna steaks
4 tblspns corn oil
lemon juice, to serve

SEASONING
4 tblspns yellow bean sauce
    (see NOTE)
3 tblspns sugar
½ tspn white pepper
1 tblspn finely grated fresh
    root ginger

METHOD

1 Rinse the fish and pat dry on absorbent paper.
2 Blend all the seasoning ingredients and spread evenly over both sides of the fish. Place in the refrigerator and marinate for 24 hours.
3 The next day, rinse off the marinade and pat dry. Heat the oil in a large pan and fry the fish until golden brown.
4 Serve at once with a little lemon juice.

NOTE
Yellow bean sauce is a slightly sweet paste made from fermented soya beans. It is available in cans or jars from any Chinese supermarket.

炸鮑魚排

Fried Fish Steaks

INGREDIENTS (SERVES 4)

700 g/1½ lbs plaice or
    whiting fillets
100 g/4 oz fresh white
    breadcrumbs
1 egg, beaten
corn oil, for deep frying
sweet chilli sauce, to serve

SEASONING
1 tspn salt
1 tblspn ginger wine
½ tspn white pepper

METHOD

1 Rinse the fish in cold water and pat dry with absorbent paper. Cut the fillets into four pieces.
2 Blend the seasoning ingredients in a bowl, stir in the fish and set aside for 30 minutes.
3 Place the breadcrumbs on a piece of greaseproof paper and then dip the fish slices in the beaten egg and coat evenly with the breadcrumbs.
4 Heat the oil in a deep-fat fryer and carefully add the fish slices. Deep fry the fish for 2-3 minutes until golden brown.
5 Remove with a slotted spoon and drain on absorbent paper. Serve with sweet chilli sauce.

清炒金瓜

Stir-Fried Pumpkin

INGREDIENTS (SERVES 4)

½ small pumpkin
4 tblspns corn oil

SEASONING
1 tspn salt
½ tspn white pepper
2 tblspns water

METHOD

1 Remove the seeds, but do not peel the pumpkin. Cut into 12 mm × 2.5 cm/½ × 1 inch pieces.
2 Heat the oil in a wok. Add the pumpkin and the seasoning and stir-fry over a medium heat for 3 minutes. Reduce the heat slightly and cover. Simmer for a further 4-5 minutes until the pumpkin is tender, stirring occasionally.

NOTE
This is a tasty dish and goes well with the Fried Fish Steaks. It's a good choice in late autumn, when pumpkins are in abundance.

Steamed Rice with Seafood

INGREDIENTS (SERVES 6)

275 g/10 oz spring greens
10 scallops
6 crab claws
3 Chinese mushrooms,
    soaked (see NOTES)
2 tblspns dried baby shrimps,
    soaked (see NOTES)
350 g/12 oz long-grain rice
1.2 litres/2 pints clear soup
    stock (see p. 261)

SEASONING

1 tspn salt
½ tspn white pepper
2 tblspns corn oil
½ tblspn rice wine or dry
    sherry
2 tspns sugar

METHOD

1 Wash and trim the spring greens and cut into small pieces.
2 Slice 5 of the scallops thinly, leaving the others whole. Chop the crab claws into pieces.
3 Mix all the ingredients and seasoning ingredients in a large heatproof bowl. Place the bowl in a steamer, cover and steam over boiling water for about 30 minutes, or until the rice is tender. Serve.

NOTES

1 Soak the Chinese mushrooms in warm water for 30 minutes before using, then remove and discard the stalk and slice finely.
2 Soak the dried shrimps in warm water for 30 minutes before using.

Seafood Congee

INGREDIENTS
(SERVES 4-6)
100 g/4 oz cod fillet
3 dried scallops, soaked (see
    NOTES)
1 piece of bean curd sheet,
    soaked (see NOTES)
75 g/3 oz short-grain rice
1.5 litres /2½ pints water
2 hard-boiled eggs, chopped
1 tspn salt
50 g/2 oz cooked peeled
    prawns
50 g/2 oz crab meat
2 clams, shelled and diced
1 egg
2 sticks of twisted doughnuts
    or Yiu-tiao, thinly sliced
    (see NOTE on p. 301)
1 tblspn chopped fresh
    parsley
parsley sprigs, to garnish

SEASONING

½ tspn white pepper
1 tblspn sesame oil
1 tblspn rice wine or dry
    sherry

METHOD

1 Cut the fish into bite-sized pieces, finely slice the soaked scallops and dice the soaked bean curd.
2 Place the rice, cod, scallops and bean curd in a large pan. Add the water and bring to the boil. Cover and simmer gently over a low heat for 30 minutes.
3 Add the hard-boiled eggs and salt, and simmer for a further 5 minutes.
4 Mix the prawns, crab meat and clams with the seasoning ingredients and stir into the soup. Cook for a further 10 minutes.
5 Place the egg, doughnuts or Yiu-tiao and chopped parsley in a bowl. Pour the cooked broth over the top, beat lightly and serve, garnished with parsley sprigs.

NOTES

1 Congee is a porridge made principally from boiled rice, which is often eaten for breakfast in China.
2 To soak the dried scallops, cover with boiling water and soak for 1 hour, then drain.
3 To soak the dried bean curd sheet, place it in cold water for about 10 minutes, till soft. Drain, and wrap in a tea-towel.

Sweet and Sour Squid

INGREDIENTS (SERVES 4)

450 g/1 lb squid
2 red chillis
1 green pepper
5 tblspns corn oil
1 tblspn grated fresh root
   ginger
2 tblspns cornflour
2 tspns sesame oil

SEASONING

1 tblspn ginger wine
1 tspn salt
3 tblspns sugar
4 tblspns white vinegar
50 ml/2 fl oz clear soup stock
   (see p. 261)

METHOD

1 Pull away the head and entrails from the squid.
Feel inside the body and remove the transparent
cartilage. Peel off and discard the mottled skin from
the body and rinse the squid under running water.
2 Cut the squid into thin 5 cm/2 inch square pieces.
Make tiny slits along each edge, approximately 6
mm/¼ inch long. Place in a bowl, cover with boiling
water and set aside for 2 minutes. Drain.
3 Cut the chillis diagonally and remove the seeds
(see NOTE). Cut the pepper into cubes, discarding the
seeds and core.
4 Heat the oil in the wok, add the ginger and chillis
and stir-fry for 10 seconds. Add the green pepper,
squid and seasoning ingredients. Cook, stirring for 5
minutes.
5 Blend the cornflour with a little water and stir into
the squid with the sesame oil. Bring back to the boil,
cook for ½ minute and serve.

NOTE

Chillis can be very hot. Take care preparing them;
wear rubber gloves if liked and take care not to rub
your eyes. The chillis' seeds are especially hot. Unless
you enjoy very hot food, it's probably advisable to
remove them.

Five-Willow Fish

INGREDIENTS (SERVES 2)

1 whole lemon sole or plaice
3 red chillis
3 tblspns corn oil
2 tblspns grated fresh root
  ginger
175 ml/6 fl oz clear soup
  stock (see p. 261)
2 tblspns cornflour
1 tblspn malt vinegar

SEASONING A
1 tblspn ginger wine
½ tspn white pepper

SEASONING B
½ tblspn chopped pork fat
1 tblspn sliced Chinese
  mushrooms (see NOTE)
3 tblspns white vinegar
1 garlic clove, crushed
½ tspn white pepper
1 tspn salt
2 tspns sugar

METHOD

1 Clean the fish if not already gutted. Trim the tail and cut away the fins. Rinse under cold water and pat dry with absorbent paper.
2 Mix together seasoning **A** and spread evenly over the fish. Set aside for 20 minutes.
3 Thinly slice the chillis, removing the seeds. Heat the oil in the wok and fry the chillis and grated ginger for 5 seconds. Add the soup stock and seasoning **B** and bring to the boil.
4 Gently lower the fish into the wok, cover and simmer for 5 minutes, turning over halfway through cooking.
5 Blend the cornflour with the malt vinegar and add to the wok. Stir gently, taking care not to disturb the fish and cook for 2-3 minutes.
6 Remove the fish and place on a serving plate. Pour the sauce over and serve at once.

NOTE
Chinese mushrooms are only available dried and should be soaked for 30 minutes before use. Remove stalk and slice after soaking.

Fish Jelly

INGREDIENTS
(SERVES 4-6)

1 Chinese mushroom
  (see NOTE above)
600 g/1¼ lbs cod cutlets
1 carrot
225 ml/8 fl oz clear soup
  stock (see p. 261)
1 tblspn dried agar-agar
2 tblspns canned sweetcorn
parsley sprigs, to garnish

SEASONING
1 tspn salt
1 tspn rice wine or dry sherry
1 tspn ginger wine
½ tspn white pepper

METHOD

1 Soak the Chinese mushroom in warm water for 30 minutes. Remove and discard the stalk.
2 Bone and skin the fish cutlets and cut into thin pieces, about 2.5 × 5 cm/1 × 2 inches. Place in a steamer and steam over a high heat for 8-10 minutes until cooked.
3 Peel the carrot. Use aspic cutters to cut into pretty shapes.
4 Place the soup stock in a saucepan and bring to the boil. Add the carrot and simmer for 10 minutes.
5 Remove the carrot with a slotted spoon and set aside. Add the agar-agar, bring to the boil and simmer for 10 minutes. Strain the soup through a fine muslin and mix with the seasoning ingredients.
6 Place the mushroom in the centre of a rectangular mould. Arrange the carrot pieces around the outside and scatter the sweetcorn on top. Lie the fish over the sweetcorn and then carefully pour on the soup stock.
7 Cool, and then refrigerate for 24 hours. To unmould the jelly, place the mould up to the rim in a basin of boiling water. Leave for 5-10 seconds, then up-end onto a serving plate and the jelly should come away. If not, repeat this process. Serve, garnished with parsley.

炸脆皮蝦球

Crispy Fried Prawn Balls

INGREDIENTS (SERVES 6)

900 g/2 lbs cooked peeled
    prawns
100 g/4 oz fresh white
    breadcrumbs
1 tblspn cornflour
1 egg yolk, beaten
corn oil, for deep frying
spring onions and tomatoes,
    to garnish

SEASONING

1 tblspn ginger wine
3 tblspns cornflour
½ tspn white pepper
1 tspn sugar
2 tspns sesame oil
1 egg white
1 tspn salt

METHOD

1 Chop the prawns finely and then mince with a cleaver or heavy knife until they resemble a paste. Mix thoroughly with all the seasoning ingredients.

2 Place the breadcrumbs and cornflour on separate sheets of greaseproof paper.

3 Take a small handful (about 1 rounded tblspn) of the prawn mixture and roll into a ball between your hands. Dip the ball into the beaten egg and then roll first in the cornflour and then in the breadcrumbs, coating firmly and evenly. Continue until all the mixture has been used up.

4 Heat the oil in a deep-fat fryer and fry the prawn balls, a few at a time, until golden brown. Remove with a slotted spoon and drain on absorbent paper. Serve, garnished with spring onions and tomatoes.

Prawn and Clam Rice Noodles

INGREDIENTS
(SERVES 4-6)

25 g/1 oz dried baby shrimps, optional
100 g/4 oz cooked chicken, thinly sliced
175-250 g/6-9 oz thin dried rice noodles
350 g/12 oz raw King prawns
150 g/5 oz clams
4 tblspns corn oil
1 spring onion, finely chopped
2.3 litres/4 pints clear soup stock (see p. 261)
150 g/5 oz bean sprouts
2 shredded mushrooms (see NOTE p. 45)
1 tspn salt
2 or 3 lettuce leaves
1 tspn white pepper

SEASONING
1 tspn cornflour
2 tspns ginger wine

METHOD

1 Place the dried baby shrimps in a bowl, cover with warm water and soak for 30 minutes, if using. Drain.
2 Blend the seasoning ingredients in a bowl, add the chicken and marinate for 10 minutes. Drain.
3 Place the noodles in a bowl, cover with boiling water and soak for 10 minutes until soft. Drain.
4 Shell the prawns and remove the thin 'vein' or intestinal cord that runs down the spine (see Step 1, p. 55).
5 Rinse the clams in cold water and then place in a large pan and cover with boiling water. Cook rapidly for 2-3 minutes, shaking the pan occasionally, until the clams have opened. Drain thoroughly, discarding any that have not opened. Gently loosen the flesh from the shell with a sharp knife. Remove any grit or loose seaweed.
6 Heat the oil in a wok or frying pan. When hot, add the chopped spring onion and dried baby shrimps if using. Stir-fry for 2 minutes.
7 Add the soup stock, prawns, clams, marinated chicken, bean sprouts, shredded black mushrooms and salt. Bring to the boil and simmer for 5 minutes. Add the noodles and boil for a further 1 minute.
8 Mix together the lettuce and pepper, and serve over the noodle mixture.

Noodles with Fish and Pork

INGREDIENTS (SERVES 6)

100 g/4 oz pork fillet, sliced
3 Chinese mushrooms
225 g/8 oz cod steak
6-8 tblspns cornflour
700 g/1½ lbs rice noodles
6 tblspns oil
2 spring onions, chopped
1.2 litres/2 pints clear soup stock (see p. 261)
2 tspns salt
1 tspn rice wine or dry sherry
100 g/4 oz cooked prawns
125 ml/4 fl oz water
2 eggs, beaten
sliced gherkin to garnish

SEASONING A
½ tblspn soy sauce
1 tspn ginger juice
SEASONING B
3 tblspns cornflour
1 tspn white pepper
1 tblspn sesame oil

METHOD

1 Combine seasoning **A** ingredients in a bowl and add the pork fillet. Marinate for 1 hour.
2 Rinse the mushrooms and soak in warm water for 30 minutes until softened. Remove stalks and cut into shreds.
3 Cut the fish into large pieces, and coat each piece generously with the cornflour. Pat the pieces flat with a rolling pin.
4 Place the noodles in a bowl and cover with boiling water. Soak for 3-5 minutes, then drain. Plunge into a bowl of cold water, and stir to separate the strands.
5 Heat the oil in a large wok or frying pan. Add the spring onions and fry for a few seconds. Add the stock, salt, wine, mushrooms, and pork fillet. Bring to the boil.
6 Blend seasoning **B** in a bowl with the water. Add the pieces of fish to the wok, then stir in the seasoning.
7 Drain the noodles and add to the wok together with the prawns. Bring back to the boil, stirring all the time, then remove from the heat. Leave for 5 minutes to cool slightly before adding the beaten eggs. Serve immediately garnished with gherkin slices.

蒜粒豉香花龍魚

Red Snapper with Black Bean Sauce

INGREDIENTS (SERVES 4)

4 small red snappers
6 tblspns corn oil
2 red chillis, seeded and
  finely sliced
2 tblspns fermented black
  beans, mashed (see
  NOTES)
6 garlic cloves, crushed
3 tblsns water
parsley sprigs, to garnish

SEASONING

2 tblspns light soy sauce
½ tblspn rice wine or dry
  sherry
1 tspn salt
2 tspns sugar

METHOD

1 Clean and gut the fish and trim the tail and gills.
Pat dry with absorbent paper.
2 Heat the oil in a large frying pan or wok and
carefully add the fish. Fry for 2 minutes, turn the fish
over and fry the other side for 1 minute. Remove.
3 Add the chillis, black beans, garlic and seasoning
ingredients and bring to the boil, stirring. Return the
fish to the pan, add the water and cover. Simmer for 3
minutes and turn on to a serving plate. Garnish with a
little parsley and serve at once.

NOTES

1 The silver-grey fish pictured are commonly
available in China, but are not obtainable fresh in this
country. Red snapper, however, is a similar size and
works very well in this recipe.
2 Fermented black beans are commonly used in fish
recipes. Since they are very salty, they should be
thoroughly rinsed before using.

蝦仁炒蛋

Prawn Omelette

INGREDIENTS (SERVES 4)

450 g/1 lb raw King prawns
  (see NOTE)
2 tspns plain flour
6 eggs
4 tblspns corn oil
chopped chives and
  shredded carrots, to
  garnish

SEASONING A
½ tblspn ginger wine
1 tblspn cornflour
large pinch of white pepper

SEASONING B
1 tspn rice wine or dry sherry
2 tspns salt

METHOD

1 Shell the prawns and remove the thin 'vein' or intestinal cord that runs down the spine (see small picture 1, right).
2 Mix seasoning **A** in a bowl, add the prawns and marinate for 15 minutes.
3 Scald the prawns with boiling water and set aside for 5 minutes. Drain and dust with the plain flour.
4 Beat the eggs, add seasoning **B** and stir in the prawns.
5 Heat the oil in a large wok or frying pan, pour in the egg mixture and fry over a medium heat until the egg sets.
6 Slide onto a serving plate and garnish with chives and carrot shreds.

NOTE
Cooked prawns could also be used for this recipe, either peeled or unpeeled. Follow method, but do not scald with boiling water, simply dust with plain flour after marinating.

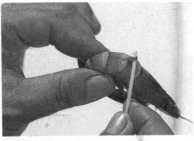

炸菊花大蝦

Fried Prawns with Black Sesame Seeds

INGREDIENTS (SERVES 4)

12 raw King prawns
1 tspn cornflour
4 eggs
2-3 tblspns rice flour
125 ml/4 fl oz corn oil
1 tblspn black sesame seeds

SEASONING A
½ tspn salt
1 tblspn ginger wine

SEASONING B
1 tspn ground cinnamon
½ tspn salt
1 tspn white pepper

METHOD

1   Remove the heads and shells of the prawns but leave their tails intact. Remove the intestinal cord (see Step 1, p. 55). Cut each one in half.
2   Mix seasoning **A** with the cornflour in a bowl and add the prawns. Stir well to mix.
3   Beat the eggs and add enough rice flour to make a smooth batter.
4   Heat the oil in a saucepan. Dip the prawns in the batter and then carefully drop into the hot oil. Fry for 2 minutes. Remove with a slotted spoon.
5   Heat 1 tblspn of the oil in a separate pan. When hot, re-fry the prawns with the black sesame seeds for 1 minute. Add seasoning **B**. Mix well and serve.

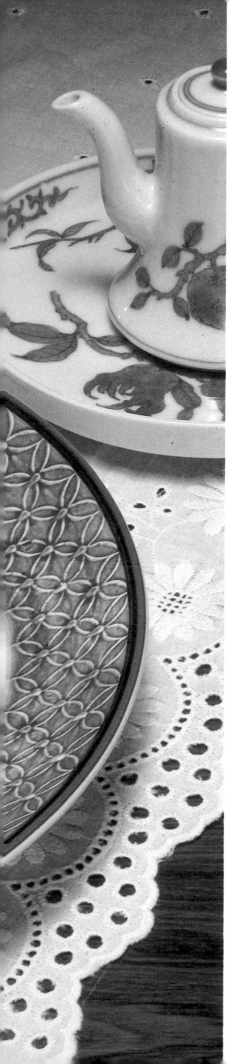

Drunken Prawns

INGREDIENTS (SERVES 4)

12 raw King prawns
2 thin slices fresh root ginger
300 ml/½ pint rice wine or
dry sherry

SEASONING
1 tspn salt
1 tspn white pepper

METHOD

1   Trim the feelers and legs of the prawns and
remove the thin 'vein' or intestinal cord that runs
down the spine with a pair of scissors (see small
picture 1, above).
2   Bruise the ginger slices with a cleaver or heavy
rolling pin (see NOTE) and place in a large pan with
the prawns.
3   Add the rice wine and slowly bring to the boil.
4   Simmer the prawns for 1 minute or until they turn
pink.
5   Remove the prawns with a slotted spoon and
arrange on a plate. Sprinkle with the seasoning and
serve.

NOTE
Bruising the ginger (crushing it slightly with a heavy
object) helps to release its juices and flavour.

串烤鲜鱿
Roast Squid

INGREDIENTS (SERVES 4)

3 squid, about 700 g/1½ lbs
   in weight
2 garlic cloves, crushed
1 large carrot
3 spring onions
1 tblspn corn oil

SEASONING

½ tspn salt
½ tspn white pepper
2 tspns rice wine or dry
   sherry

METHOD

1 Pull away the head and entrails from the squid.
Feel inside the body and remove the transparent
cartilage. Peel off and discard the mottled skin from
the body and rinse the squid under running water. Pat
dry with absorbent paper.
2 Mix the seasoning ingredients in a bowl and add
the squid. Marinate for 20 minutes.
3 Remove the squid from the marinade and rub the
inside of the bodies with the crushed garlic.
4 Cut the carrot lengthways into 6 long thin strips.
Cut off the roots and tops of the spring onions, peel
away any discoloured leaves.
5 Insert two carrot strips and a spring onion into the
body cavity of the squid. Arrange on a roasting tin and
brush with the oil. Bake at 190°C/375°F/Gas Mark 5 for
20 minutes.
6 Cut into sections, arrange on a serving plate and
serve.

糟香炸鳗

Fried Eel with Red Bean Sauce

INGREDIENTS (SERVES 4)

400 g/14 oz eel
3 tblspns red bean sauce (see
   NOTE)
2 tblspns water
100 g/4 oz potato flour
125 ml/4 fl oz corn oil
salt and pepper to serve

SEASONING

1½ tblspns sugar
½ tblspn grated fresh root
   ginger
½ tspn white pepper

METHOD

1 Rinse the eel in cold water and pat dry with
absorbent paper. Cut in half, remove the central bone
and cut into lengthways pieces.
2 Mix the red bean sauce, the seasoning ingredients
and the water in a large bowl. Add the eel pieces and
marinate for 2 hours.
3 Remove the eel, scrape off any excess marinade
and coat each piece evenly with the potato flour.
4 Heat the oil in a wok, add the eel and fry for 6-8
minutes, turning the pieces over occasionally.
5 Remove with a slotted spoon and drain on
absorbent paper. Serve hot with plenty of salt and
pepper.

NOTE

Red bean sauce or sweet bean sauce can be bought
from most Chinese supermarkets. When not available,
use Hoisin sauce.

Fish Fluff with Lettuce

INGREDIENTS (SERVES 4)

1 wood ear mushroom
½ iceberg lettuce
450 g/1 lb white fish steak
   e.g. cod, haddock, halibut
1 tblspn rice flour
1 egg
corn oil, for deep frying
50 g/2 oz bamboo shoots
100 g/4 oz minced pork
1 cooked potato, diced
50 g/2 oz salted peanuts,
   crushed

SEASONING A

½ tspn salt
1 tblspn finely grated fresh
   root ginger
½ tspn ground cinnamon

SEASONING B

1 tblspn light soy sauce
½ tspn salt
½ tspn white pepper
1 tspn sesame oil

METHOD

1   Soak the mushroom in warm water for 30 minutes. Drain, remove the stalk and roughly chop into pieces.
2   Separate the lettuce leaves, rinse them in cold water and shake dry. Arrange in a salad bowl.
3   Skin and bone the fish and cut into small cubes. Mix seasoning **A** in a bowl, add the fish and stir to blend thoroughly. Set aside for 30 minutes.
4   Beat together the rice flour and egg and stir into the marinated fish.
5   Heat the oil in deep-fat fryer, add spoonfuls of the fish mixture and fry for 4-5 minutes until well browned. Remove with a slotted spoon and drain on absorbent paper.
6   Chop the bamboo shoots and mix with the chopped mushroom and minced pork. Heat 3 tblspns of oil in a wok and stir-fry the mixture for 1 minute. Add the potato and seasoning **B** and stir to mix.
7   Stir in the fish mixture and cook until heated through.
8   Turn on to one half of a large serving plate, with the chopped peanuts to the other side. Serve immediately.

NOTE

The way to eat this tasty dish, is to take a leaf of lettuce, place a spoonful of Fish Fluff in the centre and add a sprinkling of chopped peanuts. Roll up and eat with your fingers.

魷魚羹

Squid Broth

INGREDIENTS (SERVES 4)

1 large dried squid
2 Chinese mushrooms
350 g/12 oz fish paste (see NOTE)
900 ml/1½ pints clear soup stock (see p. 261)
50 g/2 oz lean pork, finely sliced
25 g/1 oz bamboo shoots, sliced
1 carrot, grated
4 tblspns cornflour
4 tblspns water

SEASONING A
½ tspn salt
½ tblspn ginger wine
2 tblspns chopped celery
1 tspn light soy sauce
1 tspn sugar

SEASONING B
1 tspn salt
1 tblspn light soy sauce

SEASONING C
3 tspns sesame oil
2 tblspns malt vinegar

METHOD

1 Soak the dried squid in cold water overnight. Soak the dried Chinese mushrooms in warm water for 30 minutes.
2 Drain squid and cut into pieces. Pat dry on absorbent paper. Mix the fish paste with seasoning **A** and add squid. Mix together thoroughly.
3 Bring a large saucepan of water to the boil. Drop the fish paste-coated squid into it, a few pieces at a time, and cook until they float and the coating is firm. Remove with a slotted spoon and set aside.
4 Drain the mushrooms and shred finely. Bring the stock to the boil and add seasoning **B**. Boil for 3 minutes and add the pork, bamboo shoots and carrot, together with the cooked squid. Bring to the boil again, then lower the heat and simmer for 5 minutes.
5 Blend the cornflour with the water and stir into the soup. Bring to the boil and cook until thickened, then stir in seasoning **C** and serve at once.

NOTE
To make the fish paste, put 350 g/12 oz raw cod or plaice into a food processor and mince. Add ½ an egg white, 1 tblspn cornflour and ½ tspn chilli powder and process again until everything is well mixed.

炸蚵餅

Fried Shellfish Patties

INGREDIENTS (SERVES 4)

275 g/10 oz shelled clams
½ tblspn cornflour
1 bunch spring onions
50 g/2 oz white cabbage
150 g/5 oz lean pork, minced
400 g/14 oz plain flour
1 tspn salt
125-150 ml/4-5 fl oz water
corn oil, for deep frying

SEASONING A
½ tspn salt
1 tspn white pepper

SEASONING B
3 garlic cloves, finely chopped
3 tblspns light soy sauce
1 tblspn sweet chilli sauce

METHOD

1 Wash and drain the clams thoroughly. Toss with the cornflour.
2 Trim and chop the spring onions and finely shred the cabbage. Mix these vegetables with the pork, clams and seasoning **A**. Set aside.
3 Sift flour and salt into a large bowl and add sufficient water to make a fairly thick, coating batter.
4 Heat the oil in a deep-fat fryer. Place about 1 tblspn of the batter in a ladle and cover with 3 tblspns clam mixture. Cover with another 1 tblspn of the batter, then lower ladle into oil. Fry until golden brown, then remove and drain on absorbent paper. Keep warm while cooking remaining patties in the same way.
5 Blend seasoning **B** and serve with the patties.

麻辣魚塊

Hot Salmon Steaks

INGREDIENTS (SERVES 2)

2 salmon steaks
2 tblspns cornflour
4 tblspns corn oil
2 red chillis, seeded and
    finely sliced

SEASONING

1 garlic clove, crushed
2 tblspns dark soy sauce
1 tblspn rice wine or dry
    sherry
½ tspn sugar
1 tspn white pepper
3 tblspns water

METHOD

1   Wipe dry the fish and dust with the cornflour.
2   Heat the oil in a frying pan and add the fish steaks.
Fry for 2 minutes, turn them over and fry for a further 2
minutes until just tender.
3   Drain all the surplus oil from the frying pan into a
small frying pan or wok. Add the chillis and seasoning
ingredients. Bring to the boil, stirring.
4   Pour the chilli seasoning over the fish and cook
over a low heat for 5 minutes.
5   Serve immediately, with the sauce spooned over
the fish.

滷肥肝

Fish Steaks with Red Sauce

INGREDIENTS (SERVES 4)

2 cod or halibut steaks
4 tblspns corn oil

SEASONING
1 tblspn red bean sauce (see NOTE)
1 tblspn water
½ tblspn sugar

METHOD

1   Blend the seasoning ingredients thoroughly in a bowl. Add the fish, turning to coat both sides thoroughly. Marinate for 1-2 hours and then drain.
2   Heat the oil in a wok or frying pan, add the fish slices, and fry over medium heat until both sides are browned slightly. Serve.

NOTE
Red bean sauce adds a distinct and delicious piquancy to this dish. If it is unavailable, use Hoisin sauce.

醬瓜肉

Steamed Dried Fish

INGREDIENTS (SERVES 4)

1 dried fish
1 tblspn rice wine or dry sherry
2 tblspns finely grated fresh root ginger
3 tblspns white vinegar

METHOD

1   Trim off the tail and gills of the fish and soak in water for 1 hour.
2   Rinse the fish, and pat dry with absorbent paper. Rub thoroughly with the wine.
3   Spread the grated ginger over the fish and place in a steamer. Pour 5 cm/2 inches water into a large saucepan and bring to the boil. Set the steamer over the saucepan, cover with a tight-fitting lid and steam over a high heat for 40 minutes. Remove from heat.
4   Cut the fish into bite-sized pieces and serve the vinegar as a dipping sauce.

NOTE
Dried fish are commonly available in Chinese supermarkets. Buy garoupa or sea-eel, if available.

MEAT AND POULTRY

Although meat does not feature as prominently in Chinese cuisine as it does in the West, there are still hundreds of exciting and authentic meat and poultry dishes to choose from and it would be a shame not to include at least one of these in a Chinese meal.

The cooking methods employed for meat cooking are gentle and quick. Steaming is very common and even whole chickens and ducks can be steamed. Stir-frying, where the meat has been chopped or sliced in advance and is then cooked with a variety of vegetables, is popular as well, since it is quick and economical. Look out also for twice-cooked dishes. Here meat is first lightly cooked (either by boiling, steaming or stir-frying) to seal in flavour, and then cooked again, normally by deep-frying or stir-frying, when extra and stronger seasoning is added. The result is a rich, distinctive flavour and a delicious crispy texture.

Apart from poultry, the most popular meat in Chinese cuisine is undoubtedly pork. This extremely versatile meat appears in all sorts of Chinese dishes – cooked by itself as an impressive centrepiece, stir-fried with vegetables or simmered with noodles. Beef is also popular in parts of China and in Peking and north China, lamb dishes can also be found.

When buying meat for Chinese dishes, bear in mind that the delicate, quick cooking methods, such as stir-frying, often require tender cuts of meat – rump or sirloin steak for beef dishes and pork fillet or escalopes for pork ones. Boned chicken breasts, now widely available in supermarkets, are convenient when sliced chicken meat is required. However, you could always bone a whole chicken, in which case use the carcass for Chicken Stock (see p. 149).

辣味牛肉

Hot Beef

INGREDIENTS (SERVES 4)

350 g/12 oz rump steak
3 tblspns water
4 tblspns corn oil
2 or 3 chillis, seeded and
    finely chopped
1 tspn chopped dried orange
    peel (see NOTE)

SEASONING
3 garlic cloves, sliced
1 tspn salt
1 tblspn soy sauce
½ tblspn rice wine or dry
    sherry
2 tspns cornflour
1½ tblspns corn oil

METHOD

1   Slice the beef into thin slices, cutting against the grain.
2   Blend the seasoning ingredients with the water in a bowl and add the slices of beef. Marinate for 30 minutes. Drain.
3   Heat the oil in a wok or frying pan. Add the chillis and dried orange peel and fry over a medium heat for a few seconds. Add the beef and stir-fry over a high heat for 2 minutes. Serve.

NOTE
Dried orange peel is available from Chinese delicatessens. (You can use fresh peel instead, but the flavour is less concentrated.) To prepare, soak the dried peel in warm water till soft, then chop.

京醬牛柳

Beef Slices in Sauce

INGREDIENTS (SERVES 4)

350 g/12 oz rump steak
6 tblspns corn oil
broccoli stalks, to garnish

SEASONING A
1 tblspn soy sauce
½ tblspn chopped garlic
½ tblspn rice wine or dry
    sherry
½ tspn salt
1 tspn black bean sauce
1 tblspn cornflour
3 tblspns water

SEASONING B
1 tblspn cornflour
1 tspn sesame oil
1 tblspn soy sauce
1 tblspn water

METHOD

1   Slice the beef against the grain into thick slices.
2   Blend seasoning **A** in a bowl, add the slices of beef and marinate for 30 minutes. Drain.
3   Blend seasoning **B** ingredients in another bowl.
4   Heat the oil in a wok or frying pan. Add the beef and stir-fry over a high heat for 3-4 minutes. Remove from the heat. Pour in seasoning **B** and bring to the boil, stirring all the time. Garnish with slices of cooked broccoli stalks and serve.

Beef and Tomato Soup

INGREDIENTS (SERVES 6)

600 g/1¼ lbs stewing steak
2 large tomatoes
1.2 litres/2 pints water
12 mm × 2.5 cm/½ × 1 inch
   piece fresh root ginger
275 g/10 oz bean sprouts,
   rinsed
2 tspns rice wine or dry
   sherry

SEASONING
1-2 tspns salt
2 tspns light soy sauce

METHOD

1 Cut the beef into large 4 cm/1½ inch cubes and cut the tomatoes into wedges.
2 Bring the water to the boil and add the ginger and beef. Simmer for 1 hour or until the meat is just tender. Add the tomatoes and cook for a further 15 minutes.
3 Stir in the bean sprouts and rice wine and simmer for a further 5 minutes. Add the seasoning and stir.
4 Remove the slice of ginger and serve piping hot.

Shredded Chicken and Pea Broth

INGREDIENTS (SERVES 4)

225 g/8 oz boned chicken
   breasts, skinned
2 tblspns light soy sauce
2 tblspns cornflour
175 g/6 oz garden peas (see
   NOTE)
2 tblspns vegetable oil
1 tspn salt
350 ml/12 fl oz water
½ tspn white pepper
½ tspn sugar

METHOD

1 Slice the chicken breasts into thin 6 mm × 2.5 cm/¼ × 1 inch shreds.

2 Mix the soy sauce with 1 tspn of the cornflour in a bowl. Stir in the chicken and set aside for 20 minutes.

3 Place the peas in a bowl, cover with boiling water and scald for 3 minutes. Drain.

4 Heat the oil in a large flameproof casserole. Stir in the peas, the salt and 225 ml/8 fl oz water. Set over a high heat and bring to the boil.

5 Add the shredded chicken and bring back to the boil, stirring constantly to keep the chicken shreds separated.

6 Reduce heat, cover and simmer very gently for 15 minutes.

7 Blend the remaining cornflour with the remaining water to make a smooth paste and stir into the casserole with the pepper and sugar. Cook for a few minutes until the soup thickens and then serve.

NOTE

Frozen peas can be used if fresh garden peas are not available. They do not need scalding, but defrost first before cooking.

Chicken Balls with Lettuce

INGREDIENTS (SERVES 4)

2 boned chicken breasts,
  skinned
25 g/1 oz pork fillet
½ tspn salt
½ tspn sugar
1½ tspns rice wine or dry
  sherry
4 tblspns cornflour
1 Cos or round lettuce
900 ml/1½ pints chicken
  stock (see p. 149)
corn oil, for deep frying

METHOD

1 Very finely chop the chicken and pork. Place in a bowl and add the salt, sugar and rice wine. Form into walnut-sized balls and roll in the cornflour.
2 Break the lettuce into separate leaves and rinse in cold water. Bring the stock to the boil and drop the lettuce leaves in. Bring back to the boil. As soon as the water begins to boil again, remove the lettuce and arrange on a serving platter, reserving the stock.
3 Heat the oil in a deep-fat fryer and fry the chicken balls until they are golden. Remove with a slotted spoon, and drain on absorbent paper. Place on top of the lettuce. Season the soup with a little salt and pour over chicken balls.

五香雞塊

Five-Spice Chicken Pieces

INGREDIENTS (SERVES 6)

1 chicken, about 1.1 kg/2½
   lbs in weight
2 tspns salt
4 tblspns corn oil
cucumber slices and carrot
   flowers, to garnish

SEASONING

2 tblspns rice wine or dry
   sherry
2 tblspns soy sauce
1 spring onion, finely
   chopped
½ star anise
½ tspn Szechuan
   peppercorns (see NOTE)
125 ml/4 fl oz water

METHOD

1   Using a cleaver or meat axe cut the chicken into large pieces. Sprinkle with the salt.
2   Blend the seasoning ingredients in a bowl.
3   Heat the oil in a wok or frying pan, add the chicken pieces and fry until golden. Pour the seasoning over the chicken, bring to the boil then reduce the heat. Cook uncovered over a low heat for about 20 minutes, or until the chicken is cooked.
4   Arrange the chicken in a serving dish. Garnish with cucumber slices and carrot flowers, and serve.

NOTE

Szechuan peppercorns are available from Chinese delicatessens. They are not really peppercorns at all, but dried berries from a citrus shrub, with a pungent aroma and spicy flavour.

Steak, Chinese Style

INGREDIENTS (SERVES 6)

4 slices rump or sirloin steak,
    about 800 g/1¾ lbs in
    weight
75 ml/3 fl oz water
50 g/2 oz butter

SEASONING

3 tblspns soy sauce
1 tblspn chopped garlic
½ tspn salt
1½ tspns black pepper
2 tspns sugar
1 tblspn ginger wine
2 tblspns corn oil
1 tspn cornflour

METHOD

1 Tenderize the beef by beating it with a meat hammer or heavy rolling pin.
2 Blend the seasoning ingredients with the water in a large bowl. Add the beef and marinate for 1 hour.
3 Melt the butter in a frying pan, add the steak and fry over a medium-high heat until both sides are browned. Serve.

麻辣手撕雞

Hand-Torn Chicken with Spicy Sauce

INGREDIENTS (SERVES 6)

1 large chicken, about 1.5
  kg/3¼ lbs in weight
2 tomatoes and parsley
  sprigs, to garnish

SEASONING

2 tblspns sesame seed paste
  (see NOTE)
2-3 garlic cloves, crushed
1 tblspn sugar
½ tspn salt

METHOD

1 Rinse the chicken and pat dry with absorbent paper.
2 Place the chicken in a large steamer. Pour 5 cm/2 inches water into a large saucepan and bring to the boil.
3 Set the steamer containing the chicken over the saucepan. Cover with a tight-fitting lid and steam the chicken over a medium heat for 45-60 minutes, adding more water to the saucepan if necessary. The chicken is cooked when the flesh is no longer pink and the meat juices run clear when pierced with a knife. If these are still pink, continue steaming for a further 15-20 minutes.
4 Remove the chicken and pour the remaining steaming liquid into a measuring jug. Make up to 125 ml/4 fl oz liquid with a little water if necessary.
5 When the chicken is cool enough to handle, use your hands to tear the flesh from the bones. Arrange on a large serving platter.
6 Mix the seasoning ingredients with the reserved steaming liquid, heat gently and pour over the chicken pieces.
7 Garnish with slices of tomato and sprigs of parsley and serve with mustard or a sweet chilli sauce.

NOTE

Sesame seed or tahini paste is available from most health food shops as well as Chinese delicatessens. Stir thoroughly before using.

雞茸粟米

Chicken and Sweetcorn Chowder

INGREDIENTS (SERVES 4)

100 g/4 oz boned chicken
  breast, skinned
2 egg whites
½ tspn salt
900 ml/1½ pints chicken
  stock (see p. 149)
400 g/14 oz can sweetcorn,
  drained
2 tblspns cornflour
3 tblspns water
parsley sprig, to garnish

SEASONING

2 tspns light soy sauce
pinch of sugar

METHOD

1 Finely chop the chicken and place in a bowl. Add the seasoning ingredients and stir to mix.
2 Lightly beat the egg whites until frothy. Add the salt and stir into the chicken mixture.
3 Bring the chicken stock to the boil and add the sweetcorn. Cook for 5 minutes and then reduce the heat and add the chicken. Simmer gently for 15 minutes or until the chicken is cooked, stirring occasionally.
4 Blend the cornflour with the water to make a smooth paste. Stir into the soup and cook for a few minutes until the soup thickens.
5 Garnish with parsley and serve.

軟兜豬排

Pork Chops in Spicy Sauce

INGREDIENTS (SERVES 6)

6 pork loin chops, weighing
    about 800 g/1¾ lbs
corn oil, for deep frying
spring onion flowers, to
    garnish (see NOTE)

SEASONING
1 garlic clove, crushed
2 tblspns soy sauce
1 tblspn ginger wine
1 tspn cornflour
1 tblspn sesame oil
¼ tspn salt
½ tspn white pepper
1 tspn sugar

METHOD

1 Tenderize the pork chops by beating them with a
meat hammer or heavy rolling pin. Score them slightly
using a sharp knife.
2 Blend the seasoning ingredients in a bowl. Add
the pork chops and marinate for 30 minutes. Drain.
3 Heat the oil in a deep-fat fryer and deep fry the
pork chops for 5-7 minutes. Remove with a slotted
spoon and serve garnished with spring onion flowers.

NOTE
To make spring onion flowers, cut out 6.5-cm/2½-
inch lengths of spring onion. Make star-shaped cuts,
about 2.5-cm/1-inch deep, into both ends. Drop the
spring onions into iced water. They will curl within
½-1 hour.

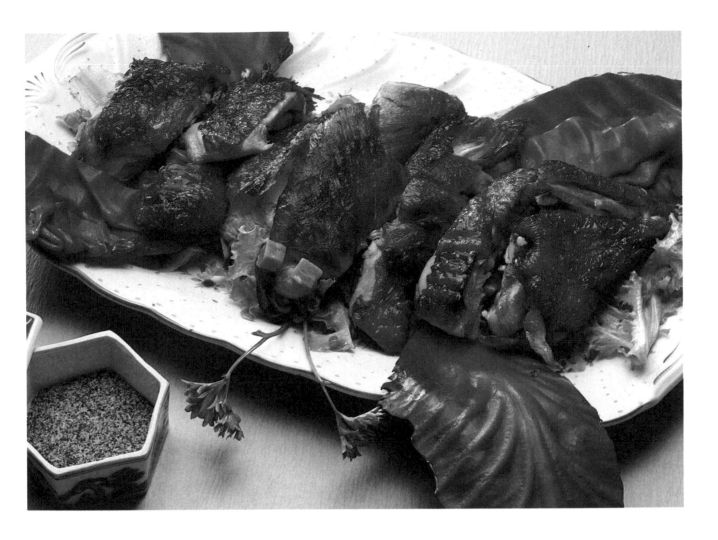

Fried Eight Pieces

INGREDIENTS (SERVES 6)

1 chicken, about 1.1 kg/2½ lbs in weight
corn oil, for deep frying
1 tspn sesame oil
red cabbage leaves, to garnish

SEASONING A

1 spring onion, cut into 3 pieces
3 slices fresh root ginger
1 star anise, crushed
4 tblspns soy sauce
1 tblspn rice wine or dry sherry
1 egg white
1 tblspn cornflour

SEASONING B

2 tspns salt
2 tspns Szechuan peppercorns (see NOTE)

METHOD

1 Using a cleaver or meat axe, cut the chicken into eight pieces.
2 Blend seasoning **A** ingredients in a bowl and add the chicken pieces. Marinate for about 1 hour. Drain.
3 Heat a wok or frying pan over a low heat and add seasoning **B** ingredients. Stir-fry until the salt turns slightly brown. Place in a mortar and pestle or coffee grinder and crush to a fine powder.
4 Heat the corn oil in a deep-fat fryer, and deep-fry the chicken pieces for 3 minutes. Remove with a slotted spoon, sprinkle with the sesame oil and garnish with the cabbage leaves. Serve with seasoning **B**.

NOTE
This mixture of dry-roasted salt and Szechuan peppercorns (which are not true peppercorns but dried berries) is served all over China as a dip for deep-fried foods.

Pork, Clam and Fuzzy Melon Soup

INGREDIENTS (SERVES 4)

1 large fuzzy melon (see
  NOTES)
50 g/2 oz pork fillet
275 g/10 oz clams
1 tblspn finely grated fresh
  root ginger
900 ml/1½ pints water
½ piece laver (see NOTES)
1 tspn sesame oil

SEASONING

1 tspn rice wine or dry sherry
1 tspn salt
1 tspn white pepper

METHOD

1   Peel the fuzzy melon and remove the stalk. Cut
lengthways into eight pieces and cut away the seeds,
then slice the melon diagonally in 12 mm/½ inch
pieces.
2   Cut the pork fillet into thin pieces and clean the
clams thoroughly.
3   Place the pork, ginger and water in a large
saucepan and bring to the boil. Add the clams, bring
back to the boil and add the fuzzy melon. Simmer for
10 minutes.
4   Tear the laver into small pieces and add to the
soup. Add the seasoning ingredients and stir to mix.
5   Sprinkle the sesame oil on top and serve at once.

NOTE

1   Fuzzy melon is a very popular Chinese summer
vegetable. It is normally available in Chinese
supermarkets, but if not, use a large cucumber
instead.
2   Laver is dried pressed seaweed, coming in wafer-
thin sheets. It's available from most Chinese
supermarkets.

Pork and Dried Fish Clear Soup

INGREDIENTS (SERVES 4)

50 g/2 oz bamboo shoots
100 g/4 oz pork fillet
275 g/10 oz dried salt fish
  (see NOTES)
5 cm/2 inch piece fresh root
  ginger, finely shredded
600 ml/1 pint boiling water
2 tspns rice wine or dry
  sherry

SEASONING

½ tspn white pepper
1 tspn sugar

METHOD

1   Cut the bamboo shoots into small pieces and slice
the pork fillet thinly. Place in a bowl, cover with
boiling water and set aside for 5 minutes. Drain.
2   Rinse the salt fish in cold water. Cut into 2.5 cm/1
inch pieces.
3   Arrange the bamboo shoots, pork, fish and ginger
in large bowl. Add the boiling water. Place over a pan
of boiling water, cover and steam for 40 minutes. Stir
in the rice wine.
4   Sprinkle with the seasoning ingredients just before
serving.

NOTES

1   Dried salt fish is regularly available at Chinese
supermarkets. The most common variety is dried
yellow fish.
2   This soup can be boiled rather than steamed.
However, it will become opaque, not transparent as
shown here.

貢丸湯

Meat Ball Soup

INGREDIENTS (SERVES 4)

12 Chinese meat balls (see NOTE)
2 celery stalks
900 ml/1½ pints chicken stock (see p. 149)
1 tspn salt
½ tspn white pepper

METHOD

1   Wash the meat balls. Using a sharp knife, score a criss-cross pattern on each one.
2   Wash and trim the celery, and cut into small cubes.
3   Place the stock and the meat balls in a saucepan, bring to the boil and boil for 3 minutes. Remove from the heat.
4   Add the diced celery, salt and pepper, and serve immediately.

NOTE
Buy the Chinese meat balls from any Chinese supermarket. They can be bought fresh, but are more commonly available in sealed packets.

清蒸猪排

Steamed Pork Chops

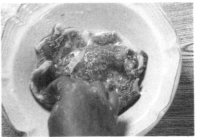

INGREDIENTS (SERVES 4)

4 pork escalopes, about 600 g/1¼ lbs in weight

SEASONING
1 tblspn ginger wine
1 tblspn salt
½ tspn white pepper
1 tblspn cornflour
2 tspns sesame oil
3 tblspns water

METHOD

1   Tenderize the meat by beating it lightly with a meat hammer or heavy rolling pin. Using a sharp knife, score slightly.
2   Blend the seasoning ingredients in a bowl. Add the pork chops, turning to ensure they are evenly coated. Marinate for 30 minutes.
3   Place the chops on a heatproof plate in a large steamer. Pour 5 cm/2 inches boiling water into a large saucepan. Set the steamer containing the pork chops over the saucepan. Cover with a tight-fitting lid and steam the pork chops over high heat for 12 minutes or until they are cooked. Remove from the heat.
4   Arrange on a serving dish and serve.

Chicken Wings with Abalone

INGREDIENTS (SERVES 4)

1 small can abalones
(see NOTE)
12 chicken wings
3 dried scallops, soaked in
cold water for 2 hours
2 canned asparagus spears,
to garnish, optional

SEASONING

1 tblspn finely grated fresh
root ginger
1 tspn white pepper
1 tspn salt
1 tspn sugar

METHOD

1 Drain the canned abalones and reserve the juice.
Take two of the abalones and cut into 6 slices.
2 Place the chicken wings in a bowl, cover with
boiling water and scald for 10 minutes. Drain.
3 Cut the soaked scallops into thin slices.
4 Place the abalone slices, the chicken wings and
the scallops in a deep bowl. Mix the reserved abalone
juice with the seasoning ingredients and pour over the
abalones and chicken. Place in a large steamer and set
over a pan of boiling water. Cover and steam for 30
minutes.
5 Serve, garnished with asparagus spears, if liked.

NOTE

Abalones are a popular delicacy in China. They are
molluscs with a delicate fishy taste and a similar
texture to scallops. Canned abalones are available
from Chinese supermarkets. Remaining abalones can
be kept in a sealed container with a little fresh water in
the refrigerator for up to 1 week.

原汁玉米雞

Chicken with Sweetcorn

INGREDIENTS (SERVES 4)

400 g/14 oz boned chicken
   breasts, skinned
225 g/8 oz broccoli
1½ tblspns corn oil
225 g/8 oz canned
   sweetcorn
1 egg white, lightly beaten
1½ tblspns cornflour
2 tblspns water
radish slices, to garnish

SEASONING

1 tblspn rice wine or dry
   sherry
2 tspns salt
½ tspn white pepper
½ tspn sugar
125 ml/4 fl oz water

METHOD

1   Cut the chicken breasts into small cubes and place in a bowl. Add the seasoning ingredients and stir thoroughly.

2   Place the bowl in a steamer over a pan of boiling water. Cover and steam over a high heat for 10 minutes or until the chicken is cooked, stirring occasionally.

3   Meanwhile, break the broccoli into florets and place in a large bowl. Cover with boiling water and blanch for 3 minutes. Drain and keep warm.

4   Drain the chicken and keep warm. Reserve the liquid from the bowl.

5   Heat the oil in a wok. Add the sweetcorn and the reserved chicken liquid. Bring to the boil and beat in the egg white. Stir constantly for 30 seconds.

6   Mix the cornflour with the water to form a paste. Stir into the sweetcorn mixture and cook for a few minutes, stirring, until the sauce thickens.

7   Arrange the broccoli around the outside of a plate and pile the chicken in the centre. Pour the sweetcorn sauce over the top and garnish with radish slices.

蔴油蜜汁雞

Chicken with Sesame Oil and Honey

INGREDIENTS (SERVES 6)

1 chicken, about 1.4 kg/3½
  lbs in weight
4 Chinese mushrooms,
  optional
2 tblspns vegetable oil
125 ml/4 fl oz water
2 tblspns sesame oil
lettuce and tomatoes, to
  garnish

SEASONING

4 tblspns light soy sauce
3 tblspns clear honey
1 tblspn rice wine or dry
  sherry
½ tspn ground ginger
1 tspn salt

METHOD

1 Using a cleaver or meat axe, cut the chicken into
bite-sized pieces.
2 Mix the seasoning ingredients in a bowl and add
the chicken. Marinate for 1 hour.
3 Soak the mushrooms, if using, in warm water for
30 minutes.
4 Drain the chicken, reserving the marinade. Heat
the vegetable oil in a wok and add the chicken pieces.
5 Stir-fry over a high heat until chicken begins to
brown. Add the water and bring to the boil.
6 Stir in the reserved marinade and the sesame oil
and simmer gently for 40 minutes.
7 Meanwhile, remove the stalks of the soaked
mushrooms and steam, over a pan of boiling water for
20 minutes.
8 Serve the chicken with the steamed mushrooms,
garnished with lettuce and tomatoes.

Velvet Chicken

INGREDIENTS (SERVES 4)

175 g/6 oz boned chicken
   breast, skinned
4 egg whites
5 tblspns water
3 tspns cornflour
450 ml/¾ pint corn oil
50 g/2 oz cooked ham, sliced
½ cucumber, quartered and
   sliced
8 straw mushrooms
3 tblspns chicken stock
   (see p. 149)
1 tspn salt

SEASONING
½ tspn salt
1½ tspns rice wine or dry
   sherry

METHOD

1 Slice the chicken thinly and place in a bowl. Beat 1 egg white with 1 tblspn water and the seasoning ingredients and stir into the chicken. Set aside for 15 minutes.
2 Beat the remaining egg whites with 1 tblspn water and beat into the chicken mixture. Continue beating for 5 minutes.
3 Blend 2 tspns of the cornflour with 1 tblspn water and stir into the chicken mixture. Mix thoroughly.
4 Heat the oil in a large wok. Add the coated chicken pieces and fry for 5 minutes. Remove the chicken with a slotted spoon and drain.
5 Drain off all but 2 tblspns of the oil and re-heat. Add the ham, cucumber and mushrooms and stir-fry for 2 minutes. Blend the remaining 1 tspn of cornflour with 1 tblspn water and stir into the mixture with the chicken stock and salt. Cook for 1 minute until thick and bubbly, then return the chicken to the pan and cook for a further minute.
6 Sprinkle in remaining water, stir and serve immediately.

Chinese-style Hot Pot

INGREDIENTS (SERVES 6)

900 g/2 lbs stewing lamb
1 section of peeled sugar
   cane (see NOTES)
225 g/8 oz water chestnuts
   (see NOTES)
1 star anise
½ tblspn rice wine or dry
   sherry
1.2 litres/2 pints water

SEASONING
1½ tspns salt
2 tspns sugar

METHOD

1   Trim the lamb and cut into 5 cm/2 inch thick
strips. Scald in boiling water for 1 minute. Drain and
rinse in cold water.
2   Cut the sugar cane into 2.5 cm/1 inch sections.
Peel the water chestnuts, if fresh, or drain canned
ones.
3   Place the meat, sugar cane, water chestnuts, star
anise and rice wine in a large flameproof casserole.
Add the water and bring to the boil. Cover and simmer
for 1½-2 hours or until the meat is tender.
4   Add seasoning and serve.

NOTES
1   Sugar cane is available from Chinese, Indian and
West Indian supermarkets.
2   Fresh water chestnuts are occasionally available
from Chinese supermarkets. If you cannot get hold of
them, use canned ones instead which are widely
available from most supermarkets.

Shredded Chicken with Bean Sprouts

INGREDIENTS (SERVES 4)

225 g/8 oz boned chicken
   breasts, skinned
1 egg white
2 tspns cornflour
100 g/4 oz bean sprouts
5 tblspns corn oil
raspberries and celery tops,
   to garnish

SEASONING

1½ tspns salt
½ tspn white pepper

METHOD

1   Shred the chicken into thin pieces and place in a bowl. Lightly beat the egg white, add the cornflour and stir into the chicken.
2   Rinse the bean sprouts in cold water and drain.
3   Heat the oil in the wok. Add the chicken and stir-fry over a high heat for 45-60 seconds. Remove with a slotted spoon and set aside.
4   Drain all but 2 tblspns of the oil. Reheat the wok, add the bean sprouts and stir-fry for a few seconds. Add the seasoning ingredients and stir well.
5   Return the chicken and cook, stirring for 15 seconds. Serve garnished with celery tops and raspberries

Crystal Paper-wrapped Chicken

INGREDIENTS (SERVES 4-6)

600 g/1¼ lbs boned chicken
   breasts, skinned
1 egg white
corn oil, for deep frying
lemon slices, to garnish

SEASONING

3 tblspns light soy sauce
1 tspn rice wine or dry
   sherry
1 tblspn finely grated fresh
   root ginger
½ tspn sugar

METHOD

1   Cut the chicken into rectangles about 2 × 4 cm/¾ × 1½ inches.
2   Mix the seasoning ingredients with the egg white and stir into the chicken pieces. Marinate for 3 hours in a cool place, stirring occasionally.
3   Cut a sheet of cellophane into about 12 (15 cm/6 inch) squares. Place a spoonful of the chicken mixture at the corner of each square and wrap up, twisting the ends to seal.
4   Heat the oil in a deep-fat fryer and deep-fry the parcels for 3 minutes.
5   Serve the chicken in the wrappers, garnished with slices of lemon.

Boiled Chicken with Spring Onions

INGREDIENTS (SERVES 4)

2 chicken legs
1 bunch spring onions
5 cm/2 inch piece fresh root
    ginger
50 ml/2 fl oz corn oil

SEASONING
1 tspn salt
½ tspn white pepper

METHOD

1   Place the chicken legs in a saucepan or flameproof casserole. Add sufficient water to cover the chicken and bring to the boil. Simmer for 15 minutes and then remove the pan from the heat and leave, covered, for 20 minutes.

2   Remove the chicken pieces from the stock, skin and strip away the flesh from the bones. Arrange the meat on a serving plate.

3   Trim the spring onions and cut lengthways and then across into 7.5 cm/3 inch pieces. Peel the ginger and cut into fine shreds. Place both in a bowl and mix with the seasoning ingredients.

4   Heat the oil in a wok, add the spring onions and ginger and stir-fry for 30 seconds. Pour the contents of the wok over the shredded chicken and serve.

NOTE
The chicken stock will make a good basis for a soup. Place in a rigid container and refrigerate for up to 3 days or freeze for up to 3 months.

Chicken with Wood Ear Mushrooms

INGREDIENTS
(SERVES 4-6)

25 g/1 oz wood ear
   mushrooms
4 chicken pieces
4 tblspns dark soy sauce
corn oil, for deep frying
2 spring onions, thinly sliced
2.5 cm/1 inch piece fresh
   root ginger, cut into 3
   slices
450 ml/¾ pint chicken stock
   (see p. 149)
2 tblspns cornflour
parsley sprigs and baby corn-
   on-the-cobs, to garnish

SEASONING
1 tblspn rice wine or dry
   sherry
2 tblspns light soy sauce
1 tspn dark soy sauce
1 tspn sugar
1 tspn salt

METHOD

1   Soak the wood ear mushrooms in warm water for 30 minutes. Drain and thinly slice.
2   Rub the chicken pieces evenly with the dark soy sauce and marinate for 30 minutes.
3   Heat the oil in a large wok or deep fryer and deep fry the chicken pieces, two at a time, until well browned. Remove the chicken and set aside; drain the oil from the wok.
4   Heat 1 tblspn of oil in the wok and fry the spring onions, wood ear mushrooms and ginger slices for 30 seconds.
5   Remove the ginger and discard. Add the chicken, the chicken stock and the seasoning ingredients. Stir thoroughly, cover and simmer over a low heat for 25 minutes.
6   Remove the chicken and cool slightly. When cool enough to handle, pull away the meat from the bones and arrange on a serving plate.
7   Remove the mushrooms from the wok with a slotted spoon and scatter over the chicken.
8   Blend the cornflour with a little water and stir into the wok. Bring to the boil, stirring, and cook for a few minutes until the sauce thickens slightly.
9   Pour the sauce over the chicken and garnish with the parsley and baby corn-on-the-cobs. Serve.

Spicy Braised Chicken

INGREDIENTS (SERVES 6)

1 whole chicken, about 1.4
   kg/3 lbs in weight
50 ml/2 fl oz corn oil
600 ml/1 pint water
½ tblspn sesame oil
2 tspns salt
lettuce leaves and radishes,
   to garnish

SEASONING A
10 garlic cloves
5 red chillis, seeded and
   finely chopped (see NOTE)
2.5 cm/1 inch fresh root
   ginger, sliced
1 spring onion, finely
   chopped

SEASONING B
3 tblspns light soy sauce
1 tblspn rice wine or dry
   sherry

METHOD

1   Using a heavy cleaver or meat axe, cut the chicken into bite-sized pieces.
2   Using a coffee grinder or mortar and pestle, grind seasoning **A** to form a paste.
3   Heat the corn oil in a wok and stir-fry the paste for 1 minute. Add the chicken pieces and fry over a medium-high heat until golden brown. Drain excess oil.
4   Add the water and seasoning **B** to the chicken, stir thoroughly and bring to the boil. Simmer gently for about 1 hour.
5   Spoon chicken out onto a serving plate and sprinkle with the sesame oil and salt. Garnish with lettuce leaves and sliced radishes and serve.

NOTE
This is quite a hot dish, perhaps too spicy for those who prefer milder flavours. If you prefer to play it safe, use only 2 or 3 chillis.

Quick and Easy Roast Pork

INGREDIENTS (SERVES 4)

600 g/1¼ lbs pork fillet
4 tblspns corn oil
sesame oil, to serve

SEASONING
1 tblspn soy sauce
2 tblspns chilli sauce (see NOTES)
1 spring onion, finely chopped
1.2 cm/½ inch fresh root ginger, chopped
¼ tspn five-spice powder
4 tblspns sugar
125 ml/4 fl oz water
1 tblspn rice wine or dry sherry

METHOD

1   Using a sharp knife, score the pork on both sides in several places.
2   Place the seasoning ingredients in a bowl and blend thoroughly. Add the pork, turning to ensure it is evenly coated. Marinate for at least 4 hours. Drain.
3   Heat the oil in a wok or frying pan until medium-hot. Add the pork, and fry for about 5 minutes turning to brown all sides. Remove from the heat and drain.
4   Place the pork in a roasting pan and bake at 220°C/425°F/Gas Mark 7 for 15 minutes. Remove from the oven and allow to cool.
5   When the meat is cold, sprinkle with the sesame oil, slice thinly and serve.

NOTES
1   This dish is perfect for summer meals and picnics. In northern China, cold platters are often served at banquets.
2   Chilli sauce is available from many supermarkets and from Chinese delicatessens.

Marinated Pork

INGREDIENTS (SERVES 4)

2 tblspns rice wine or dry sherry
600 g/1¼ lbs pork fillet
1½ tblspns salt

SEASONING
3 garlic cloves, finely chopped
6 tspns sesame oil

METHOD

1   Rub the rice wine over the pork fillet and then rub with the salt until it is all absorbed. Place in a non-metal bowl and leave to marinate in the refrigerator for 24 hours.
2   Rinse the pork lightly, and place in a large steamer. Place 5 cm/2 inches boiling water in a large saucepan, set the steamer over the saucepan and cover with a tight-fitting lid. Steam for 20-25 minutes or until pork is tender and cooked through.
3   Slice the pork thinly. Blend the seasoning ingredients and serve as a dipping sauce with the sliced pork.

White Cooked Chicken

INGREDIENTS (SERVES 6)

2.5 litres/4½ pints water
4 slices fresh root ginger
1 whole chicken, about 1.4
  kg/3 lbs in weight
Chinese parsley, to garnish
  (see NOTE)

SEASONING
1 tblspn finely grated fresh
  root ginger
2 spring onions, finely
  chopped
1 tblspn corn oil
1 tspn salt

METHOD

1   Place the water in a large saucepan. Add the ginger and bring to the boil. Add the chicken, bring back to the boil and cook rapidly for 10 minutes. Reduce the heat, cover and simmer over a low heat for 20 minutes. Remove the pan from the heat and set aside, covered, until the chicken is cool.
2   Drain the chicken and using a meat cleaver or heavy knife, chop the chicken into large pieces. Arrange on a serving plate and garnish with the parsley.
3   Make a dipping sauce by blending all the seasoning ingredients in a bowl. Serve with the chicken.

NOTE
Chinese parsley is sometimes known as flat-leafed parsley and is available from Chinese and Indian supermarkets. It has a similar flavour to our own parsley, which may be used instead.

Braised Duck

INGREDIENTS (SERVES 4-6)

1 whole duck, about
  1.4 kg/3 lbs in weight
2 tblspns dark soy sauce
4 tblspns corn oil
3 spring onions, sliced
2-3 red chillis, seeded and
  sliced
2 courgettes, roughly
  chopped
2 tblspns cornflour

SEASONING
2 tblspns light soy sauce
4 slices fresh root ginger
2 star anise
2 tspns rice wine or dry
  sherry

METHOD

1   Rub the duck with the dark soy sauce and then chop into bite-sized pieces.
2   Heat the oil in a wok or frying pan, add the duck and fry for 2-3 minutes until golden brown on all sides. Remove with a slotted spoon and place in a large saucepan with the spring onions, chillis and seasoning ingredients.
3   Add sufficient water to cover, bring to the boil and then reduce heat and simmer, covered, for 1¼ hours. Add the courgettes and continue cooking for 20-30 minutes or until the duck is tender.
4   Blend the cornflour with a little water and stir into the pan. Cook until the sauce has thickened and then serve at once.

Barbecued Chicken with Sweet Bean Sauce

INGREDIENTS (SERVES 6)

4 tblspns rice wine or dry
  sherry
1 chicken, about 1.4 kg/3 lbs
  in weight
1 tblspn corn oil
6-8 tblspns sweet or red bean
  sauce, to serve

SEASONING A

4 tblspns sweet or red bean
  sauce
1 tspn salt
1½ tspns sugar
1 tspn chopped fresh root
  ginger

SEASONING B

4 tblspns soy sauce
4 tblspns sugar

METHOD

1 Pour the rice wine slowly over the chicken, rubbing it in with your fingers.
2 Blend seasoning **A** and rub the cavity of the chicken with this mixture. Close the cavity with a skewer.
3 Place the chicken in a steamer and steam, covered, over boiling water for 40 minutes, turning the chicken once halfway through cooking.
4 Remove the chicken from the steamer, and rub with the oil.
5 Blend seasoning **B** ingredients together in a saucepan, and heat gently. Keep hot.
6 Place the chicken on a spit, brush with a little of seasoning **B** and cook either over charcoal or in a very hot oven (220°C/425°F/Gas Mark 7) for 30-45 minutes, basting frequently with the seasoning.
7 Using a cleaver or meat axe, cut the chicken into pieces, and arrange on a serving dish. Pour some sweet bean sauce on top and serve.

一品雞排

Chicken Cutlets

INGREDIENTS (SERVES 6)

6 boned chicken breasts,
    skinned
3 eggs
100 g/4 oz lean minced pork
2 tspns cornflour
100 g/4 oz golden
    breadcrumbs
corn oil, for deep frying
2 large tomatoes, to garnish

SEASONING A

4 tblspns rice wine or dry
    sherry
2 tspns salt

SEASONING B

2 garlic cloves, crushed
1 tspn ground ginger
1 tspn salt
½ tspn sesame oil

METHOD

1 Beat the chicken breasts out lightly with a meat
hammer or heavy rolling pin. Mix seasoning **A** in a
bowl and add the chicken, turning to coat each piece
evenly. Marinate for 20 minutes.

2 Beat one of the eggs and mix with the minced
pork, the cornflour and seasoning **B**. Spread the
mixture over the chicken pieces.

3 Beat the other two eggs and place the
breadcrumbs on a sheet of greaseproof paper. Dip
each coated chicken fillet in the beaten egg and then
in the breadcrumbs.

4 Heat the oil in a deep-fat fryer and deep-fry the
chicken for 5-10 minutes or until golden brown and
cooked through. Drain on absorbent paper and then
arrange on a serving plate. Garnish with tomato slices
and serve with a tomato sauce, if liked.

果汁牛肉

Beef in Fruit Juice

INGREDIENTS (SERVES 4)

400 g/14 oz sirloin or rump
    steak
100 g/4 oz fresh pineapple
1 tblspn dried orange peel
    (see NOTE p. 73)
6 tblspns corn oil
1 tblspn cornflour
3 tblspns water
strawberries and spring
    onion curl, to garnish (see
    NOTE p. 82)

SEASONING

2 garlic cloves, crushed
3 tblspns fresh orange juice
1 tblspn dark soy sauce
½ tblspn rice wine or dry
    sherry
1½ tblspns sugar
1 tspn salt

METHOD

1   Cut the steak, against the grain, into long thin strips.
2   Roughly chop the pineapple into small pieces and finely chop the dried orange peel.
3   Blend the seasoning ingredients in a small bowl. Heat the oil in a wok, add the seasoning and stir-fry for 1 minute.
4   Add the steak and stir-fry vigorously over a high heat for 2 minutes.
5   Stir in the pineapple and cook for 30 seconds.
6   Blend the cornflour with the water and stir into the beef mixture. Cook for a few minutes until the sauce thickens and then turn onto a serving plate.
7   Garnish with strawberry halves and a spring onion curl. Serve at once.

麻辣蘆筍雞

Spicy-Hot Chicken with Asparagus

INGREDIENTS (SERVES 4)

350 g/12 oz boned chicken
 breasts, skinned
450 g/1 lb fresh asparagus

SEASONING
4 garlic cloves, finely
 chopped
2 tblspns sesame oil
2 tblspns light soy sauce
2 tblspns hot chilli oil
1 tblspn sugar
2 tspns white vinegar
pinch of salt

METHOD

1 Cut the chicken into 2.5 × 5 cm/1 × 2 inch strips.
Remove the woody stems from the asparagus and cut
into 5 cm/2 inch lengths.
2 Place the chicken and asparagus in a saucepan,
just cover with boiling water and simmer for 5-10
minutes or until the chicken is cooked and the
asparagus is tender.
3 Drain and arrange the chicken and asparagus on a
serving plate.
4 Mix the seasoning ingredients together in a
serving bowl. Spoon a little over the chicken and
asparagus and serve the remainder separately, as a
dipping sauce.

Chicken and Pea Casserole

INGREDIENTS (SERVES 6)

600 g/1¼ lbs boned chicken
   breast, skinned
40 g/1½ oz butter
1 small onion, thinly sliced
1 × 400 g/14 oz can chopped
   tomatoes
600 ml/1 pint chicken stock
   (see p. 149)
175 g/6 oz frozen peas
1 tblspn cornflour

SEASONING

1 tspn rice wine or dry sherry
½ tspn white pepper
1½ tspns salt
1 tspn sugar

METHOD

1   Cut the chicken into 1 × 5 cm/½ × 2 inch pieces
and place in a small pan. Cover with boiling water and
leave for 1 minute. Drain.

2   Melt the butter in a large, flameproof casserole.
Add the onion and fry for 2-3 minutes until lightly
brown.

3   Add the chicken, chopped tomatoes and chicken
stock. Bring to the boil and add the seasoning
ingredients. Reduce the heat, cover and simmer for 1
hour.

4   Add the peas and cook for a further 10 minutes.
Blend the cornflour with a little cold water and stir into
the casserole. Cook for 2-3 minutes until the sauce
thickens and serve.

Chicken with Cucumber

INGREDIENTS (SERVES 4)

1 cucumber
2 tspns salt
2 tspns sesame oil
450 g/1 lb boned chicken
   breast, skinned
1 pack of pea-starch noodles
   (see NOTE)

SEASONING
1½ tspns chopped fresh root
   ginger
1½ tspns chopped garlic
1 tblspn hot chilli oil
1 tblspn sesame oil
3 tblspns soy sauce
1 tblspn vinegar
2 tspns sugar
2 tblspns sesame paste
1 tspn salt

METHOD

1 Slice the cucumber thinly then cut the slices in half. Sprinkle with the salt and marinate for 10 minutes. Rinse off the salt, pat dry and mix with the sesame oil. Arrange on a platter.
2 Place the chicken breasts in boiling water, and cook for 15 minutes. Drain and cool. When cool, use your fingers to shred into small pieces.
3 Place the pea-starch noodles in cold water. Bring to the boil, remove from the heat, and leave to stand for 30 minutes. Drain and chop roughly. Arrange on top of the cucumber slices, and place the shredded chicken on top.
4 Blend the seasoning ingredients together and sprinkle over the chicken.

NOTE
Pea-starch noodles also known as bean thread noodles or transparent vermicelli, are available from Chinese delicatessens. Made not from a grain but from ground mung beans, they are always served as part of another dish, never on their own.

Grilled Chicken Pieces

INGREDIENTS (SERVES 6)

600 g/1¼ lbs boned chicken
   breasts, skinned
1 egg, beaten
6 tblspns cornflour
4 tblspns corn oil
125 ml/4 fl oz chicken stock
   (see p. 149)
4 tblspns tomato sauce
1 tspn sugar
1 tspn Worcestershire sauce
1 tspn sesame oil
lemon slices and lettuce
   leaves, to garnish

SEASONING

1 tblspn rice wine or dry
   sherry
1 tblspn light soy sauce
1 tspn salt
½ tspn white pepper

METHOD

1 Cut the chicken into 2.5 × 5 cm/1 × 2 inch pieces
and beat out slightly with a meat hammer or heavy
rolling pin.
2 Blend the seasoning ingredients in a bowl, add the
chicken and marinate for 30 minutes.
3 Drain the chicken and dip first in the beaten egg
and then in the cornflour.
4 Brush lightly with the oil and grill under a low heat
for 10-15 minutes. Turn the pieces over and grill for a
further 5 minutes or until the chicken is very tender.
5 Place the chicken stock and any meat juices from
the grill pan in a saucepan. Add the tomato sauce,
sugar, Worcestershire sauce and sesame oil and
bring to the boil.
6 Pour the sauce over the chicken and garnish with
lemon slices and lettuce leaves.

Barbecued Beef

INGREDIENTS (SERVES 6)

600 g/1¼ lbs rump steak
2 green peppers
125 ml/4 fl oz clear soup
   stock (see p. 261)

SEASONING A
1 tblspn Hoisin or barbecue
   sauce
1 tblspn light soy sauce
½ tblspn ginger wine
1 tspn cornflour
2 tspns sugar
½ tspn black pepper

SEASONING B
3½ tblspns smooth peanut
   butter
1 tblspn Hoisin or barbecue
   sauce
2 garlic cloves, crushed
1 tspn salt
2 tblspns finely chopped
   parsley
½ tspn black pepper

METHOD

1 Cut the steak across the grain into thin 5 cm/2 inch long slices.

2 Blend seasoning **A** in a bowl. Add the steak and set aside for 20 minutes.

3 Cut the peppers in half, remove the seeds and then cut into small chunks. Place in a saucepan of boiling water and boil for 2 minutes. Drain.

4 Drain the meat and then thread alternate pieces of pepper and steak onto 6 large or 12 small bamboo sticks.

5 Grill or barbecue for 5 minutes, turning the sticks occasionally.

6 Mix together seasoning **B** and the stock in a saucepan and bring to the boil. Simmer for 1 minute and then turn into a serving bowl.

7 Serve as a dipping sauce with the meat and pepper kebabs.

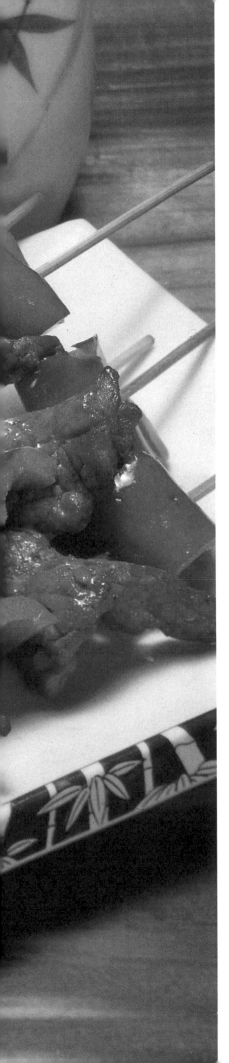

Chicken in the Pot

INGREDIENTS (SERVES 4)

1 large chicken, about 1.8 g/4
 lbs in weight
5 star anise
450 ml/¾ pint water

SEASONING
225 ml/8 fl oz dark soy sauce
225 ml/8 fl oz rice wine or dry
 sherry
150 g/5 oz rock sugar
 (see NOTE)

METHOD

1   Using a cleaver or meat axe, chop the chicken into bite-sized pieces and place in a bowl.
2   Blend the seasoning ingredients to make a rich marinade and pour 10 tblspns over the chicken. Marinate for 1 hour.
3   Place the chicken in its marinade in a large flameproof casserole with the star anise, water and the remaining marinade. Bring to the boil and then cover and simmer gently for 45-60 minutes or until chicken is tender.

NOTE
Rock sugar or sugar crystals are pale yellow or amber in colour and are not quite as sweet as normal sugar. If rock sugar cannot be found at a Chinese store, use 75 g/3 oz demerara instead.

墨魚 燜 排骨

Pork Spareribs with Dried Squid

INGREDIENTS (SERVES 6)

2 large dried squid, soaked
(see NOTE)
450 g/1 lb pork spareribs
2.5 cm/1 inch piece fresh
root ginger
2 spring onions
white pepper
parsley, to garnish

SEASONING
3 tblspns light soy sauce
1 tblspn rice wine or dry
sherry
1 tblspn sugar
1 tspn salt

METHOD

1 Peel away the skin from the soaked squid and discard the head and tentacles. Cut into 2.5 × 5 cm/1 × 2 inch pieces.
2 Chop the spareribs into 2.5 cm/1 inch pieces. Bruise the ginger by patting firmly with a heavy cleaver or rolling pin. Slice the spring onions.
3 Place the squid, spareribs, ginger and spring onions together with the seasoning ingredients, in a large saucepan or flameproof casserole. Cover with water and bring to the boil. Simmer for about 1 hour or until the stock has reduced by half.
4 Stir in a little pepper and garnish with parsley. Serve piping hot.

NOTE
Dried squid is available from Chinese supermarkets all year. It should be kept in a dry place and used within a few months of purchase. Dried squid needs to be soaked for 24 hours in cold water before using in a recipe.

115

子芋燗鴨

Stewed Duck with Taros

INGREDIENTS (SERVES 4)

½ large duck, about 600 g/
   1¼ lbs in weight
450 g/1 lb taros (see NOTE)
corn oil, for deep frying
3 spring onions, sliced
600 ml/1 pint clear soup
   stock (see p. 261)
2 tspns sesame oil

SEASONING A
4 tblspns light soy sauce
2 tblspns ginger wine
2 tspns sugar

SEASONING B
2 tblspns light soy sauce
1 tspn sugar
½ tspn salt
½ tspn white pepper

METHOD

1   Rinse the duck and dry on absorbent paper. Cut into bite-sized pieces, using a cleaver or meat axe.
2   Mix together seasoning **A** in a large bowl, add the duck and marinate for 30 minutes. Drain, reserving the marinade.
3   Soak the taros in boiling water for 10 minutes and then peel. Cut into large chunks.
4   Heat the oil in a deep fat fryer and deep fry the taros for 5 minutes. Remove with a slotted spoon.
5   Heat 2 tblspns oil in a wok and stir-fry the duck for 3 minutes. Remove. Add 4 more tblspns of oil to the wok and stir-fry the spring onions for a few seconds.
6   Add the duck pieces, the reserved marinade, the taros, the seasoning **B** ingredients and the soup stock. Bring to the boil and then simmer over a low heat for 30 minutes.
7   Sprinkle with sesame oil just before serving.

NOTE
Taros are a root vegetable with a slightly sweet flavour. They are available from most Chinese, Indian and West Indian supermarkets, but if not, use sweet potatoes.

Spicy Chicken

INGREDIENTS (SERVES 4)

600 g/1¼ lbs boned chicken
   breasts, skinned
3 tblspns sesame oil
1 red chilli, seeded and finely
   chopped
2 spring onions, chopped
2 tblspns corn oil
baby tomatoes and corn-on-
   the-cobs, to garnish

SEASONING A

1 garlic clove, finely chopped
1 tspn grated fresh root
   ginger
½ tspn white pepper

SEASONING B

2 tblspns light soy sauce
2 tspns white vinegar
1 tspn sugar
1 tspn salt

METHOD

1 Place the chicken in boiling water and cook for 5 minutes. Drain and thickly slice.
2 Heat the sesame oil in a wok, add the chilli and spring onions and gently stir-fry for a few seconds. Remove and set aside.
3 Heat the corn oil in the wok and add the chicken and seasoning **A**. Stir-fry for 1 minute and then stir in seasoning **B**. Cook for a further 2 minutes, stirring all the time.
4 Arrange the chicken on a serving plate and sprinkle the chilli and spring onions over the top. Garnish with baby tomatoes and corn-on-the-cobs and spoon the cooking sauce over.

簡易家常焗鶏

Easy Roast Chicken

INGREDIENTS
(SERVES 4-6)

1 chicken, about 1.4 kg/3 lbs
in weight

SEASONING
4 spring onions, finely
chopped
2 slices fresh root ginger
3 star anise
1½ tblspns salt
1 tblspn rice wine or dry
sherry
2 tblspns peppermint leaves,
chopped (see NOTE)

METHOD

1 Mix the seasoning ingredients together in a bowl,
and stuff into the body cavity of the chicken.
2 Wrap the chicken in aluminium foil, place in a
roasting pan and bake at 200°C/400°F/Gas Mark 6 for
1½ hours. Serve.

NOTE
Peppermint leaves are sometimes available in the
summer from good greengrocers. If not, use any type
of garden mint, preferably fresh, although dried could
be used if necessary.

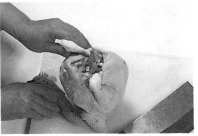

炸鶏腿

Deep-Fried Drumsticks

INGREDIENTS (SERVES 4)

4 chicken drumsticks
100 g/4 oz plain flour
corn oil, for deep frying

SEASONING A

2 tblspns ginger wine
2 tspns five-spice powder
2 tblspns light soy sauce
1 tspn sugar
1 tspn salt
½ tspn white pepper

SEASONING B

3 tblspns Worcestershire
    sauce
½ tspn salt
½ tspn white pepper

METHOD

1   Blend seasoning **A** in a bowl and add the chicken drumsticks. Marinate for 1 hour, turning occasionally.
2   Drain the chicken and coat lightly with the flour.
3   Heat the oil in a deep fat-fryer and deep-fry the chicken legs for 4-5 minutes until cooked and golden brown. The chicken is cooked when meat juices run clear.
4   Blend seasoning **B** to make a dipping sauce and turn into a serving bowl.
5   Wrap a little foil around the joint end of the chicken drumstick and serve with the dipping sauce.

檸檬雞片

Lemon Chicken

INGREDIENTS (SERVES 4)

275 g/10 oz boned chicken
    breasts, skinned
1 egg yolk
7 tblspns cornflour
3 tblspns plain flour
corn oil, for deep frying
2 tblspns water
3 tblspns chicken stock
    (see p. 149)

SEASONING A
½ tblspn rice wine or dry
    sherry
1½ tblspns light soy sauce
1 tspn cornflour

SEASONING B
3 tblspns lemon juice
3 tblspns sugar
½ tspn salt
1 tspn sesame oil

METHOD

1   Cut the chicken into 2.5 × 5 cm/1 × 2 inch strips.
2   Blend seasoning **A** and stir in the chicken pieces. Marinate for 1 hour. Drain.
3   Mix 6 tblspns of the cornflour with the plain flour and coat the chicken pieces evenly.
4   Heat the oil in a deep-fat fryer and deep-fry the chicken slices for 30 seconds. Remove with a slotted spoon and set aside.
5   Mix the remaining cornflour with the water. Heat 1 tspn of oil in a frying pan, add the cornflour mixture together with the chicken stock and seasoning **B**. Cook over a medium heat until slightly thickened.
6   Reheat the oil in the deep fat, fry the chicken slices for about 10-20 seconds. Remove and arrange on a serving plate and pour the lemon sauce over.

Chicken with Gammon

INGREDIENTS (SERVES 6)

1 large chicken, about
   1.6 kg/3½ lbs in weight
900 ml/1½ pints water
1 small onion, very finely
   chopped
1 tspn finely chopped fresh
   root ginger
100 g/4 oz smoked gammon
   slices
2 tblspns corn oil
1 tspn cornflour

SEASONING
1 tspn salt
1½ tspns rice wine or dry
   sherry

METHOD

1   Place the chicken in a large saucepan or casserole, add the water and the onion and ginger. Bring to the boil, cover and simmer for 40 minutes or until the chicken is cooked.

2   Drain, reserving 125 ml/4 fl oz of the liquid. Allow the chicken to cool and then slice.

3   Arrange alternate slices of chicken and gammon on a platter and place in a steamer to keep warm.

4   Heat the oil in a small pan and add the reserved chicken liquid. Bring to the boil and add the seasoning ingredients.

5   Mix the cornflour with a little water and add to the chicken stock. Cook for a few minutes until the mixture thickens, and then pour over chicken and gammon and serve.

NOTE
Keep any remaining stock from the chicken for soups or casseroles.

滷 牛 肝

Spiced Ox Liver

INGREDIENTS (SERVES 4)

1 pack of spices (see NOTE)
2.5 cm/1 inch piece fresh
  root ginger, sliced
600 ml/1 pint water
275 g/10 oz ox or pig's liver
1 tblspn sesame oil

SEASONING

3 tblspns light soy sauce
2 tblspns rice wine or dry
  sherry
1 tblspn rock sugar
  (see NOTE p. 114)
1 tspn salt
½ tspn white pepper

METHOD

1 Wrap the spices and the sliced ginger in a piece of muslin, knotting the end.
2 Place the water in a saucepan, bring to the boil and then boil the spice pack for 30 minutes.
3 Add the liver together with the seasoning ingredients. Bring to the boil and then reduce the heat, cover and simmer gently for 40 minutes. Remove from the heat and leave, covered, for 10 minutes.
4 Remove the liver and brush with the sesame oil. Allow to cool and then slice thinly. Serve with a salad.

NOTE

A pack of spices is a common provision at Chinese supermarkets. It contains liquorice, five-spice powder, star anise, dried orange peel, fennel and cinnamon.

滷 牛 腱

Spiced Brisket

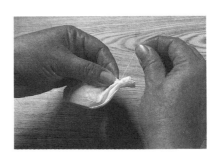

INGREDIENTS (SERVES 6)

450 g/1 lb beef brisket
1 pack of spices (see NOTE
  above)
1.2 litres/2 pints water

SEASONING

4 tblspns dark soy sauce
1 tblspn rock sugar
  (see NOTE p. 114)
3 tblspns rice wine or dry
  sherry
pinch of salt
pinch of white pepper

METHOD

1 Rinse the joint of meat and then scald in boiling water for 2 minutes.
2 Wrap the pack of spices in a piece of muslin, knotting the end. Place the water in a large saucepan and bring to the boil. Add the spice pack and boil for 30 minutes.
3 Add the brisket to the liquid and bring back to the boil. Reduce the heat, cover and simmer for 1½ hours. Remove the pan from the heat and set aside, covered, for 20 minutes.
4 Remove the joint, reserving the cooking liquid and slice thinly.
5 Place the seasoning ingredients in a large frying pan. Add 125 ml/4 fl oz of the reserved liquid and bring to the boil. Add the slices of brisket and simmer until the liquid has evaporated and the pan is almost dry. Serve.

Stuffed Green Peppers

INGREDIENTS (SERVES 4)

4 small green peppers
1 tblspn cornflour
6 tblspns corn oil
175 ml/6 fl oz clear soup
   stock (see p. 261)
pineapple cubes, to garnish

STUFFING

225 g/8 oz minced pork
1 egg white, lightly beaten
2 tspns sesame oil
2 tblspns cornflour
½ tspn salt
25 g/1 oz water chestnuts,
   finely chopped
1 tblspn carrot, grated
1 spring onion, chopped

SEASONING

2 tblspns soy sauce
1 tblspn sugar

METHOD

1   Wash the green peppers and pat dry with
absorbent paper. Cut in half lengthwise, and remove
the seeds and core. Sprinkle the inner surface of the
peppers with the cornflour.
2   Mix the stuffing ingredients thoroughly.
3   Stuff the pork mixture into each pepper as tightly
as possible.
4   Heat the oil in a wok or frying pan, and fry the
peppers, stuffing side down, for 2 minutes. Turn the
peppers over and fry for a further 1 minute.
5   Blend the seasoning ingredients and add to the
pan, shaking the pan carefully to ensure the seasoning
is evenly distributed. Continue frying for 1 more
minute.
6   Pour in the soup stock, cover and simmer for 5-8
minutes.
7   Arrange on a serving dish and garnish with
pineapple cubes.

Quick Fried Chicken and Pork

INGREDIENTS (SERVES 4)

12 Chinese mushrooms,
    optional
100 g/4 oz boned chicken
    breasts, skinned
100 g/4 oz lean pork
1 egg white
2 tspns cornflour
4 tblspns corn oil
3 tblspns chicken stock
(see p. 149)
carrot and bamboo shoot
    slices, to garnish

SEASONING

2 garlic cloves, crushed
1½ tspns rice wine or dry
    sherry
½ tspn sugar
1 tspn salt

METHOD

1   Place the mushrooms in a bowl, cover with warm
water and soak for 30 minutes. Drain; remove stalks
and squeeze out excess liquid.
2   Cut the chicken and pork into bite-sized pieces.
Place in two separate bowls. Beat the egg white with
1 tspn of the cornflour and divide between the chicken
and pork. Stir.
3   Heat 2 tblspns of oil in a wok and add the chicken.
Stir-fry vigorously for 4 minutes and remove.
4   Add another 1 tblspn oil to the wok, heat and add
the pork. Stir-fry for 7-8 minutes or until cooked
through. Push the pork up the sides of the wok, add
the remaining oil to the centre. Add the chicken and
cook for 30 seconds, and then stir in with the pork.
5   Blend the remaining cornflour with a little cold
water, stir in the chicken stock and the seasoning
ingredients. Stir into the chicken and pork and bring
to the boil, stirring. Cook until slightly thickened and
then turn onto a serving plate. Garnish with the
mushrooms and the sliced carrots and bamboo
shoots.

胡蘿蔔燜牛肉

Stewed Beef with Carrots

INGREDIENTS (SERVES 4)

700 g/1½ lbs braising beef
2-3 carrots
1 piece of dried orange peel,
   soaked (see NOTE)
1 spring onion, chopped
1 tblspn grated fresh root
   ginger
2 star anise
450 ml/¾ pint water

SEASONING

3 tblspns soy sauce
¼ tspn salt
1 tblspn rice wine or dry
   sherry

METHOD

1   Cut the beef into 5 cm/2 inch cubes. Place in
boiling water and scald for 1 minute, then remove
with a slotted spoon and rinse again.
2   Peel the carrots and cut them into chunks. Drain
and rinse the dried orange peel.
3   Place all the ingredients, including the seasoning
ingredients, in a saucepan with the water, cover and
bring to the boil. Reduce the heat and simmer for
1-1½ hours or until the meat is tender. Add more
water, if necessary, while the meat is cooking. Serve
at once.

NOTE

The orange peel should be soaked in warm water for
20 minutes before using.

羅漢果燉牛肉丸湯

Stewed Beef Balls

INGREDIENTS (SERVES 4)

600 g/1¼ lbs lean minced
   beef
1 onion, peeled and
   quartered
1.2 litres/2 pints clear soup
   stock (see p. 261)
2 tspns sugar

SEASONING A

½ tspn white pepper
1 tspn chopped spring
   onions
½ tspn dried orange peel,
   soaked (see NOTE above)
¼ tspn salt
1 tblspn ginger wine
2 tblspns cornflour
½ tspn five-spice powder

SEASONING B

¾ tspn salt
2 tspns rice wine or dry
   sherry

METHOD

1   Blend the beef with seasoning **A** and marinate for
30 minutes. Form into balls about 4 cm/1½ inches in
diameter.
2   Place the meat balls, onion, soup stock, sugar and
seasoning **B** in a saucepan or wok. Cover and bring to
the boil. Reduce heat and simmer for 1½ hours,
adding more water if necessary during cooking. Serve
immediately.

鶏肝串烤

Roasted Pork and Chicken Liver Rolls

INGREDIENTS (SERVES 4)

225 g/8 oz chicken livers
350 g/12 oz pork fillet
4 tblspns corn oil

SEASONING A
1 tblspn plum sauce
pinch of salt

SEASONING B
1 tblspn Hoisin or barbecue
  sauce
1 tblspn light soy sauce
1 tblspn ginger wine
2 tspns sugar
½ tspn salt
½ tspn white pepper

METHOD

1 Rinse and trim the chicken livers. Pat dry and cut into thin slices. Blend seasoning **A** in a bowl, add the chicken livers and marinate for 30 minutes.
2 Slice the pork into strips about 12 mm × 7.5 cm/½ × 3 inches. Blend seasoning **B**, add the pork and marinate for 30 minutes.
3 Place slices of chicken liver inside the slices of pork. Roll up and secure with a wooden cocktail stick.
4 Heat half the oil in a wok. Add the pork and chicken liver rolls and fry gently, for 4 minutes. Turn the rolls over, add the remaining oil and fry for a further 4 minutes.
5 Remove and serve immediately.

洋蔥十錦

Assorted Shreds

INGREDIENTS (SERVES 4)

4 tblspns corn oil
100 g/4 oz lean pork, cut into
  thin strips
1 carrot, cut into thin strips
5 cm/2 inch piece dried bean
  curd, cut into thin strips
½ red pepper, seeded and
  cut into thin strips
½ green pepper, seeded and
  cut into thin strips
1 onion, cut into thin rings

SEASONING
1 tspn salt
½ tspn white pepper
1 tspn sugar

METHOD

1 Heat the oil in a wok. Stir-fry the pork strips for 5 minutes, add the carrot, bean curd and red and green pepper and fry for 2 minutes.
2 Add the onion and seasoning ingredients and fry for a further 3-4 minutes or until the vegetables are tender but still crisp. Serve at once.

Bird's Nest Chicken

INGREDIENTS (SERVES 4)

350 g/12 oz boned chicken
    breasts, skinned
2 large potatoes
100 g/4 oz cornflour
½ tspn salt
corn oil, for deep fat frying
2 spring onions, chopped
1 tblspn finely grated fresh
    root ginger
10 straw mushrooms
    (see NOTE)
1 small green pepper, seeded
    and chopped
50 g/2 oz water chestnuts,
    chopped
1 carrot, diced

SEASONING A

1 egg white
1½ tblspns cornflour
1 tblspn light soy sauce

SEASONING B

2 tblspns light soy sauce
1 tblspn rice wine or dry
    sherry
1½ tspns cornflour
pinch of salt
pinch of sugar
½ tspn sesame oil

METHOD

1   Dice the chicken and marinate in seasoning **A** for
30 minutes.
2   Cut the potato into very, very fine strips
(alternatively grate the potato coarsely). Rinse in cold
water and pat dry thoroughly.
3   Mix the potato with the cornflour and salt and
spread this mixture around the inside of a large
colander or wire net basket. Place a slightly smaller
colander inside, so that the potato mixture is pressed
between the two wire baskets.
4   Take a large deep-fat fryer, large enough to take
the 'potato' basket, and add sufficient oil to come
about halfway up the fryer. Do not overfill as the oil
will bubble up.
5   Heat the oil, and when hot, lower the 'potato'
basket into the oil and deep fry until the potato turns
golden-brown. Drain thoroughly and gently ease the
baskets apart, so that you are left with a potato nest.
6   Place 3 tblspns of oil in a wok and add the spring
onions, root ginger, mushrooms and the prepared
vegetables. Stir-fry for 3 minutes and add the
marinated chicken and seasoning **B**.
7   Cook for a few minutes until the mixture thickens
and is hot and bubbly and then pour into the potato
nest. Serve at once.

NOTE
Straw mushrooms are only available in cans and are
sold from almost any Chinese supermarket. Button
mushrooms can be substituted if liked.

Deep-Fried Chicken with Straw Mushrooms

INGREDIENTS
(SERVES 4-6)

1 chicken, about 1.4 kg/3 lbs
  in weight
3 tblspns plain flour
4 tblspns cornflour
corn oil, for deep frying
2 cans straw mushrooms (see
  NOTE on p. 133)
2 tblspns corn oil
1 tspn salt
50 ml/2 fl oz water
prawn crackers, to garnish

SEASONING

4 tblspns soy sauce
2 tblspns rice wine or dry
  sherry
2 tspns sugar

METHOD

1 Cut the chicken into 2.5 cm/1 inch cubes. Blend the seasoning ingredients in a bowl. Add the chicken pieces and marinate for 3 hours. Drain.
2 Mix the plain flour and 2 tblspns of the cornflour in a large bowl. Add the chicken pieces and toss to coat lightly.
3 Heat the oil in a deep-fat fryer and deep-fry the chicken pieces for 5 minutes. Remove the chicken and drain. Arrange on a serving dish.
4 Drain the straw mushrooms, rinse in cold water and pat dry with absorbent paper.
5 Heat 2 tblspns oil in a wok or frying pan add the straw mushrooms and stir-fry for 1 minute. Add the salt.
6 Blend the remaining 2 tblspns cornflour with the water, and add to the straw mushrooms. Heat until slightly thickened, stirring all the time, then pour over the chicken.
7 Garnish with the prawn crackers.

Braised Chicken with Chestnuts

INGREDIENTS (SERVES 4)

225 g/8 oz boned chicken
  breasts, skinned
2 tblspns corn oil
12 mm/½ inch piece fresh
  root ginger, sliced
125 ml/4 fl oz chicken stock
  (see p. 149)
100 g/4 oz dried chestnuts,
  soaked (see NOTE)

SEASONING A
2 tblspns light soy sauce
1 tspn sugar

SEASONING B
3 tblspns dark soy sauce
1 tspn rice wine or dry sherry
½ tspn salt
1 tspn sugar

METHOD

1   Cut the chicken into large bite-sized pieces and
marinate in seasoning **A** for 30 minutes.
2   Heat the oil in a wok, add the ginger and stir-fry for
20 seconds.
3   Add the marinated chicken and stir-fry for 10
seconds. Stir in seasoning **B** together with the chicken
stock. Cover and simmer over a low heat for 10
minutes.
4   Add the soaked chestnuts and continue to simmer
for 30 minutes. Turn onto a serving plate and serve at
once.

NOTE
Dried chestnuts should be soaked in cold water for 24
hours before using.

醤 豬 排

Saucy Pork Chops

INGREDIENTS (SERVES 4)

600 g/1¼ lbs pork loin chops
4 tblspns corn oil
1 spring onion, finely
    chopped
225 ml/8 fl oz water

SEASONING
3 tblspns black bean sauce
1 tblspn sugar
1¼ tspns salt
3 tblspns soy sauce
½ tblspn rock sugar (see
    NOTE)
1 tblspn ginger wine

METHOD

1 Tenderize the pork chops by beating them with a meat hammer or heavy rolling pin.
2 Heat the oil in a wok or frying pan, add the spring onion and stir-fry for 2 minutes. Add the seasoning ingredients with the water, and bring to the boil. Boil for 1 minute.
3 Place the pork chops in the wok or pan, and bring back to the boil over a medium-low heat. Simmer for 3 minutes, then reduce the heat, cover and simmer for a further 20-25 minutes or until the pork is tender. Serve at once.

NOTE
Rock sugar is available from Chinese delicatessens, but amber coffee sugar crystals or demerera sugar could be substituted.

糟 香 豬 排

Red-Spiced Spareribs

INGREDIENTS (SERVES 4)

800 g/1¾ lbs pork spareribs
    (see NOTE)
3 tblspns water
4 tblspns corn oil
3 garlic cloves, crushed
1 spring onion flower, to
    garnish (see p. 82)

SEASONING
2 tblspns red bean sauce (see
NOTE p. 61)
1 tblspn sugar
1 tblspn rice wine or dry
    sherry

METHOD

1 Cut the spareribs into 2.5 cm/1 inch pieces using a meat cleaver or heavy knife.
2 Blend the seasoning ingredients in a bowl with the water, add the pork pieces and marinate for 30 minutes. Drain.
3 Heat the oil in a wok or frying pan. Add the chopped garlic, and stir-fry over high heat for a few seconds. Add the spareribs, and stir-fry for 2-3 minutes until lightly browned. Reduce the heat, cover and simmer for 6 minutes. Remove the lid, increase the heat slightly and stir-fry for 3 minutes. Garnish with a spring onion flower, and serve.

NOTE
Make sure to ask your butcher for Chinese-style spareribs, rather than the American-style ribs which are a slightly different cut.

Cold Spicy Diced Chicken

INGREDIENTS (SERVES 4)

2 boned chicken breasts,
   skinned
6 dried bean curd sheets
75 g/3 oz roasted cashew
   nuts
100 g/4 oz broccoli florets
carrot flowers, to garnish

SEASONING

1 tblspn soy sauce
1 tspn sugar
1 tblspn hot chilli oil
½ tspn Szechuan
   peppercorns, crushed
1 tspn sesame paste
1 tspn sesame oil
¼ tspn salt

METHOD

1   Place the chicken breasts in a shallow pan, cover with boiling water, and cook gently for about 10 minutes or until they are cooked. Drain and cool thoroughly. Cut into small cubes.
2   Soak the dried bean curd sheets in cold water for 30 minutes until soft. Drain and then pat dry. Cut into small pieces and mix with the diced chicken. Stir in the cashew nuts.
3   Blend the seasoning ingredients in a bowl, and add to the chicken mixture, stirring thoroughly.
4   Place the broccoli florets in a large bowl. Cover with boiling water and blanch for 3 minutes. Drain.
5   Arrange the broccoli around the outside of a serving dish, and pile the chicken mixture into the centre.
6   Garnish with carrot flowers and serve.

Shredded Cold Chicken with Hot Sauce

INGREDIENTS (SERVES 4)

350 g/12 oz boned chicken
   breast, skinned
lettuce leaves, orange slices,
   cherry tomatoes and
   parsley sprigs, to garnish

SEASONING
1½ tspns sugar
1 tblspn salt
2 tblspns sesame paste
2 tblspns English mustard
   paste
4 garlic cloves, crushed

METHOD

1   Place the chicken in a steamer or large colander. Put 5 cm/2 inches boiling water in a large saucepan. Set the chicken over the saucepan, cover with a tight-fitting lid and steam for 30 minutes. Remove the chicken from the steamer and allow to cool.

2   When it is cool enough to handle, shred into long, thin pieces, and arrange on a serving dish.

3   Blend the seasoning ingredients in a bowl, adding a little water or chicken stock to thin, if necessary. Pour over the chicken, or serve as a dipping sauce along with the chicken. Serve with lettuce, orange slices, parsley sprigs and cherry tomatoes.

煎牛肉碎餅

Chinese-Style Beef Patties

INGREDIENTS (SERVES 4)

600 g/1¼ lbs lean beef, roughly chopped
50 g/2 oz pork fat
1 small carrot, roughly chopped
1 celery stalk, chopped
½ small onion, chopped
1½ tspns chopped dried orange peel, soaked (see NOTE)
4 tblspns corn oil

SEASONING
½ tspn salt
½ tspn black pepper
1 tblspn ginger wine
1½ tspns sugar
1 tblspn oil
1 tblspn cornflour

METHOD

1   Place the beef, pork fat, carrot, celery, onion, orange peel and the seasoning ingredients in a food processor and mince to make a smooth paste.
2   Divide the mixture equally into eight balls, and form into patties, compressing them with your hands.
3   Heat the oil in a wok or frying pan and fry the patties over a medium heat until both sides are well browned.

NOTE
Soak the dried orange peel in warm water for 20 minutes before using.

咖喱牛腩

Chinese Curried Beef

INGREDIENTS (SERVES 4)

600 g/1¼ lbs beef brisket or shin
1 spring onion plus 1 tblspn chopped spring onion bulb
1 tblspn grated fresh root ginger
2 star anise
4 tblspns corn oil
½ onion, sliced
2-3 tspns Chinese curry powder (see NOTE)
½ tblspn chopped red pepper
1½ tspns salt
1 tblspn rice wine or dry sherry
1 tblspn sugar
200 ml/7 fl oz milk
2 tblspns cornflour
2 tblspns water

METHOD

1   Cut the beef into large pieces.
2   Immerse the beef in boiling water for 1 minute, drain and pat dry with absorbent paper.
3   Put the beef, whole spring onion, grated ginger and star anise in a pan and just cover with water. Bring to the boil, and simmer very gently uncovered, for 2-2½ hours, or until the meat is tender. (The juice remaining in the pan when the cooking is completed should be no more than 125 ml/4 fl oz.)
4   Heat the oil in a wok or frying pan. Add the chopped spring onion bulb and stir-fry for 1 minute. Add the onion, curry powder and chopped red pepper, and stir-fry for 2 minutes.
5   Add the beef with the juice from the pan, together with the salt, rice wine, sugar and milk. Simmer for 1 minute. Remove from the heat. Blend the cornflour with the water and add to the meat mixture. Return to the heat and bring back to the boil, stirring constantly. Serve.

NOTE
Make sure to use Chinese curry powder – not an Indian one. Chinese curry powder can be bought from Chinese supermarkets.

滷鷄腿

Spiced Chicken Legs

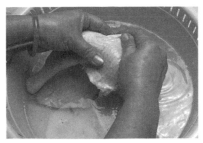

INGREDIENTS (SERVES 4)

1.2 litres/2 pints water
6 spring onions, cut into 12
  mm/½ inch sections
4 chicken legs
Maraschino cherries and
  parsley sprigs, to garnish

SEASONING
12 mm/½ inch piece of fresh
  root ginger, cut into thin
  slices
1 pack of spices containing
  star anise, chilli pepper,
  fennel and cinnamon
75 ml/3 fl oz soy sauce
1 tspn salt
1½ tblspns rock sugar

METHOD

1 Place the water in a saucepan. Add the spring
onions and the seasoning ingredients and bring to the
boil. Boil for 30 minutes.
2 Rinse the chicken legs, and add to the saucepan.
Cook over a medium-heat for 10 minutes, and then
remove the pan from the heat.
3 Leave the chicken in the liquid for 5 minutes and
then arrange on a serving dish. Garnish with parsley
sprigs and Maraschino cherries and serve.

蔴醬鷄絲

Chicken Shreds with Sesame Paste

INGREDIENTS (SERVES 4)

2 cooked chicken legs or 2
  cooked chicken breasts
5 cm/2 inch piece agar-agar
  (about 20 g/¾ oz in
  weight) (see NOTE)
125 ml/4 fl oz water
1 small cucumber, cut into
  thin strips
Maraschino cherry, to
  garnish

SEASONING
2 tblspns sesame paste (see
  NOTE p. 81)
1 tblspn chilli oil
1 tblspn soy sauce
¾ tspn salt
2 tblspns sesame oil

METHOD

1 Using your fingers, tear the chicken meat into
shreds.
2 Soak the agar-agar in warm water for 5 minutes,
and then tear into pieces with your fingers and
squeeze dry.
3 Blend the seasoning ingredients together in a bowl
with the water.
4 Arrange the cucumber strips on a serving dish,
and place the shredded agar-agar and chicken on top.
Pour the seasoning over the top, garnish with a
Maraschino cherry and serve.

NOTE
If fresh agar-agar is unobtainable it might be possible
to buy the dried variety which comes in strips. If this
too is unavailable, it's still possible to follow this
recipe, but without the agar-agar garnish.

咖喱鷄

Chinese Curried Chicken

INGREDIENTS (SERVES 4)

2 large chicken legs
4 tblspns corn oil plus oil for
    deep frying
1 tblspn chopped spring
    onion bulb
½ tblspn grated fresh root
    ginger
1 garlic clove, chopped
2 chillis, seeded and finely
    chopped or 1 tblspn
    cayenne pepper
1 small onion, cut into
    wedges
3-5 tblspns Chinese curry
    powder (see NOTE)
1 large carrot, cut into large
    cubes
1 large potato, cut into large
    cubes
225 ml/8 fl oz milk
225 ml/8 fl oz water

SEASONING

1½ tspns salt
1 tblspn sugar
1 tblspn rice wine or dry
    sherry

METHOD

1   Using a cleaver or meat axe, cut the chicken into bite-sized pieces.
2   Heat the 4 tblspns of oil in a wok or frying pan. Add the chopped spring onion, ginger, garlic and chillis or cayenne and fry for a few seconds.
3   Add the onion and stir-fry for 3 minutes. Add the curry powder and stir well.
4   Add the chicken pieces, and stir-fry over a medium-high heat for 3 minutes. Reduce the heat, cover and simmer gently for 10 minutes, turning the chicken pieces over occasionally.
5   Heat the oil in a deep-fat fryer. When the oil is very hot, add the cubed carrot and potato. Deep-fry for about 3 minutes, or until they are browned. Remove with a slotted spoon and drain.
6   Add the carrots and potatoes to the pan with the chicken and continue simmering for a further 5-10 minutes, until almost dry.
7   Add the milk, water and the seasoning ingredients. Bring to the boil and simmer, uncovered for 3-5 minutes, turning the chicken pieces occasionally.

NOTE

Use Chinese curry powder for this recipe – available from most Chinese supermarkets.

糟味鷄塊

Chicken with Red Fermented Sauce

INGREDIENTS (SERVES 4)

6 chicken wings
350 ml/12 fl oz water
4 tblspns corn oil
½ tblspn grated fresh root
  ginger
celery tops, to garnish

SEASONING
1 tblspn red bean sauce
1 tblspn rice wine or dry
  sherry
1 tblspn sugar

METHOD

1 Using a cleaver or meat axe, cut the chicken wings into large pieces.
2 Blend the seasoning ingredients in a bowl with 225 ml/8 fl oz water. Add the chicken and marinate for 30 minutes. Drain.
3 Heat the oil in a wok or frying pan, add the ginger and stir-fry over a high heat for 10 seconds.
4 Add the chicken, and stir-fry for 1 minute. Add remaining water. Lower the heat to medium-low, cover and simmer for 5 minutes, stirring occasionally. Garnish with celery tops, and serve.

豉汁鷄球

Steamed Chicken with Black Beans

INGREDIENTS (SERVES 4)

2 small chicken breasts,
  boned

SEASONING
1 tblspn fermented black
  beans (see NOTE)
2 tspns cornflour
1 tblspn water
½ tblspn chopped garlic
1 tspn sugar
1 tspn salt
1 tblspn sesame oil
1 tblspn rice wine or dry
  sherry

METHOD

1 Using a cleaver or meat axe, cut the chicken into large pieces.
2 Rinse the black beans, and crush them lightly with the back of a heavy knife.
3 Blend the cornflour with the water then stir in the remaining seasoning ingredients. Add the crushed beans and mix well. Add the chicken stirring thoroughly and marinate for 20 minutes.
4 Place the chicken on a heatproof plate, and set inside a steamer or large colander. Place 5 cm/2 inches boiling water in a large saucepan. Set the steamer over the saucepan, cover with a tight-fitting lid and steam for 5 minutes over a high heat. Serve.

NOTE
Fermented black beans, also called salted beans, are available from Chinese delicatessens. They are fermented with salt and spices in order to preserve them, and are very salty. They should be soaked or rinsed in cold water before using.

Simmered Spring Chickens

INGREDIENTS (SERVES 4)

2 spring chickens
2 tblspns soy sauce
225 g/8 oz spinach
5 tblspns sesame oil
1 slice fresh root ginger
2 spring onions, halved
½ tspn Szechuan
   peppercorns
1 tblspn sugar
¾ tspn salt
450 ml/¾ pint boiling water
3 tblspns corn oil

METHOD

1   Place the spring chickens in a large bowl, pour the soy sauce over the top and marinate for 30 minutes. Drain, reserving the soy sauce.
2   Wash and drain the spinach.
3   Heat the oil in a wok or frying pan and fry the spring chickens, browning them on all sides. Remove and place in a flameproof casserole.
4   Add the reserved soy sauce, ginger, spring onions, Szechuan peppercorns, sugar, ½ tspn salt and the boiling water to the spring chickens. Bring to the boil and simmer, covered, over a very low heat for 2 hours.
5   Heat the corn oil in a wok or frying pan and sprinkle in the remaining ¼ tspn salt. Add the spinach, and stir fry for 1-2 minutes. Remove from the pan and arrange around the spring chickens. Serve.

Chicken Stock

INGREDIENTS

600 g/1¼ lbs uncooked
   chicken bones, eg legs,
   wings, carcass etc.
   (see NOTE)
1.2 litres/2 pints water
6 slices fresh root ginger
4 spring onions, trimmed but
   left whole

METHOD

1   Place the chicken bones in a large pan, cover with
boiling water and boil for 5 minutes. Drain the water.
2   Add the water together with the ginger and spring
onions. Bring to the boil slowly and simmer over a low
heat for 1 hour.
3   Strain the stock through a fine sieve. Use straight
away or keep refrigerated for up to 3 days. The stock
can also be frozen for up to 6 months.

NOTE

Cooked chicken bones also make a fine stock. Follow
the above recipe from Step 2. Alternatively, use a
chicken stock cube for 450-600 ml/¾-1 pint of liquid.

Chopping Meat

Where large pieces of
chicken are required, cut into
12 mm × 2.5 cm/½ × 2 inch
strips.

Use a chopper or heavy knife
to cut chicken into small 6
mm/½ inch cubes.

For escalopes, beat the meat
firmly with the back of a meat
chopper or heavy rolling pin.

For ultra-quick stir-frying,
finely shred chicken into thin
strips.

To mince chicken coarsely,
cut into fine strips and then
roughly chop.

To mince chicken finely,
chop as for coarsely minced
chicken, but re-chop several
more times.

VEGETABLES AND SALADS

A large percentage of Chinese people are vegetarian – some through necessity, because meat and fish are scarce and thus expensive, some through choice, because of their religion. The Chinese vegetarian diet is in fact extremely healthy, since a huge range of vegetables are grown in China and protein is provided through the popular Chinese ingredient, bean curd.

The vegetables of China are the key to the exotic tastes and textures that make Chinese meals so unique and delicious. Root vegetables (like taros), fresh bamboo shoots, crisp water chestnuts and the huge variety of Chinese cabbages and greens are just some of the exciting vegetables used frequently in Chinese cooking. Mushrooms and fungi, which add not only a delicate flavour, but more important still, a distinct texture to a meal, are also extremely important in Chinese cooking, as are the various seaweeds, like black moss and laver, which add a slightly glutinous texture and a faint 'sea' flavour to a dish.

Flexibility is one of the marks of Chinese cookery and Chinese cooks will always use fresh ingredients to hand. Consequently, when a recipe calls for a fresh vegetable that is unavailable, the cook will not hesitate to replace the specified vegetable with another fresh ingredient, in order to retain the essential freshness of the dish. This attitude is helpful for the Western cook, since many common vegetables can be substituted for the rarer Chinese varieties. For instance, sweet potatoes can be used instead of taros, while spring greens can be used instead of Chinese broccoli. When it comes to cooking Chinese vegetables, a little ingenuity in the true Chinese tradition, will give you greater scope and much more variety.

Stuffed Cucumber

INGREDIENTS (SERVES 4)

6 Chinese mushrooms
1 large cucumber
1 tblspn cornflour
50-75 g/2-3 oz water
   chestnuts
1 small carrot
½ a salted cabbage root
1 bean curd
5 tblspns corn oil
1½ tspns sesame oil
1.2 litres/2 pints clear soup
   stock (see p. 261)

SEASONING A
⅔ tspn salt
½ tspn mustard powder
1 tblspn cornflour
1 egg white

SEASONING B
1 tspn salt
½ tspn white pepper

METHOD

1   Soak the Chinese mushrooms in boiling water for 20 minutes. Drain. Cut off and discard the stalks.
2   Cut off and discard the end parts of the cucumber. Peel and chop into 2.5-cm/1-inch round sections. Scoop out the seeds. Wash the cucumber rings and wipe dry on absorbent paper. Dust the inside with the cornflour.
3   Peel the water chestnuts and carrot. Remove outer pieces of cabbage root. Wash all these ingredients then chop them very finely, together with the Chinese mushrooms.
4   Blanch the bean curd in boiling water for 3 minutes. Mash it and drain off the water. Blend with the chopped ingredients, together with seasoning **A**. Mix everything together thoroughly.
5   Heat the oil in a wok and stir-fry the mixture for 2 minutes. Pack into the cucumber rings.
6   Tip the oil from the wok into a frying pan and fry the stuffed cucumber rings over a medium heat until lightly browned. Pour the soup stock over them and bring to the boil. Lower the heat and simmer very gently for 20 minutes. Add seasoning **B** and the sesame oil. Transfer to a serving dish and serve.

Stuffed Chinese Mushrooms

INGREDIENTS (SERVES 4)

16-20 large Chinese
   mushrooms
1 tblspn cornflour
1 bean curd
2 tblspns water chestnuts
1 small carrot
¼ a salted vegetable
4 tblspns corn oil
16-20 green beans

SEASONING A
½ tspn white pepper
½ tspn salt
1 tspn sugar
1 tblspn cornflour

SEASONING B
1½ tblspns light soy sauce
1 tspn sugar
3 tblspns clear soup stock
   (see p. 261)
⅓ tspn salt

METHOD

1   Soak the Chinese mushrooms in boiling water for 20 minutes. Drain. Cut off and discard the stalks, then coat the inner sides with the cornflour.
2   Wash the bean curd, water chestnuts, carrot and salted vegetable. Peel the water chestnuts and the carrot, then chop all the vegetables very finely and mix them together with seasoning **A**.
3   Heat the oil in a wok and stir-fry the chopped ingredients for 1½ minutes. Remove from the oil with a slotted spoon.
4   Divide the stuffing between the mushrooms pressing it into them firmly. Wash the beans and cook in boiling water for 2-3 minutes. Press one into the top of each stuffed mushroom.
5   Pour the oil from the wok into a large frying-pan. Put the mushrooms into the pan, stuffing side down in a single layer. Fry for a few minutes, then turn over carefully. Add seasoning **B**, bring to simmering point and simmer, covered, for 1 minute. Serve.

153

菇香莱粳

Broth of Mushrooms and Cabbage

INGREDIENTS (SERVES 4)

5-6 Chinese mushrooms
1 small cabbage
100 g/4 oz long-stem
  mushrooms
1 tblspn shredded preserved
  vegetable
4 tblspns corn oil
1 tblspn finely chopped
  spring onion
900 ml/1½ pints clear soup
  stock (see p. 261)
2 tblspns cornflour mixed
  with 2½ tblspns water

SEASONING

1⅓ tspns salt
1 tspn sugar
⅔ tspn white pepper

METHOD

1 Soak the Chinese mushrooms in boiling water for 20 minutes. Drain. Cut off and discard the stalks and shred the caps.
2 Cut off and discard the root and any withered leaves from the cabbage. Shred the remainder and wash. Cut off and discard the muddy roots from the long-stem mushrooms and wash clean. Wash the shredded preserved vegetables.
3 Heat the oil in a wok and stir-fry the Chinese mushrooms and the spring onion for 2 minutes. Add the shredded cabbage and the seasoning and stir for 1 minute. Add the stock, bring to the boil, lower the heat and simmer, covered until the cabbage is tender – about 10 minutes. Add the long-stem mushrooms and cook, stirring, for 1 minute more.
4 Stir in the cornflour mixture and cook until the mixture thickens. Sprinkle the shredded preserved vegetable over the surface of the broth. Serve.

Black Moss with Vegetables and Dried Bean Curd Knots

INGREDIENTS (SERVES 4)

1 tblspn black moss
1 carrot
4 tblspns corn oil
1 tblspn finely chopped
  spring onion
100 g/4 oz dried bean curd
  knots (see NOTES)
¼ tspn bicarbonate of soda
150 ml/¼ pint clear soup
  stock (see p. 261)
10 straw mushrooms
1 tblspn cornflour mixed with
  2 tblspns water

SEASONING

1 tspn salt
1 tspn sugar
½ tspn white pepper

METHOD

1 Soak the black moss in water for 10 minutes. Drain. Peel the carrot and dice.
2 Heat the oil in a wok and stir-fry the spring onion until beginning to brown. Add the bean curd knots, bicarbonate of soda and the soup stock and bring to the boil. Boil for 3 minutes.
3 Add the seasoning, straw mushrooms, drained black moss and diced carrot and cook for 2 minutes more. Stir in the cornflour mixture and cook until the sauce thickens. Serve at once.

NOTES

1 To make bean curd knots, soak bean curd sheets in cold water until soft. Pat dry in a clean cloth and cut into 10 × 2.5-cm/4 × 1-inch strips. Tie into knots and drop back into cold water for 5 minutes more, (see small picture 3, right).
2 Add 1 sliced, large white turnip to make the dish more substantial.

圍園春濃

Cream of Green Peas

INGREDIENTS (SERVES 4)

1 × 410g/14 oz can green
  peas, drained
1 tomato
8 button mushrooms
6 tblspns corn kernels
250 ml/8 fl oz clear soup
  stock (see p. 261)
250 ml/8 fl oz milk
2½ tblspns cornflour
1½ tblspns single cream
2-3 grains orange comfit

SEASONING

1½ tspns salt
⅓ tspn white pepper

METHOD

1 Purée the drained peas. Wash the tomato and
chop. Wash the button mushrooms and dice. Wash
the corn kernels.
2 Mix these ingredients with the drained green peas
and the soup stock in a saucepan. Bring to the boil
over a medium heat and simmer for a few minutes,
stirring. Stir in the milk and the seasoning.
3 Mix the cornflour with the cream and stir into the
pea mixture. Simmer for 3 minutes, stirring all the
time to keep the mixture thick and creamy.
4 Chop the orange comfit and sprinkle it over the
soup.

NOTE

Substitute 25 g/1 oz chopped almonds for the orange
comfit.

鳳 梨 盅

Pineapple Cup

INGREDIENTS (SERVES 4)

1 large fresh pineapple
100 g/4 oz gluten puff
75 g/3 oz baby corn shoots
50 g/2 oz water chestnuts
50 g/2 oz green beans
75 g/3 oz taro
1 tblspn corn oil
600 ml/1 pint clear soup
   stock (see p. 261)

SEASONING

1½ tspns salt
½ tblspn sugar
½ tspn white pepper

METHOD

1   Scrub the pineapple and cut off the top part to make a lid. Scoop out the pulp, taking care not to pierce through the skin. Place the pineapple container in a large pan of water and bring to the boil. Simmer for 3 minutes, then remove the pineapple and rinse it under cold water.

2   Soak the gluten puff in cold water for 20 minutes. Chop roughly.

3   Wash the baby corn shoots and chop in half. Peel the water chestnuts and wash them together with the green beans. Chop taro into pieces and stir-fry in the oil for 3-4 minutes.

4   Put the gluten puff, corn, water chestnuts, green beans, fried taro, soup stock and seasoning into the pineapple cup. Place in a dish and put this into a steamer. Steam over boiling water for 30 minutes. Serve at once.

157

鉄板豆腐

Fried Bean Curds with Onions

INGREDIENTS (SERVES 4)

3 cakes bean curds
1 onion
3 red chillis
4 garlic cloves, crushed
2 tblspns Hoisin sauce
4 tblspns corn oil
1 tblspn cornflour mixed with
   2 tblspns water
3 spring onions

SEASONING A
1½ tspns salt
1 tblspn soy sauce
½ tblspn sugar
3 tblspns clear soup stock
   (see p. 261)

SEASONING B
½ tblspn dry sherry
½ tblspn brown vinegar
1 tspn black pepper

METHOD

1   Put the bean curds into a saucepan and cover with water. Bring to the boil over a medium heat for 3-5 minutes. Then drain and cut into 2.5-cm/1-inch cubes.
2   Peel the onion and cut off the ends. Slice thinly. Wash the chillis and chop finely.
3   Blend seasoning **A** with the chopped chillis, crushed garlic and Hoisin sauce. Heat the oil in a wok and stir-fry this mixture for a few seconds, then add the bean curd cubes. Stir over a medium heat until they are well coated with the sauce, then lower the heat and simmer, covered for 5-10 minutes.
4   Remove the lid and add the sliced onion and seasoning **B**. Turn up the heat and cook, stirring, for 1½ minutes.
5   Stir in the cornflour mixture to thicken and serve sprinkled with the spring onion cut in diagonal slices.

NOTE
If you have an iron plate, heat it until it is very hot and serve this dish on it. The ingredients should 'hiss' as you spoon them onto the iron plate.

Congee of Green Beans

INGREDIENTS (SERVES 4)

100 g/4 oz green beans
3 tblspns millet
900 ml/1½ pints water

SEASONING
1 tspn salt
4 tblspns sugar

METHOD

1 Wash the green beans and millet. Drain well.
2 Bring the water to the boil and add the beans and millet. Lower the heat and simmer until the mixture has thickened – about 1 hour. Stir in the seasoning and serve at once.

NOTE
Green beans can be used to make a drink which is said to relieve hypertension. Wash a good handful and put into a thermos jug. Pour in boiling water, screw on the lid and leave for 15 minutes. Strain and drink the liquid.

Soup of Lily Petals with Lotus Seeds

INGREDIENTS (SERVES 4)

50 g/2 oz dried lily (or 75-100 g/3-4 oz fresh)
100-150 g/4-5 oz dried lotus seeds (or 275 g/10 oz fresh)
900 ml/1½ pints water
50 g/2 oz rock sugar powder

METHOD

1 Soak dried lily overnight, then wash under cold running water. (If using fresh, just wash.)
2 Soak dried lotus seeds in cold water for 4 hours, then wash under cold running water. (If using fresh, just wash.)
3 Pour the water into a saucepan. Add the drained lily and lotus seeds and the rock sugar powder. Bring to the boil, then lower the heat and simmer for 40 minutes. Serve at once.

NOTE
Lily and lotus seeds both make cooling tonics that provide particularly refreshing summer drinks.

撥魚麵湯

Soup of Dough Slices

INGREDIENTS (SERVES 4)

3 large Chinese mushrooms
150-225 g/5-8 oz wheat flour
½ tspn salt
1 egg
water (see recipe)
50 g/2 oz fungus
1 carrot
100 g/4 oz Chinese greens
900 ml/1½ pints clear soup
    stock (see p. 261)

METHOD

1 Soak the Chinese mushrooms in boiling water for 20 minutes. Drain. Cut off and discard the stalks and slice the caps.
2 Mix the wheat flour with the salt, then beat in the egg and sufficient water to make a very thick batter. Leave it to stand for 20 minutes, then beat again thoroughly.
3 Wash the fungus and slice it. Peel and slice the carrot and wash and shred the Chinese greens, using only the green parts.
4 Put all the vegetables in a large pan with the soup stock. Bring to the boil, then add spoonfuls of the batter, keeping the soup boiling all the time. When you have added all the batter to the pan, simmer for 5 minutes more then serve.

NOTE
For those who include fish in their diet, a few cooked, peeled prawns can be added to the soup

玉米湯

Cream of Corn Soup

INGREDIENTS (SERVES 4)

900 ml/1½ pints clear soup
    stock (see p.261)
50 g/2 oz plain flour
450 g/1 lb corn kernels
1 carrot
4 tblspns green peas
1½ tspns salt
2 tblspns sugar
1 tspn black pepper
2 tblspns single cream
1 slice bread, toasted

METHOD

1 Put about a third of the soup stock into a saucepan and stir in the flour, keeping the mixture smooth.
2 Liquidize the corn kernels with the rest of the soup stock and gradually stir this into the mixture in the pan, keeping it smooth and free from lumps.
3 Peel the carrot and chop into cubes. Add to the soup with the peas, salt and sugar and simmer for 5 minutes. Just before serving, stir in the pepper and cream and sprinkle the toast, cut into cubes, over the surface.

鳳尾生雲

Clear Soup of Bamboo Shoots

INGREDIENTS (SERVES 4)

150 g/5 oz pickled bamboo
  shoots
900 ml/1½ pints clear soup
  stock (see p. 261)

SEASONING
1½ tspns salt
½ tspn white pepper

METHOD

1 Wash the pickled bamboo shoots and chop off the ends. Tear the remainder of the shoots into long shreds.
2 Bring the soup stock to the boil, add the bamboo shoots and seasoning, bring back to the boil and simmer for 3 minutes.

NOTE
Use tender bamboo shoots for this dish. It is a particularly refreshing soup for a summer evening. The torn shreds of bamboo shoots resemble birds' tails, which is how it gets its more romantic name of Cloudbuilt Phoenix Tails.

菇香呈祥

Golden Mushrooms in Ginger Juice

INGREDIENTS (SERVES 4)

450 g/1 lb button mushrooms
salt
125 ml/4 fl oz plus 2 extra
  tblspns corn oil
2 tblspns soy sauce
½ tblspn ginger juice
½ tblspn cornflour mixed
  with 1 tblspn water

SEASONING
⅔ tspn salt
1 tblspn sugar
⅓ tspn white pepper

METHOD

1 Wash the button mushrooms in water mixed with a little salt. Dry on absorbent paper and make slanting cuts round the caps.
2 Heat the 125 ml/4 fl oz of oil in a wok and stir-fry the mushrooms until they have turned golden. Remove with a slotted spoon and soak in the soy sauce for 20 minutes.
3 Heat the remaining 2 tblspns oil in a clean pan and stir-fry the ginger juice for ½ minute. Add the mushrooms and the seasoning and stir-fry for a few minutes. Add the cornflour paste, let the sauce thicken and serve.

Vegetarian Shark's Fins

INGREDIENTS (SERVES 4)

25 g/1 oz fungus
1 bundle transparent
   vermicelli
4 Chinese mushrooms
2 green-stemmed flat
   cabbages
2 tblspns shredded bamboo
   shoot
2 tblspns shredded carrot
4 tblspns corn oil
2 tblspns water
900 ml/1½ pints clear soup
   stock (see p. 261)

SEASONING A

1½ tspns salt
1 tblspn light soy sauce
½ tspn white pepper

SEASONING B

1 tblspn cornflour mixed with
   2 tblspns water and 1 tspn
   sesame oil

METHOD

1 Soak the fungus in cold water for 1 hour.
2 Soak the vermicelli in boiling water for 20
minutes. Drain and cut into even sections using
scissors.
3 Soak the Chinese mushrooms in boiling water for
20 minutes. Drain, cut off and discard the stalks and
shred the caps.
4 Cut away the root and withered outer leaves from
the cabbages. Wash the leaves and chop into shreds.
5 Drain the fungus, then remove the stalk and chop
the remainder into shreds.
6 Heat the oil in a wok and stir-fry all the prepared
ingredients together with the 2 tblspns water. Add
seasoning **A** and stir-fry for 2 minutes more.
7 Pour in the stock and bring to the boil. Stir in
seasoning **B** and cook, stirring until the mixture
thickens slightly. Serve at once.

NOTE

1 The cooked transparent vermicelli resembles
shark's fins, which is why the recipe has its name.
2 You can substitute 225 g/8 oz bean sprouts (see
small picture 3, right) for the fungus.

Long-Stem Mushrooms with Sesame Oil

INGREDIENTS (SERVES 4)

450 g/1 lb long-stem
   mushrooms
salt
⅓ tblspn black sesame seeds
3 tblspns corn oil
1 tblspn ginger juice or 1½
   tblspns ginger wine

SEASONING A

1 tspn salt
½ tblspn sesame oil

SEASONING B

½ tblspn cornflour mixed
   with 3 tblspns water

METHOD

1 Pick out any hard stems from the mushrooms (if
using fresh ones), then chop off the root ends. Wash
the mushrooms with water mixed with a little salt,
then drain and wash again under cold running water.
Drain well.
2 Pick out and discard any impurities in the black
sesame seeds. Stir-fry the remainder with 1 tblspn oil
over a gentle heat for 2 minutes. Tip onto a plate and
rinse out the pan.
3 Put the oil and ginger juice or wine into the pan.
Add the mushrooms and stir-fry for a minute or so.
Add seasoning **A** and stir-fry for 2 minutes more.
4 Stir in seasoning **B**, and when the mixture has
thickened, remove from the heat. Sprinkle with the
black sesame seeds and serve.

洋葱濃湯
Onion Soup

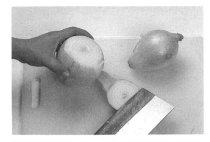

INGREDIENTS (SERVES 4)

2 small onions
1 slice bread
4 tblspns corn oil
600 ml/1 pint water

SEASONING
1½ tspns salt
½ tblspn sugar
½ tspn black pepper

METHOD

1 Peel the onions and cut off ends. Shred the remainder finely.
2 Toast the bread lightly and cut into cubes.
3 Heat the oil in a pan and stir-fry the onions until well browned. Add the water and bring to the boil. Lower the heat and simmer for 30 minutes. Add the seasoning and serve with the croûtons sprinkled on the surface.

NOTE
If you want a creamy soup, use cream instead of oil to stir-fry the onions.

茄汁豆酥
Beans with Tomato Sauce

INGREDIENTS (SERVES 4)

275 g/10 oz peeled broad
   beans
100 g/4 oz wheat flour
⅓ tspn salt
⅓ tspn white pepper
1 egg white
4 tblspns corn oil
50 ml/2 fl oz water
1 pan of corn oil for deep
   frying
½ tblspn crushed garlic
3 tblspns tomato sauce or
   ketchup
4 tblspns water

SEASONING
2 tblspns sugar
1 tblspn vinegar
1 tspn salt

METHOD

1 Wash the beans and drain. Steam for 5 minutes.
2 Make a smooth batter with the wheat flour, salt, pepper, egg white, 1 tblspn oil and water. Add the beans to this and mix to coat them thoroughly.
3 Heat the oil for deep frying and drop in spoonfuls of the bean mixture, frying them until they are golden brown. Remove and drain on absorbent paper. Keep warm.
4 Heat the remaining 3 tblspns oil in a wok and stir-fry the garlic for 1 minute. Add the tomato sauce, water and seasoning and bring to the boil. Add the fried beans to this sauce, stirring to coat them evenly. Serve at once.

169

素酸辣湯

Hot and Sour Soup

INGREDIENTS (SERVES 4)

4 Chinese mushrooms
1 tblspn dried black moss
3-4 red chillis
100 g/4 oz long-stem
   mushrooms
2 cakes of square bean curds
1 carrot
50 g/2 oz sour cabbage
6 tblspns corn oil
900 ml/1½ pints clear soup
   stock (see p. 261)
2 tblspns cornflour mixed
   with 4 tblspns water
1 egg, beaten

SEASONING A

2 tblspns dark soy sauce
1½ tspns salt
½ tspn white pepper

SEASONING B

4 tblspns brown vinegar
1 tblspn white vinegar
2 tspns sesame oil
1 tblspn chopped parsley

METHOD

1   Soak the Chinese mushrooms in boiling water for 20 minutes. Drain. Cut off and discard the stalks and shred the caps.
2   Soak the black moss for 20 minutes. Drain.
3   Wash the chillis and shred finely. Cut off and discard the roots from the long-stem mushrooms and wash.
4   Shred the bean curds. Peel the carrot and shred finely. Wash the sour cabbage and shred finely.
5   Heat the oil in a wok and stir-fry the Chinese mushrooms for 1 minute. Add all the other shredded ingredients and the long-stem mushrooms. Stir well, then add the soup stock and seasoning **A**. Bring to the boil and simmer for 2 minutes.
6   Stir in the cornflour mixture and bring to the boil, again, stirring until the soup thickens. Turn off the heat and leave for 1 minute, then stir in the beaten egg. Pour into a soup bowl and stir in seasoning **B**. Serve at once.

NOTE

If you cannot get long-stem mushrooms, use bean sprouts instead.

麻醬豆腐

Bean Curds with Sesame Sauce

INGREDIENTS (SERVES 4)

4 cakes of square bean curds
900 ml/1½ pints water
1 tblspn finely chopped
   spring onion

SEASONING

1½ tblspns sesame sauce
1 tblspn sesame oil
1½ tblspns soy sauce
½ tspn salt
4 tblspns cold boiled water
1 tspn sugar

METHOD

1   Put the bean curds into a large saucepan with the water and bring to the boil for 1 minute. Drain and place in a deep plate.
2   Blend the seasoning together and pour it over the bean curds. Sprinkle with the spring onion and serve.

NOTE

For a different taste, add a small bunch of cedar shoots (see small picture 1 right) to the ingredients in this recipe. Rinse them in cold water, then drop into a pan of boiling water for 2 minutes and serve separately.

牡丹富貴

Stewed Cabbage with Mixed Vegetables

INGREDIENTS (SERVES 4)

2-3 Chinese mushrooms
50 g/2 oz bamboo shoot
1 medium Chinese cabbage
900 ml/1½ pints clear
  soup stock (see p. 261)
1½ tblspns carrot (diced)
1½ tblspns corn kernels
1½ tblspns green beans
1½ tblspns preserved
  vegetable

SEASONING
1½ tspns salt
½ tspn white pepper

METHOD

1   Soak the Chinese mushrooms in boiling water for 20 minutes. Drain. Cut off and discard the stalks. Shred the bamboo shoot and soak in cold water.
2   Cut off and discard any old or withered leaves and the root part from the cabbage. Wash the leaves and shred them.
3   Put the soup stock into a large saucepan with the cabbage. Sprinkle all the other vegetables on top. Add the seasoning, bring to boiling point over a medium heat, then lower the heat and simmer very gently for 30 minutes. Serve at once.

NOTE
If you like you could sprinkle 2 finely chopped spring onions over the soup just before serving.

韭花銀芽

Chive Flowers with Bean Sprouts

INGREDIENTS (SERVES 4)

50 g/2 oz chives with flowers
350 g/12 oz bean sprouts
4 tblspns corn oil

SEASONING
⅔ tspn salt
1 tblspn light soy sauce
½ tspn white pepper

METHOD

1 Wash the chives. Discard any old or withered stems and chop the remainder into 2.5-cm/1-inch pieces.
2 Chop off the ends of the bean sprouts. Wash the remainder clean and dry in a clean cloth.
3 Heat the oil in a wok and stir-fry the chives and bean sprouts with the seasoning over a high heat for 1 minute. Serve at once.

NOTES
1 This is a fresh attractive-looking dish which is also very nutritious.
2 Although the chives shown here are rather broader-stemmed than those commonly grown in the U.K., ordinary chives would be perfectly suitable for this recipe and the one below. Pick them just as the flower buds have appeared.

炸韭菜结

Fried Chive Knots

INGREDIENTS (SERVES 4)

100 g/4 oz wheat flour
⅓ tspn salt
2 tblspns potato starch
2 eggs, beaten
approx 175 ml/6 fl oz water
225 g/8 oz chives (without flowers)
1 pan of corn oil for deep frying

SEASONING
3 tblspns dark soy sauce
½ tblspn chilli sauce
½ tblspn sugar
1 tspn garlic powder

METHOD

1 Mix together the wheat flour, salt and potato starch in a large bowl. Make a well in the centre and tip in the beaten eggs. Stir, adding the water gradually, to incorporate the flour, keeping the mixture smooth. Add sufficient water to make a batter the consistency of thick cream.
2 Discard any old or withered leaves from the chives and wash the remainder. Scald a handful of chives in boiling water to soften them.
3 Divide the remainder of the chives into bundles of 3. Fold these into 7.5-cm/3-inch long sections and bind them together with the softened chives.
4 Coat the bundles of chives in the batter, making sure they are evenly covered. Fry a few at a time in the hot oil until golden brown. Drain on absorbent paper while you cook the remainder.
5 Cut the knots into diagonal slices and serve with the seasoning mixed together in a small bowl.

盛世太平火鍋

Dish of the Flourishing

INGREDIENTS (SERVES 4)

8 Chinese mushrooms
2 bundles vermicelli
½ a salted or preserved
  vegetable
350 g/12 oz spinach
1 bamboo shoot
4 tblspns corn oil
2 tblspns finely chopped
  shallot
1 tblspn light soy sauce
1.5 litres/2½ pints clear soup
  stock (see p.261)
10 pieces triangular shaped
  fried bean curds
100 g/4 oz dried bean curds
100 g/4 oz fungus slices

SEASONING
2 tspns salt
1 tspn white pepper

METHOD

1 Soak the Chinese mushrooms in boiling water for 20 minutes. Drain. Cut off and discard the stalks. Soak the vermicelli in cold water for 20 minutes. Drain and cut into 2.5-cm/1-inch sections.
2 Wash the salted or preserved vegetable. Discard outer skin, then cut into thin slices.
3 Discard any old or withered leaves from the spinach. Scrape off the dirt and rootlets from the spinach root, but do not chop off the root itself. Wash the spinach well and chop.
4 Wash the bamboo shoot and cut into slices.
5 Heat the oil in a wok and stir-fry the shallot until browned. Add the soy sauce, soup stock, fried bean curds, dried bean curd, the fungus, bamboo shoot and salted vegetable slices, the Chinese mushrooms and half of the seasoning. Bring to the boil.
6 Add the vermicelli and spinach with the rest of the seasoning and boil for 2 minutes more. Transfer to an earthenware pot and serve.

NOTE
This dish is so-called because very good weather conditions are necessary to produce all the vegetables at the same time.

興子旺孫暖鍋

Pot of Prosperity

INGREDIENTS (SERVES 4)

175 g/6 oz Chinese
  mushrooms
3 corn-on-the-cobs
175 g/6 oz green beans
50 g/2 oz mange tout
225 g/8 oz straw mushrooms
175 g/6 oz button mushrooms
175 g/6 oz abalone
  mushrooms
175 g/6 oz long-stem
  mushrooms
1 large onion
4-6 tblspns corn oil
75 g/3 oz plain flour
1.5 litres/2½ pints clear
  soup stock (see p.261)

SEASONING
2 tspns salt
½ tspn white pepper
1 tblspn sugar
½ tspn finely chopped fresh
  root ginger

METHOD

1 Soak the Chinese mushrooms in boiling water for 20 minutes. Drain. Cut off and discard stalks.
2 Cut off and discard the outer leaves and feathery parts of the corns. Wash the cobs and chop into 2.5-cm/1-inch sections.
3 Wash the beans and mange tout. Rub off the membranes from the beans, and top and tail the mange tout.
4 Wash all the mushrooms, then cut off and discard the stalks. Finely chop the onion.
5 Heat the oil in a wok and stir-fry the onion until lightly browned. Mix together the flour and soup, adding the liquid gradually to the flour to keep it smooth. Pour this into the pan with the onion and bring to the boil over medium heat, stirring all the time. Add the seasoning.
6 Add all the vegetable ingredients and boil for 2 minutes more. Transfer to an earthenware pot and serve.

NOTES
1 Substitute 100 g/4 oz shredded bamboo shoots for the long-stem mushrooms.
2 Substitute 100 g/4 oz fresh dark-gilled mushrooms for the abalone mushrooms.

紅乳燴豆腐

Bean Curds in Red Fermented Sauce

INGREDIENTS (SERVES 4)

2 bean curds
1 tspn salt
5 tblspns corn oil
1 red fermented bean curd
½ tblspn red juice from the
   fermented bean curd
1½ tblspns sugar

SEASONING

50-75 ml/2-3 fl oz water
½ tspn white pepper
2 tspns sesame oil

METHOD

1 Blanch bean curds in boiling water with the salt for 3 minutes. Drain and chop into dice.
2 Heat the oil in a wok. Mix the fermented bean curd with the red juice and the sugar, add to the wok and stir-fry over a medium heat, mashing the bean curd as you stir. Add the diced bean curds and the seasoning and stir everything together. Put the lid on the wok, and simmer until most of the liquid has been absorbed. Stir occasionally.

NOTE

If you prefer, you can use cheese instead of the fermented bean curd. Any type of fermented bean curd can be used in this recipe; it does not have to be the red variety.

醬爆青菽

Stir-fried Green Peppers with Bean Sauce

INGREDIENTS (SERVES 4)

4 green peppers
4 tblspns corn oil
1 tblspn cornflour mixed with
   2 tblspns water

SEASONING A
½ tblspn finely chopped
   spring onion
½ tblspn crushed garlic

SEASONING B
2 tblspns hot bean sauce
1 tspn finely chopped red
   chilli
½ tblspn sugar
1 tblspn dark soy sauce
5 tblspns clear soup stock
   (see p. 261)

METHOD

1 Wash the green peppers. Discard the stalk and seeds, then chop into 2.5-cm/1-inch sections.
2 Heat the oil in a wok and stir-fry seasoning **A** until lightly coloured. Add seasoning **B** and stir-fry for 1-2 minutes.
3 Add the green peppers to the wok and stir-fry over a high heat for 1 minute. Pour in the cornflour mixture and stir until the sauce thickens. Serve at once.

NOTE

Add other vegetables such as shredded fungus, bamboo shoots and spiced bean curds to add variety, but do not use too many ingredients or you will spoil the clear taste of the dish.

金鈎掛玉牌

Golden Hooks with Jade Plates

INGREDIENTS (SERVES 4)

225 g/8 oz yellow bean
   sprouts
2 cakes bean curd
2.5 × 4-cm/1 × 1½-in slice
   fresh root ginger, peeled
600 ml/1-pint clear soup
   stock (see p. 261)

SEASONING
1½ tspns salt
½ tspn white pepper

METHOD

1 Cut off and discard the end parts of the bean
sprouts. Wash the remainder and the bean curd.
2 Crush the ginger slightly with the edge of the
chopper; this makes it easier to peel and also releases
the juices.
3 Put all the ingredients except for the seasoning
into a pan and bring to the boil over medium heat.
Lower the heat and simmer for 30 minutes. Remove
the ginger, add the seasoning and serve.

NOTES
1 This is a delicately flavoured dish that is
particularly refreshing in the summer.
2 The recipe is so-called because yellow bean
sprouts look like golden hooks and the bean curds like
jade plates – to the imaginative!

豉汁蒸白蒋

Steamed Water Chestnuts with Black Bean Sauce

INGREDIENTS (SERVES 4)

250 g/12 oz water chestnuts
150 ml/5 fl oz corn oil
2 tblspns black fermented
   beans
½ tblspn crushed garlic
3 tblspns green beans

SEASONING
½ tspn salt
½ tspn sugar
1 tspn white pepper

METHOD

1 Peel the water chestnuts and wash them. Fry in
hot oil for 2 minutes. Remove with a slotted spoon
and drain off the oil, reserving 1 tblspn in the pan.
2 Stir-fry the fermented beans and garlic until the
garlic has browned. Wash the green beans and add
them to the pan, stir-frying them for 1 minute.
3 Mix the stir-fried ingredients with the water
chestnuts in a bowl. Place this in a steamer and
steam over boiling water for 15-20 minutes. Add the
seasoning and serve.

NOTE
Fermented beans have a salty taste, whilst water
chestnuts are quite sweet. Season this dish carefully,
therefore, tasting it to make sure it is to your liking.

苦 海 慈 航

Stuffed Bitter Gourds

INGREDIENTS (SERVES 4)

6 Chinese mushrooms
1 bitter gourd
1 tblspn cornflour
3 tblspns green beans
100 g/4 oz water chestnuts
8 pieces spiced bean curds
6 tblspns corn oil

SEASONING A

½ tspn salt
1 tblspn cornflour
½ tblspn sesame oil
⅓ tspn five-spice powder
½ tspn sugar

SEASONING B

1½ tblspns light soy sauce
3 tblspns clear soup stock
　(see p. 261)
½ tblspn crushed garlic
1 tblspn black fermented
　beans
1 tblspn sugar
½ tspn salt

METHOD

1　Soak the Chinese mushrooms in boiling water for 20 minutes. Drain. Cut off and discard the stalks.
2　Cut off and discard the stalk and top part from the bitter gourd, then chop it into sections. Scoop out the seeds and put the rings into a large pan of water. Bring to the boil and boil for 2 minutes. Drain and spread cornflour round the insides. Put on a plate.
3　Wash the green beans and cook them for 5 minutes in boiling water. Drain and cover with cold water.
4　Peel the water chestnuts and chop them finely with the spiced bean curds and the Chinese mushrooms caps. Mix in seasoning **A**.
5　Heat 4 tblspns oil in a wok and stir-fry the chopped ingredients for 1½ minutes. Remove from the wok with a slotted spoon and press into the bitter gourd rings. Put the plate into a steamer and steam over boiling water for 25 minutes.
6　Heat the remaining 2 tblspns oil in a wok. Drain the green beans and stir-fry with seasoning **B** for 30 seconds. Spoon over the bitter gourds and serve.

NOTE

If you like, you could put the steamed bitter gourd into hot clear soup stock and serve this as a soup dish.

清炒節瓜

Stir-Fried Fuzzy Melons

INGREDIENTS (SERVES 4)

2 large or 4 small fuzzy
    melons
5 tblspns corn oil
1 tblspn ginger juice
1 tblspn water
1 tspn salt
green stems of 2 spring
    onions
2 tspns sherry

METHOD

1   Peel the fuzzy melons and chop into slices.
2   Heat 4 tblspns oil in a wok and add the ginger
juice. Fry for 1 minute, then add the melon slices. Stir
for 1 minute more, then add the water and salt and
simmer over a medium heat, covered, for 3 minutes.
Stir from time to time. Transfer to a serving dish.
3   Chop the spring onion stems and stir-fry them
briefly in the remaining 1 tblspn oil. Sprinkle over the
fuzzy melons, add the sherry and serve.

NOTE
Ginger juice is a flavouring agent and also a
tenderizer. It is made from fresh ginger. If you cannot
buy it, grate some fresh ginger and press it through a
sieve to extract the juice.

小 家 碧 玉

Stir-Fried Angled Luffa

INGREDIENTS (SERVES 4)

2 angled luffas
4 tblspns corn oil
1 tblspn cornflour mixed with
    2 tblspns water
1½ tspns sesame oil

SEASONING A
½ tblspn finely chopped
    spring onions
½ tspn crushed garlic

SEASONING B
1 tspn salt
2 tblspns water

METHOD

1   Peel the angled luffas. Wash them and chop into
triangular pieces.
2   Heat the oil in a wok and stir-fry seasoning **A** until
lightly coloured. Add the luffa together with
seasoning **B**, stir, then simmer for 1½ minutes,
stirring from time to time.
3   Add the cornflour paste, stirring until the mixture
thickens. Just before serving, stir in the sesame oil.

NOTE
To make this dish more filling, you can add 1 piece of
dried bean curd sheet and 50g/2 oz fungus as shown
in the top small picture (right). Soak both these
ingredients for 1 hour in cold water, then shred and
stir-fry them for 3-4 minutes before adding the angled
luffa.

185

蠔油莱心燴鮑魚菇

Abalone Mushrooms and Green Vegetables in Oyster Sauce

INGREDIENTS (SERVES 4)

3-4 green-stemmed flat
　cabbages
275 g/10 oz abalone
　mushrooms
4 tblspns corn oil
125 ml/4 fl oz clear soup
　stock (see p. 261)
1 tblspn cornflour mixed with
　1½ tblspns water
½ tspn sesame oil

SEASONING

1 tspn salt
1 tblspn oyster sauce
1½ tblspns sugar

METHOD

1　Cut off and discard the root and any withered leaves from the cabbages. Wash them and cut in half.
2　Cut off and discard the stalks from the mushrooms. Wash and slice into large pieces.
3　Blanch the cabbage and mushrooms separately in boiling, salted water for 1 minute. Drain and plunge into cold water. Leave to cool, then drain again.
4　Heat the oil in a wok and stir-fry the cabbage and mushrooms. Add the seasoning, then the soup stock. Bring to the boil.
5　Stir in the cornflour mixture to thicken the sauce. Just before serving, stir in the sesame oil.

NOTES

1　Plunging the cabbage and mushrooms into cold water after blanching helps to preserve their colour.
2　Substitute 225 g/8 oz straw mushrooms for the abalone mushrooms.

三鮮豆苗

Stir-fried Spinach with Fresh Vegetables

INGREDIENTS (SERVES 4)

450 g/1 lb spinach
6 straw mushrooms
1 carrot
1 bamboo shoot
5 tblspns corn oil
1 tspn cornflour mixed with 2
   tspns water

SEASONING
1 tspn salt
½ tspn white pepper

METHOD

1 Discard the stalks and any old leaves from the spinach. Wash it well and shake off the water.
2 Wash the straw mushrooms and chop in half. Peel the carrot; slice it and the bamboo shoot.
3 Heat the oil in a wok and stir-fry the mushrooms, carrot and bamboo shoot for 3 minutes. Add the spinach and seasoning and stir-fry for 30 seconds more. Stir in the cornflour mixture to thicken the dish and serve at once.

NOTE
The spinach most usually used in this dish is also called pea shoots. It can be stir-fried on its own as a nourishing vegetable. If you cannot get pea shoots, use ordinary spinach.

佛手飄香

Chayotoes with Red Chilli Peppers

INGREDIENTS (SERVES 4)

2 small chayotoes
3-4 red chillis
4 tblspns corn oil
4 tblspns water
1 tspn sherry

SEASONING
1 tspn salt
½ tspn white pepper

METHOD

1 Peel the chayotoes, then carefully cut away the white tissues. Cut in half and remove the seeds. Wash and slice.
2 Wash the red chillis and chop into fine slices.
3 Heat the oil in a wok and stir-fry the chillis until beginning to brown. Add the chayoto slices with the seasoning. Stir and add the water. Simmer, covered, for 1½ minutes.
4 Stir the ingredients, add the sherry and serve.

NOTE
If chayoto is unavailable, substitute 4-5 small courgettes.

栗子燒香菇

Braised Chestnuts with Chinese Mushrooms

INGREDIENTS (SERVES 4)

150 g/5 oz dried chestnuts
50 g/2 oz Chinese
   mushrooms
2 tspns sesame oil

SEASONING
3 tblspns dark soy sauce
1 tblspn rock sugar
⅓ tspn salt
7-8 slices liquorice

METHOD

1   Soak the dried chestnuts in cold water for at least 4 hours – the longer they are soaked, the quicker they cook and the more flavour they have. Drain and remove the red membrane. Wash them under cold running water.
2   Soak the Chinese mushrooms in boiling water for 20 minutes. Drain, reserving the soaking liquid. Cut off and discard the stalks.
3   Put about 300 ml/½ pint of the water used to soak the Chinese mushrooms in a saucepan and add the chestnuts, mushrooms and seasoning. Bring to the boil, then lower the heat and simmer for about 30 minutes until nearly all the liquid has been absorbed and the chestnuts are tender. Check the pan during cooking and add more water if necessary. Serve at once.

NOTE
Substitute peppermint leaves for liquorice.

釀茄夾

Stuffed Aubergine Folders

INGREDIENTS (SERVES 4)

½ tblspn black moss
2 cakes bean curds
4 long aubergines
100 g/4 oz wheat flour
½ tspn salt
2 eggs
1 tblspn corn oil
water (see recipe)
1 pan of corn oil for deep
   frying

SEASONING A
½ tspn salt
½ tspn white pepper
1 egg white

SEASONING B
3 tblspns oyster sauce
1½ tblspns water
½ tspn salt
1 tblspn finely chopped
   spring onion
½ tblspn crushed garlic
2 tblspns corn oil

METHOD

1   Soak the black moss in cold water for 20 minutes.
2   Blanch the bean curds in boiling water for 3 minutes. Drain, cut off the hard edge and mash the remainder. Squeeze out any excess water.
3   Drain the black moss and mix with the mashed bean curd and seasoning **A**.
4   Wash the aubergines and discard the stem and top part. Chop into 15-mm/½-inch slices, then cut almost through these to make the 'folders'. Press about ½ tblspn of the bean curd mixture into each of these.
5   Mix the flour with the salt in a bowl. Make a well in the centre and tip in the eggs beaten with the tblspn corn oil. Gradually stir the flour into the eggs, adding sufficient water to make a smooth batter, the consistency of thick cream. Leave to stand for 10 minutes.
6   Mix together all the ingredients from seasoning **B** except for the oil. Heat the oil in a wok and stir-fry the ingredients for 2-3 minutes. Serve this as a sauce.
7   Dip the aubergine folders into the batter to coat them and fry them in the pan of deep oil for about 4 minutes each, until puffed up and golden. Drain on absorbent paper and serve with the sauce.

Stir-Fried Mixed Vegetables

INGREDIENTS (SERVES 4)

5 bean curd sheets
450 g/1 lb watercress
4 triangular-shaped fried
    bean curds
3-4 small red chillis (optional)
4 tblspns corn oil
½ tblspn finely chopped
    spring onion
3 tblspns clear soup stock
    (see p. 261)
1½ tblspns cornflour mixed
    with 2 tblspns water

SEASONING
1 tspn salt
½ tspn sugar

METHOD

1 Soak the bean curd sheets in cold water for about 20 minutes to soften them. Drain.
2 Discard all old or withered leaves from the watercress keeping only the tender, fresh leaves. Wash them thoroughly and drain. Chop into 2.5-cm/1-inch sections.
3 Slice the fried bean curds and chop the bean curd sheets into big pieces. Chop the chillis, if using.
4 Heat the oil in a wok and stir-fry the shallots and chillis for 3-4 minutes. Add the watercress, fried bean curds, bean curd sheets, soup stock and seasoning. Cook, stirring for 3 minutes, then add the cornflour mixture and stir until the sauce has thickened. Serve at once.

NOTE
Old leaves and stalks from the watercress can be used to make soup. It is a very nutritious vegetable, said to be good for the lungs.

Broad Beans with Mustard Sauce

INGREDIENTS (SERVES 4)

275 g/10 oz shelled broad
    beans
2 tblspns finely chopped
    spring onion

SEASONING
½ tspn salt
2 tblspns English mustard
½ tblspn sesame oil

METHOD

1 Wash the broad beans but do not peel off the skins. Cook for 5-8 minutes in simmering water until tender. Drain.
2 Mix the chopped spring onion with the seasoning and stir into the broad beans. Serve at once.

NOTE
The beans should be quite well cooked for this dish, but not so over-cooked that they turn mushy when you mix them with the other ingredients.

千　里　飄　香

Steamed Spiced Bean Curd with Green Beans

INGREDIENTS (SERVES 4)

4 cakes bean curd
50 g/2 oz green beans or
    salted vegetable
1 tblspn sesame oil

SEASONING

1½ tblspns light soy sauce
½ tspn salt
1 tspn sugar
½ tspn chilli powder

METHOD

1　Wash the bean curd and drain well. Dice.
2　Rub away the outer skin from the beans and blend them with the seasoning.
3　Put the diced bean curd on a plate and spoon the green beans on top. Steam over simmering water for 5-7 minutes. Stir in the sesame oil just before serving.

NOTE

If you use salted vegetable instead of green beans, it should be washed thoroughly and then chopped. Stir-fry the vegetable for 3 minutes before mixing with the seasoning.

木　耳　順　風

Stir-Fried Fungus with Lettuce and Pineapple

INGREDIENTS (SERVES 4)

225 g/8 oz fungus
1 head lettuce
50 g/2 oz pineapple slices,
    drained if canned
4 tblspns corn oil
1 tblspn cornflour mixed with
    2 tblspns water

SEASONING

1 tspn salt
½ tblspn sugar

METHOD

1　Chop off and discard the fungus roots. Wash the fungus, then soak in cold water for 1 hour until softened. Chop into pieces.
2　Peel the head lettuce, wash it and chop into slices.
3　Heat the oil in a wok and stir-fry all the ingredients, except the cornflour. Add the seasoning. Stir in the cornflour mixture and cook, stirring, until the mixture has thickened slightly. Remove and serve at once.

NOTES

1　This is a delicious tasting sweet and sour dish.
2　Substitute 100 g/4 oz straw mushrooms for the fungus, and 3 celery stalks for the head lettuce.

燒素肉餅

Mixed Vegetable Patties

INGREDIENTS (SERVES 4)

4 tblspns fungus
2-3 tblspns dried lily
4 tblspns shredded preserved
   vegetable
1 small onion
100 g/4 oz water chestnuts
1 bean curd
1 tblspn finely chopped
   spring onion
11 tblspns corn oil

SEASONING A

4 tblspns cornflour
½ tspn salt
½ tspn white pepper

SEASONING B

1½ tblspns light soy sauce
3 tblspns clear soup stock
   (see p.261)
½ tblspn sugar

METHOD

1   Soak the fungus in cold water for 1 hour until softened. Shred finely. Soak the dried lily in cold water for 30 minutes. Chop roughly. Wash the preserved vegetable.

2   Peel the onion and chop off the ends. Finely chop the remainder. Peel the water chestnuts and chop finely.

3   Blanch the bean curd in boiling water for 3 minutes. Drain well and mash with seasoning **A** and all the other ingredients except for the spring onion and the corn oil.

4   Heat 4 tblspns oil in a wok and stir-fry the mixture for 2 minutes. Remove and leave to go cold. Form into round cakes about 4 cm/1½ inches in diameter and 8 mm/¼ inch thick.

5   Heat 6 tblspns oil in a frying pan and fry the patties until golden brown on both sides. Arrange on a plate and sprinkle with the chopped spring onion.

6   Heat the remaining tblspn oil in a clean pan and add seasoning **B**. Bring to the boil, pour over the patties and serve.

煎茄絲餅

Aubergine Patties

INGREDIENTS (SERVES 4)

3 long aubergines
5 tblspns cornflour
75 ml/3 fl oz corn oil

SEASONING A

⅓ tspn white pepper
½ tspn chilli powder
½ tspn salt
½ tblspn finely chopped
   spring onion

SEASONING B

1 tblspn brown vinegar
1 tblspn light soy sauce
1 tblspn clear soup stock
   (see p.261)
1 tblspn crushed garlic
½ tblspn sesame oil

METHOD

1   Peel the aubergine and chop roughly. Soak in cold water for 15 minutes, then drain and steam for 7-8 minutes. Drain off any liquid and blend the aubergines with seasoning **A**. Leave to cool.

2   Stir the cornflour into the cooled aubergine, mixing them together thoroughly.

3   Heat a third of the oil in a frying pan over a medium heat. Drop in tblspns of the aubergine mixture and fry until golden brown on one side. Turn over and press the pattie flat with a fish slice. Fry until golden brown on this side. Keep adding oil to the pan as necessary until all the mixture has been cooked. Serve with seasoning **B**, mixed well together.

NOTE

Sliced cucumber and tomato makes a tasty accompaniment to this dish. If you cannot find the long aubergines shown in small picture 1, right, ordinary aubergines are perfectly suitable.

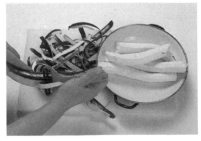

四色沙拉

Salad of Four Colours

INGREDIENTS (SERVES 4)

2 cucumbers
150 g/5 oz broad beans
½ a small pumpkin
1 large potato
⅓ tspn white pepper
50 ml/2 fl oz yoghurt dressing
 (see NOTE)

METHOD

1 Wash the cucumbers and cut off and discard the end parts. Cut in quarters lengthways and remove the seeds. Cut into chunks.
2 Wash the broad beans. Peel the pumpkin, cut into slices and remove the seeds. Wash the slices and cut into chunks. Peel the potato and wash, then cut into chunks, too.
3 Steam the broad beans, pumpkin and potato over gently boiling water for 15 minutes. Mix with the cucumber, pepper and dressing and serve.

NOTE
To make yoghurt dressing, blend 50 ml/2 fl oz mayonnaise with 1 tblspn natural yoghurt, ¼ tspn caster sugar, a large pinch of salt and ½ tblspn each finely chopped onion and celery. Beat well for about 1 minute. Keep in the regrigerator in a strong polythene bag or a bowl cover with cling film until wanted.

奶汁蘆筍

Asparagus with Milk

INGREDIENTS (SERVES 4)

150 g/5 oz white asparagus
150 g/5 oz green asparagus
125 ml/4 fl oz milk
½ tblspn cornflour
3 tblspns single cream
2 tblspns finely shredded
 carrot

SEASONING
1 tspn salt
½ tspn white pepper

METHOD

1 Scrape away any old skin from the asparagus. Wash well and chop into 4-cm/1½-inch sections.
2 Blend the milk with the cornflour, keeping it smooth and free from lumps.
3 Blanch the asparagus in boiling water for 1½ minutes. Remove the green asparagus with tongs or a slotted spoon and leave the white asparagus for 1½ minutes more. Drain and put all the asparagus onto a plate.
4 Put the milk and cornflour into a small pan with the cream and the seasoning. Bring to the boil, stirring all the time, and when the mixture has thickened pour it over the asparagus. Serve at once with the shredded carrot.

NOTES
1 Green asparagus will turn yellow if it is cooked for too long. A counsel of perfection would be to stand the asparagus upright so that the root part blanches for the full time, before turning them on their side so that the tips only blanch for 30 seconds.
2 If fresh asparagus is unobtainable, use canned asparagus.

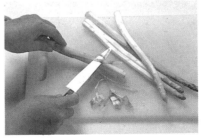

滷塌棵菜

Spiced Chinese Flat Cabbage

INGREDIENTS (SERVES 4)

450 g/1 lb Chinese flat
    cabbage
3 tblspns corn oil

SEASONING
½ tspn salt
½ tblspn sugar
2 tblspns dark soy sauce

METHOD

1   Cut off and discard any old or withered leaves
from the cabbage. Cut each one into 4 parts and wash
these thoroughly.
2   Heat the oil in a wok and stir-fry the cabbage with
the seasoning over a high heat for 1 minute. Put the
lid on the wok and simmer for 1 minute more. Stir the
cabbage and serve.

NOTE
If you prefer a thicker sauce, mix a little cornflour and
water into the cabbage.

酸辣洋葱

Hot and Sour Onions

INGREDIENTS (SERVES 4)

2 onions
2-3 red chillis
4 tblspns corn oil

SEASONING
1 tspn salt
½ tblspn sugar
1 tblspn white vinegar
½ tblspn brown vinegar
pinch of white pepper

METHOD

1   Peel the onions and cut off the ends. Cut the
onions in half and then into square pieces.
2   Wash the chillis and slice diagonally.
3   Heat the oil in a wok and stir-fry the chillis for 1
minute. Add the onions and seasoning and stir-fry
over a high heat for 2-4 minutes. The onions should
still be crunchy. Serve.

NOTE
If you like the taste of raw onion, fry it for no more
than 1 minute before serving.

糖醋高麗

Sweet and Sour Lettuce

INGREDIENTS (SERVES 4)

½ a crispy lettuce
4 tblspns corn oil
½ tblspn crushed garlic
½ tblspn chopped red chillis

SEASONING

3 tblspns sugar
4 tblspns brown vinegar
1½ tspns salt

METHOD

1 Discard outer withered leaves of the lettuce. Tear the remainder into large pieces and wash.
2 Heat the oil in a wok and stir-fry the garlic and chillis over a medium heat for about 1 minute. Raise the heat and add the lettuce. Cook for 3 minutes more, stirring all the time. Add the seasoning, stir to mix, then remove from the heat and serve.

涼拌四季豆

Cold Blended String Beans

INGREDIENTS (SERVES 4)

450 g/1 lb string beans
1 tspn salt
1 tblspn grated fresh ginger root
3 tblspns sesame sauce (see NOTES)

METHOD

1 Cut off and discard the ends and stringy pieces from the beans. Wash under cold running water. Put into a pan of boiling water with the salt and grated ginger; cook for 2½ minutes.
2 Drain the beans and plunge them straight into a pan of iced water. Leave until cold. Drain well and blend with the sesame sauce.

NOTES

1 To make sesame sauce, blend together 1½ tblspns raw sesame sauce, 2 tblspns light soy sauce, ½ tspn salt, 3 tblspns cold boiled water, 1 tspn sugar and 1 tblspn sesame oil. If making the sauce to go with noodles, add more water and salt.
2 Plunging the cooked beans into cold water will help preserve their colour. Choose even-sized beans for this dish.

Three Tastes of Turnips

INGREDIENTS (SERVES 6)

450 g/1 lb turnips
450 g/1 lb carrots

SEASONING A
1½ tblspns light soy sauce
½ tblspn sesame oil
½ tspn white pepper
½ tspn salt

METHOD A

1 Peel the turnips and the carrots. Wash and chop into large chunks.
2 Cook in boiling water until just tender. Drain and mix with seasoning **A**. Serve.

INGREDIENTS
450 g/1 lb green turnips

SEASONING B
3 tblspns light soy sauce
½ tblspn sesame oil

DRESSING
¾ tspn salt
1 tblspn sugar

METHOD B

1 Wash the turnips well, but do not peel them. Chop into big slices and slice these almost down to the root (see picture opposite), so they resemble a comb.
2 Rub the slices with the dressing, stirring them with your hands constantly. After 20 minutes, rinse and squeeze out the juice. Mix with seasoning **B**; leave for 10 minutes, then serve.

INGREDIENTS
450 g/l lb green turnips

SEASONING C
1 tblspn sugar
2 tblspns white vinegar
½ tspn white pepper

DRESSING
¾ tspn salt
1 tblspn sugar

METHOD C

1 Wash the turnips well and dry them, then shred finely.
2 Sprinkle the dressing over the turnips and leave for 30 minutes, stirring frequently with your hand. Rinse, squeeze out the juice, blend with seasoning **C** and serve.

NOTES
1 The dish in Method **B** is also known as Marinated Turnip. As it contains sesame oil it must be eaten the same day, but if you omit this ingredient, you can keep the turnip in a screw-top jar for several days.
2 The dish in Method **C** should be served as soon as it is prepared.
3 Substitute white Giant Radishes for the Turnip. English Turnips can be used in place of the Green Turnips.

咖哩豆腐

Curried Bean Curds

INGREDIENTS (SERVES 4)

2 cakes bean curd
1½ tblspns finely chopped
   shallots
4 red or green chillis
4 tblspns corn oil
about 3 tblspns curry powder
50 ml/2 fl oz water
25 g/1 oz green beans
50 ml/2 fl oz milk
1 tblspn cornflour mixed with
   1½ tblspns water

SEASONING
1½ tspns salt
1 tblspn sugar

METHOD

1   Wash the bean curd and blanch in boiling water
for 3 minutes. Drain and cut into cubes.
2   Select the best parts of the shallots as you prepare
them. Wash the chillis and chop finely.
3   Heat the oil in a wok and stir-fry the chopped
shallot for 1 minute. Add the curry powder and fry for
about 30 seconds, stirring. Add the bean curd, chillis,
water and seasoning and cook for 3-5 minutes,
covered, but stirring frequently.
4   Meanwhile cook the green beans for 5 minutes in
boiling water. Drain.
5   Gradually stir the milk into the mixture in the wok,
then add the cornflour paste and cook, stirring until
the mixture thickens. Serve at once with the green
beans sprinkled on top.

NOTE
This is a very hot dish; if you prefer a milder taste
reduce the amount of curry powder and replace the
chilli with chopped green pepper.

小炒四季

Stir-Fried String Beans

INGREDIENTS (SERVES 4)

225 g/8 oz string or runner
   beans
4 tblspns corn oil
½ tblspn shredded red chillis
1 tblspn shredded fresh root
   ginger

SEASONING
1 tspn salt
2 tspns light soy sauce
1 tspn sugar

METHOD

1   Top and tail the beans. Wash them, then slice
diagonally.
2   Heat the oil in a wok and stir-fry the chillis and
ginger over a high heat for 30 seconds. Add the beans
and seasoning and stir-fry for 1½ minutes more. Serve
at once.

NOTE
If you like, add I crushed garlic clove, stir-frying it
with the chillis.

Taro Mash

INGREDIENTS (SERVES 4)

450 g/1 lb taro
450 ml/¾ pint rich soup stock
  (see p. 261)
3 tblspns single cream

SEASONING

1½ tspns salt
½ tblspn sugar
½ tspns white pepper

METHOD

1 Peel the taro and wash thoroughly. Chop into thick slices and steam over boiling water for 25 minutes until soft. Mash thoroughly.
2 Stir the soup stock into the mashed taro and add the seasoning. Rub through a sieve.
3 Put the taro purée into a pan and slowly bring to the boil. Stir in the cream and serve at once.

NOTE
You can substitute vegetable oil for the cream. This dish is commonly served with fried noodles as a snack.

Hot Bottle Gourd Shreds

INGREDIENTS (SERVES 4)

1 bottle gourd
6 tblspns corn oil
2 tblspns shredded red chillis
1 tblspn finely chopped garlic
1 tblspn cornflour mixed with
  2 tblspns water

SEASONING
1 tspn salt
1 tspn sugar

METHOD

1 Peel the bottle gourd and wash it. Chop into slices, then shred these finely.
2 Heat the oil in a wok and stir-fry the chillis and garlic for 1 minute over a high heat. Add the shredded bottle gourd with the seasoning and stir-fry for a minute more.
3 Lower the heat and cook, stirring occasionally, until the gourd is tender. Stir in the cornflour paste and cook until the mixture has thickened. Serve at once.

NOTE
Look for a bottle gourd that feels heavy and looks fresh around the stalk.

Vegetable String Of Colours

INGREDIENTS (SERVES 4)

6 large Chinese mushrooms
2 green peppers
12 water chestnuts
1 small yam
4 spiced bean curds
1 carrot
2 cucumbers

SEASONING

1 tblspn crushed garlic
3 tblspns light soy sauce
1½ tblspns sugar
½ tspn salt
2 tblspns water
2 tblspns Hoisin sauce
1 tspn dry sherry

METHOD

1 Soak the Chinese mushrooms in boiling water for 20 minutes. Drain. Cut off and discard the stalks and cut the caps in half.
2 Wash the green peppers, cut in half and discard the seeds and stalk part. Chop into chunks. Wash the water chestnuts. Peel the yam, wash and slice.
3 Wash the spiced bean curds and chop into 8 triangular shapes. Peel the carrot, wash and slice. Wash the cucumbers, cut off the end parts and slice.
4 Put the seasoning ingredients into a small pan and bring to the boil, stirring. Take off the heat.
5 Thread the vegetables alternately onto bamboo sticks, brush with the seasoning and grill for about 5 minutes on each side. Brush continually with the seasoning during grilling.

NOTE

An alternative method of cooking is to fry the skewered vegetables in corn oil for 3-5 minutes on either side. Serve them with the seasoning as a sauce.

烤素方

Fried Vegetable Folds

INGREDIENTS (SERVES 4)

12 dried bean curd sheets
3 eggs
4 tblspns finely chopped
　spring onion
1 tspn five-spice powder
½ tspn salt
1 tblspn light soy sauce
1 pan of vegetable oil for
　deep frying

METHOD

1　Soak the bean curd sheets in cold water for 20-30 minutes to soften them. Pat dry with absorbent paper, taking care not to break or tear them.
2　Beat the eggs with the spring onions, five-spice powder, salt and the soy sauce.
3　Lay 1 of the bean curd sheets flat and brush with the beaten egg mixture. Place another sheet on top and brush with the egg mixture. Fold up as shown in the small picture 3. Repeat this brushing and folding process with the remainder of the bean curd sheets.
4　Cut the folded sheets into squares or triangles being very careful not to tear them.
5　Heat the oil and deep-fry the bean curd folds for 4-5 minutes. Remove with a slotted spoon and drain on absorbent paper before serving.

腐衣香菜

Bean Curd Rolls with Basil

INGREDIENTS (SERVES 4)

10 dried bean curd sheets
50 g/2 oz basil leaves
2 tblspns wheat flour mixed
　with 1½ tblspns water
1 pan of corn oil for deep
　frying

SEASONING
1 tspn salt
2 tspns sugar
½ tspn white pepper

METHOD

1　Soak the bean curd sheets in cold water for 20-30 minutes to soften them. Pat dry with absorbent paper, taking care not to break or tear them.
2　Pick off and discard any old or withered leaves from the basil, and wash the remainder. Dry, then chop with 4 of the bean curd sheets. Mix in the seasoning.
3　Lay 2 sheets of bean curd flat, one on top of the other. Put a third of the basil mixture on one end, then roll up the bean curd as shown in the small picture 2. Brush the end with the wheat flour paste to seal. Make 2 more rolls with the remaining 4 sheets of bean curd and the basil mixture.
4　Heat the oil and deep-fry the rolls for about 5 minutes. Remove and drain on absorbent paper and leave to cool. When cold cut into sections and serve.

NOTES
1　You could substitute white wormwood, chives or bean sprouts for the basil.
2　If you prefer, serve the rolls hot, cutting them into sections as soon as they are cooked.

213

扑 双 冬

Stir-Fried Bamboo Shoots with Chinese Mushrooms

INGREDIENTS (SERVES 4)

12 Chinese mushrooms
3 bamboo shoots
4 tblspns corn oil

SEASONING
⅔ tspn salt
2 tblspns soy sauce
½ tblspn sugar

METHOD

1 Soak the Chinese mushrooms in boiling water for 20 minutes. Drain, reserving 3 tblspns of the soaking water. Cut off and discard the stalks and cut the caps in half if they are very large.
2 Peel the bamboo shoots and cut in half. Cook in boiling water for 20 minutes, drain and plunge in cold water, leaving to cool completely. Drain and cut into 15-mm/½-inch thick slices.
3 Heat the oil in a wok and stir-fry the bamboo for 3 minutes. Add the Chinese mushrooms, seasoning and the reserved water from the Chinese mushrooms. Stir everything together, put the lid on the wok and simmer for 5 minutes. Serve.

炒 珍 珠 菜

Stir-Fried White Wormwood

INGREDIENTS (SERVES 4)

450 g/1 lb white wormwood
4 tblspns corn oil

SEASONING
1 tspn salt

METHOD

1 Tear off and discard any old or withered leaves from the white wormwood. Wash and dry, then tear into sections.
2 Heat the oil in a wok and stir-fry the white wormwood with the seasoning for 1½ minutes. Serve at once.

NOTE
If white wormwood is unavailable, use Chinese cabbage or bean sprouts instead.

Stir-Fried Chinese Red Spinach

INGREDIENTS (SERVES 4)

900 g/2 lbs Chinese red
  spinach
7 tblspns corn oil
2 tblspns chopped garlic
1 tblspn cornflour mixed with
  2 tblspns water

SEASONING
1 tspn salt
½ tspn white pepper
2 tspns sugar

METHOD

1 Tear off and discard any old or withered parts
from the spinach. Wash the remainder, rubbing it
together to clean it thoroughly.
2 Heat the oil in a wok and stir-fry the garlic for 1
minute. Add the spinach and seasoning and stir. Put
the lid on the wok and simmer the spinach until it is
well cooked and tender. Stir in the cornflour to
thicken and serve at once.

NOTE
Substitute 450 g/1 lb broccoli for the red spinach.

Sponge Gourd Pan Sticks

INGREDIENTS (SERVES 4)

1 medium sponge gourd
50-75 ml/2-3 fl oz corn oil
1 tblspn chopped preserved
  vegetable (optional)
½ tspn salt
½ tblspn finely chopped
  spring onion
6 tblspns cornflour

SEASONING
2 tblspns light soy sauce
3 tblspns clear soup stock
  (see p. 261)
½ tblspn finely chopped red
  chillis
1 tblspn finely chopped garlic
3 tblspns sesame oil

METHOD

1 Peel the sponge gourd and cut off the stalk. Wash,
chop in half and slice thinly.
2 Heat 2 tblspns oil in a wok and stir-fry the gourd
slices and preserved vegetable (if used) for a few
minutes. Remove and mix with the salt and spring
onion. When cool, mix carefully with the cornflour.
3 Heat half the remaining oil in a frying pan and fry
tablespoonfuls of the gourd mixture, pressing flat
with a fish slice. Fry over a medium heat until brown
on both sides. Repeat until the mixture is finished,
adding more oil as necessary. Serve hot with the
seasoning ingredients mixed together, as a dip.

NOTE
Instead of the sauce suggested, serve with chilli
sauce or English mustard.

高風亮節

Stir-Fried Baby Bamboo Shoots with Red Chilli

INGREDIENTS (SERVES 4)

450 g/1 lb baby bamboo
   shoots
4 red chillis
4 tblspns corn oil
½ tblspn crushed garlic
50 ml/2 fl oz clear soup stock
   (see p. 261)

SEASONING
1 tspn salt
1½ tblspns light soy sauce
1 tblspn sugar

METHOD

1 Tear off the old stalks and skins from the baby bamboo shoots and wash. Wash the chillis and slice finely.
2 Heat the oil in a wok and stir-fry the chillis and garlic for 1 minute. Add the baby bamboo shoots and the seasoning, and stir thoroughly. Pour in the soup stock and simmer, covered, until most of the liquid has been absorbed. Serve at once.

NOTES
1 Baby bamboo shoots are sweet and crispy.
2 If you would rather the dish is not too hot, substitute red peppers for the chillis.

留芳百世

Stir-Fried Taro Stalk with Peanuts

INGREDIENTS (SERVES 4)

450 g/1 lb taro stalks
6 tblspns peeled peanuts
5 tblspns corn oil
1 tblspn crushed garlic

SEASONING
1 tspn salt
1 tspn sugar
½ tblspn soy sauce

METHOD

1 Tear the taro stalks apart and peel away the stringy skin. Chop off the end part, then wash the stalks and chop into 2.5-cm/1-inch diagonal slices.
2 Put the peanuts in a strong polythene bag and crush them with the back of the chopper.
3 Heat the oil in a wok and stir-fry the garlic for 1 minute. Add the taro slices and stir-fry for 3 minutes more. Add the seasoning and the crushed peanuts, and cook, covered for 3 minutes or until the taro is tender. Stir once more and serve.

NOTE
Look for tender young taro stalks for this recipe and be sure to cook them until they are quite soft. If they are unavailable, use mange touts instead.

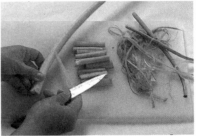

麻菇雞湯

Soup of Assorted Shreds

INGREDIENTS (SERVES 4)

25 g/1 oz dried bean curd
  sheets
50 g/2 oz fungus
5-6 Chinese mushrooms
50 g/2 oz bamboo shoot
900 ml/1½ pints clear soup
  stock (see p. 261)

SEASONING
1½ tspns salt
½ tspn white pepper

METHOD

1   Soak the dried bean curd sheets and the fungus in cold water for about 20 minutes until softened. Drain and shred finely.
2   Soak the Chinese mushrooms in boiling water for 20 minutes. Drain. Cut off and discard the stalks and shred the caps finely.
3   Peel the bamboo shoot. Wash it and shred finely.
4   Put all the shredded ingredients into a bowl (see picture opposite). Add the seasoning and carefully pour in the soup stock, taking care not to disarrange the vegetables. Steam over gently boiling water for 40 minutes. Serve straight away.

香菌鴨

Bean Curd Rolls with Mushrooms

INGREDIENTS (SERVES 4)

16 pieces of dried bean curd
  sheets
4 Chinese mushrooms
7 tblspns light soy sauce
2½ tblspns sugar
1 tspn five-spice powder
½ tspn salt
1 tblspn sesame oil
300 ml/½ pint clear soup
  stock (see p. 261)
1 tblspn rock sugar
8 pieces of liquorice or
  peppermint leaves
1 stick cinnamon

METHOD

1   Soak the dried bean curd sheets in cold water for 20-30 minutes. Pat dry with absorbent paper, taking care not to tear the sheets.
2   Soak the Chinese mushrooms in boiling water for 20 minutes. Drain. Cut off and discard the stalks and finely chop the caps. Mix with 4 tblspns soy sauce, the sugar, five-spice powder, salt and sesame oil. Put in a small pan, bring to the boil and simmer for 1 minute.
3   In a separate pan, put the soup stock, the rest of the soy sauce, rock sugar, liquorice or peppermint leaves and the cinnamon. Bring to the boil, lower the heat and simmer for 20 minutes. Discard the cinnamon stick.
4   Lay a sheet of bean curd flat and brush with the Chinese mushroom mixture. Repeat, layering and brushing 8 bean curd sheets together. Roll up, then repeat with the remaining 8 sheets of bean curd.
5   Wrap the bean curd rolls in muslin and tie with strings to secure. Steam for 25 minutes. Remove, cool slightly, then discard the string and muslin. Serve in slices with the soup stock sauce.

木耳燒素肉

Stir-Fried Glutens with Fungus

INGREDIENTS (SERVES 4)

225 g/8 oz gluten puff
2 tblspns light soy sauce
1 pan of corn oil for deep
   frying
50 g/2 oz fungus
small piece fresh root ginger
3 tblspns oil
3 tblspns clear soup stock
   (see p.261)

SEASONING
1 tspn salt
1½ tblspns sugar
½ tspn white pepper

METHOD

1 Tear the gluten puff into pieces. Mix with the soy sauce and leave for 20 minutes.
2 Heat the oil and deep fry the gluten puff for 30 seconds. Remove with a slotted spoon and drain on absorbent paper.
3 Cut off and discard the roots from the fungus. Wash and slice.
4 Peel the ginger and cut in slices.
5 Heat the 3 tblspns oil in a wok and stir-fry the fungus and ginger. Add the fried gluten puff and the seasoning. Stir-fry for a minute, then add the soup stock and simmer, covered, for 1-2 minutes more. Serve at once.

NOTE
You could add shredded cucumber and carrot to this dish to give it a bit of colour.

糟香麵筋

Marinated Glutens with Red Fermented Sauce

INGREDIENTS (SERVES 4)

225 g/8 oz gluten puff
1½ tblspns red fermented
   grain sauce or 2 red
   fermented bean curds
4 tblspns corn oil

SEASONING
1 tblspn sugar
3 tblspns clear soup stock
   (see p.261)

METHOD

1 Wash the gluten puff and dry on absorbent paper. Cut into slanting pieces.
2 Blend the red fermented grain sauce or the fermented bean curds with the seasoning, mashing them together. Add the glutens and leave for 20 minutes.
3 Heat the oil in a wok and stir-fry the marinated glutens over a medium heat for 3 minutes. Serve at once.

NOTE
Any fermented bean curd sauce could be used instead of the red fermented grain sauce.

Home-Town Style Mange Tout

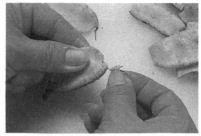

INGREDIENTS (SERVES 4)

350 g/12 oz mange tout
4 tblspns corn oil
½ tblspn finely chopped fresh
    root ginger
⅓ tblspn crushed garlic
⅓ tblspn finely chopped red
    chillis

SEASONING
1 tspn salt
½ tspn sherry

METHOD

1   Top and tail the mange tout, removing any stringy pieces. Wash.
2   Heat the oil in a wok and stir-fry the ginger, garlic and chillis for 1 minute. Add the mange tout and stir. Cook over a medium heat, covered, for 1 minute, then add the seasoning, and cook, stirring, for a further minute. Serve at once.

NOTE
Mange tout are also known as snow peas.

Stir-Fried Chinese Cabbage with Chinese Mushrooms

INGREDIENTS (SERVES 4)

5 Chinese mushrooms
50 g/2 oz dried lily flowers
1 medium Chinese cabbage
4 tblspns corn oil
½ tblspn cornflour mixed
    with 2 tblspns water

SEASONING
1 tspn salt
½ tblspn sugar

METHOD

1   Soak the Chinese mushrooms in boiling water for 20 minutes. Drain. Cut off and discard the stalks and shred the caps.
2   Cut off and discard the hard stem parts from the dried lily flowers. Tie a knot in each of the flowers, wash them and soak in cold water for about 30 minutes. Drain and squeeze dry.
3   Cut off and discard the root part and any old or withered leaves from the cabbage. Wash the leaves and cut into wide shreds.
4   Heat the oil in a wok and stir-fry the mushroom shreds for 1-2 minutes. Add the cabbage and lily flowers and stir. Lower the heat, and cook covered, until the cabbage is soft.
4   Stir in the seasoning and the cornflour paste, and cook until the mixture has thickened. Serve at once.

福壽暖鍋

Pot of Assorted Vegetables

INGREDIENTS (SERVES 4)

25 g/1 oz dried lily flowers
½ a small cabbage
1 carrot
1 turnip
½ a medium cauliflower
1 small taro
100 g/4 oz wheat flour
½ tspn salt
1 tspn chilli powder
4 eggs
50-75 ml/2-3 fl oz water
5 tblspns corn oil
3 tblspns shredded preserved
  vegetable
1.2 litres/2 pints clear soup
  stock (see p. 261)

SEASONING

1½ tspns salt

METHOD

1   Cut off and discard the hard stem parts from the dried lily flowers. Tie a knot in each of the flowers, wash them, then soak in cold water for about 30 minutes. Drain and squeeze dry.
2   Cut off and discard the root and any old or withered leaves from the cabbage. Wash the leaves and shred them.
3   Peel the carrot and turnip, wash and dice. Wash the cauliflower, cut off and discard any tough stalks and cut into small florets. Peel the taro and shred it.
4   Mix together the wheat flour, salt and chilli powder and mix to a smooth batter with the eggs, water and 1 tblspn oil. Coat the cauliflower, cabbage and taro with this batter.
5   Heat the remaining oil and fry the battered vegetables until golden brown. Remove and keep warm. Pour off all but 1 tblspn of the oil.
6   Stir fry the preserved vegetable in the oil for a few minutes, then add the seasoning, soup stock, carrot and turnip. Bring to the boil and simmer for 5 minutes. Stir in the dried lily flowers and the fried battered vegetables. Serve at once.

全福暖鍋

Family Pot

INGREDIENTS (SERVES 4)

8 Chinese mushrooms
9 pieces of dried bean curd
  sheets
10 water chestnuts
2 tblspns corn oil
1 carrot
2 pieces of fried bean curd
  sheet
2-3 water bamboos
8 seaweed rolls
9 tblspns finely chopped
  preserved vegetable
2 tblspns shredded bamboo
  shoots
6 tblspns chopped fungus
12 pieces wonton skin
1 slice fresh root ginger
1.2 litres/2 pints clear soup
  stock (see p. 261)
50 g/2 oz bean sprouts

SEASONING

1½ tblspns salt
½ tblspn sugar
2 tblspns soy sauce
½ tspn white pepper

METHOD

1   Soak the Chinese mushrooms in boiling water for 20 minutes. Drain. Cut off and discard the stalks.
2   Soak the dried bean curd sheets in cold water for 20 minutes until soft. Drain and shred 1 of them finely.
3   Peel and wash the water chestnuts and fry them in the oil for 2 minutes. Remove with a slotted spoon.
4   Peel the carrot and chop into chunks. Divide the fried bean curd sheet into 4 pieces.
5   Discard the skins from the water bamboos and cut off the stalks. Chop into chunks and wash. Wash the seaweed rolls.
6   Mix 3 tblspns of chopped preserved vegetable with the shredded dried bean curd sheet and the bamboo shoots. Mix the dried bean curd sheets into this.
7   Mix the rest of the preserved vegetable with the fungus and wrap in the wonton skins.
8   Put the ginger and soup into a large saucepan and bring to the boil. Add the carrot, Chinese mushrooms, water bamboo, water chestnuts, seaweed rolls and the dried bean curd sheet mixture. Bring to the boil and simmer gently for 20 minutes. Add the seasoning, the wonton parcels and bean sprouts, and serve.

双菇扒芥菜

Mustard Greens with Mushrooms

INGREDIENTS (SERVES 4)

450 g/1 lb mustard greens
  (or a crisp lettuce)
100 g/4 oz straw mushrooms
100 g/4 oz button mushrooms
½ tspn bicarbonate of soda
4 tblspns corn oil
½ tblspn crushed garlic
1 tspn finely chopped fresh
  root ginger
75 ml/3 fl oz clear soup stock
  (see p.261)
1 tblspn cornflour mixed with
  2 tblspns water
1 tspn sesame oil

SEASONING

1 tspn salt
2 tspns sugar

METHOD

1 Cut off and discard any withered or old parts from the mustard greens. Wash and chop into chunks.
2 Wash the straw mushrooms and the button mushrooms. Cut off and discard any muddy stalks and cut them all in half. Blanch in boiling water for 1 minute, drain (reserving the water) and plunge into cold water. Leave to cool.
3 Add the bicarbonate of soda to the boiling water used to blanch the mushrooms. Add the mustard greens and cook for 1½ minutes. Drain and rinse under cold running water.
4 Heat the oil in a wok and stir-fry the garlic and ginger for 1 minute. Add the mustard greens and half of the seasoning. Stir-fry for 1 minute, then remove with a slotted spoon.
5 Add the soup stock, and the straw and button mushrooms to the pan. Bring to the boil, stir in the rest of the seasoning and cook for 1 minute. Stir in the cornflour mixture, and when the sauce has thickened, pour it over the mustard greens. Dribble over the sesame oil and serve.

農 家 樂

The Farmer's Joy

INGREDIENTS (SERVES 4)

225 g/8 oz vermicelli
350 g/12 oz white Chinese
  cabbage
1 large fungus
1 large carrot
4 tblspns corn oil
1 tblspn chopped spring
  onion
50 ml/2 fl oz clear soup stock
  (see p.261)

SEASONING

⅔ tspn salt
1½ tblspns soy sauce
1 tspn sugar

METHOD

1 Soak the vermicelli in cold water for 15 minutes until softened. Cut into sections.
2 Cut off and discard the root and any old or withered leaves from the Chinese cabbage. Wash and chop into 2.5-cm/1-inch slices. Wash the fungus and slice.
3 Peel the carrot and chop into large slices.
4 Heat the oil in a wok and stir-fry the spring onion for 1 minute. Add the fungus and carrot slices and stir-fry for 1 minute more. Add the white cabbage and cook, stirring, for a few minutes.
5 Add the drained vermicelli, the soup stock, and the seasoning, mixing everything together well. Bring to the boil, simmer, covered for 1 minute and serve.

NOTE

Add bamboo shoot, Chinese mushrooms and bean curd sheets to this dish if you want to make it more substantial.

豆絲春濃

Stir-Fried Bean Cake Shreds with String Beans

INGREDIENTS (SERVES 4)

150-175 g/5-6 oz green bean
   starch
75-100 g/3-4 oz rice flour
water (see recipe)
50 g/2 oz string beans
50 g/2 oz fungus
50 g/2 oz bean sprouts
5 tblspns corn oil
⅔ tspn chilli powder
25 ml/1 fl oz clear soup stock
   (see p. 261)

SEASONING

1 tspn salt
1 tblspn dark soy sauce

METHOD

1 Blend the green bean starch and the rice flour
with sufficient water to make a pliable dough. Knead
it, then press it out thinly. Put it in a frying pan and
cook on both sides over a medium heat until
beginning to brown. Remove and chop into fine
shreds.
2 Top and tail the beans, removing any stringy bits.
Chop into diagonal slices. Wash the fungus and
shred. Wash the bean sprouts.
3 Heat the oil in a wok and fry the chilli powder for
30 seconds. Add the beans, fungus and bean sprouts
and stir-fry for 1 minute. Add the shredded cooked
dough and the soup stock and simmer, covered, for 1
minute. Serve at once.

脆味瓜片

Pickled Cucumber Slices

INGREDIENTS (SERVES 4)

450 g/1 lb cucumbers
2 tblspns white vinegar
3 tblspns sesame oil

SEASONING

2½ tspns salt
4 tblspns sugar

METHOD

1 Wash the cucumbers, cut off and discard end
parts and then slice finely.
2 Mix the cucumber slices with the seasoning,
mixing them together well. Put in a dish and chill.
3 Just before serving, squeeze out the excess liquid
from the cucumbers and blend with the vinegar and
sesame oil. Serve.

NOTE

You can keep the sliced cucumbers in the refrigerator
for up to 2 days. Cover with cling film or their flavour
will permeate other foods in the refrigerator.

炸 洋 蔥 餅

Fried Onion Cakes

INGREDIENTS (SERVES 4)

2 large onions
100 g/4 oz wheat flour
⅓ tspn salt
3 eggs
50 ml/2 fl oz water
9 tblspns corn oil

SEASONING
1 tspn salt
¼ tblspn paprika

METHOD

1 Peel the onion, chop off end parts, then wash and slice finely.
2 Mix together the wheat flour and salt, and then mix to a batter with the eggs, water and 1 tblspn oil.
3 Heat 4 tblspns corn oil in a wok and stir-fry the sliced onions for 2 minutes. Remove with a slotted spoon, cool slightly, then mix with the batter.
4 Heat the remaining oil in a frying pan and fry spoonfuls of the onion and batter, until golden brown on both sides.
5 Mix the salt and paprika with 1 tblspn of the oil used for frying and serve with the hot onion cakes.

NOTE
You could serve the onion cakes with tomato sauce instead of the paprika mix if you prefer.

炸 紫 菜 素 捲

Crispy Laver Rolls

INGREDIENTS (SERVES 4)

1 carrot
½ a cucumber
50 g/2 oz bamboo shoot
50 g/2 oz fungus
½ tspn salt
2 tblspns wheat flour
4½ tblspns water
3 pieces of laver
3 tblspns light soy sauce
2 tspns cornflour
½ tspn chilli powder
1½ tblspns corn oil

METHOD

1 Peel the carrot and shred finely. Wash the cucumber, peel and wash the bamboo shoot and wash the fungus. Shred all these vegetables finely. Put in a colander and sprinkle with the salt.
2 Mix the wheat flour to a paste with 1½ tblspns water.
3 Lay the pieces of laver out flat and arrange a third of the shredded vegetables on each piece as shown in the small picture 2. Roll up and seal the ends with the wheat flour paste.
4 Put the soy sauce, cornflour, chilli powder and the remaining 3 tblspns water into a small saucepan. Bring to the boil, stirring, then remove from the heat.
5 Heat the oil in a frying pan and fry the laver rolls over a medium heat for 5 minutes, turning them constantly. Remove, cut into diagonal pieces and serve with the soy sauce mixture.

凉拌海蜇

Cold Blended Jellyfish

INGREDIENTS (SERVES 4)

450 g/1 lb jellyfish, shredded
½ tspn salt
2 tblspns light soy sauce
3 tblspns shredded carrot
3 tblspns shredded Chinese
   celery or spring onion
1 tspn sugar
1 tblspn sesame oil

METHOD

1   Cover the jellyfish with cold water and leave to soak for 20 minutes. Wash under cold running water, place in a colander and scald with boiling water. Immediately plunge into cold water and leave to soak for 4-5 hours (or until you want to serve it).
2   When ready to serve, drain the jellyfish and squeeze out the water. Mix the salt and half the soy sauce into the jelly fish and leave to stand for 10 minutes. Drain again very thoroughly.
3   Mix the jellyfish with the shredded carrot and Chinese celery or spring onion. Mix in the rest of the soy sauce with the sugar and sesame oil. Serve.

NOTES

1   You can use dried, fresh or frozen jellyfish for this recipe. Dried jellyfish must be soaked in cold water until it has softened. Frozen should be thoroughly defrosted before using.
2   When scalding the jellyfish, tip spoonfuls of boiling water over it rather than plunging it into a pan of boiling water. Stir the jellyfish as you pour on the water; the shreds should roll up.

黄瓜粉皮

Cucumbers with Mung Bean Sheets

INGREDIENTS (SERVES 4)

3 cucumbers
2 tblspns crushed garlic
1 packet (about 8 slices)
   mung bean sheets

SEASONING

1 tblspn sesame oil
1½ tblspns white vinegar

DRESSING

2 tspns salt
2 tblspns sugar

METHOD

1   Wash the cucumbers; cut off the stalks and end pieces. Wipe them dry, then crush them slightly with the chopper. Chop into 2.5 cm/1-inch sections and mix with the garlic and dressing. Put into a bowl, cover with cling wrap and refrigerate for at least 4 hours.
2   Meanwhile, soak the mung bean sheets in cold water to soften them. Chop into 2.5 cm/1-inch sections.
3   Squeeze the juice from the cucumbers and mix with the strips of mung bean sheets. Stir in the seasoning and serve.

NOTES

1   If you like a hot taste, substitute chilli oil for the sesame oil and add 2 or 3 small chopped chillis.
2   Use mung bean sheets on the day that you buy them.

花生麵筋

Peanut with Gluten Puff

INGREDIENTS (SERVES 4)

150 g/5 oz raw peanuts
75 g/3 oz gluten puff
125 ml/4 fl oz water

SEASONING

2 tblspns light soy sauce
½ tspn salt
½ tblspn rock sugar powder
1 tblspn brown sugar
2 star anises

METHOD

1 Wash the peanuts thoroughly and soak them in cold water for 4 hours.
2 Put the gluten puff into a pan and cover with boiling water. Simmer until it is soft – about 5 minutes. Drain.
3 Drain the peanuts and mix with the seasoning in a saucepan. Add the water and bring to the boil. Lower the heat and simmer for 10 minutes. Add the drained gluten puff and cook for 5 minutes more. Serve at once.

NOTE

You can use cooked peanuts for this dish, in which case soak them first in boiling water containing 2-3 star anises for 1 hour (see small picture 3).

滷豆乾

Spiced Bean Curds

INGREDIENTS (SERVES 4)

1 pack of spices (see NOTES)
900 ml/1 pint water
275 g/10 oz spiced bean
curds
2 tblspns light soy sauce
½ tblspn rock sugar

METHOD

1 Boil the pack of spices in the water for 30 minutes.
2 Wash the spiced bean curds under cold running water. Add them to the pan with the soy sauce and the rock sugar. Bring to the boil, then lower the heat and simmer for 10 minutes. Remove from the heat, but leave the bean curds in the liquid until ready to serve.

NOTES

1 A pack of spices should contain star anise, fennel, dried orange peel, cinnamon and liquorice.
2 If you do not cook the spiced bean curds on the day you have bought them, put them in a pan with some salt and cover with water. Bring to the boil and cook for 3 minutes. This will preserve them for up to 3 days. Keep in the refrigerator.

炒三色丁
Stir-Fried Cubes in Three Colours

INGREDIENTS (SERVES 4)

½ a salted cabbage, cubed
½ a preserved vegetable,
    cubed
4 tblspns corn oil
50 g/2 oz bamboo shoot,
    cubed

SEASONING
1 tblspn sugar
½ tblspn light soy sauce
½ tspn white pepper
4 tblspns water

METHOD

1   Soak the salted cabbage and preserved vegetable in cold water for 20 minutes. Drain well.
2   Heat the oil in a wok and stir-fry all the vegetables together for 1 minute. Add the seasoning, cover the pan and cook for 2 minutes. Serve.

NOTES
1   This makes an ideal stuffing for steamed dumplings.
2   If you like, blend in 2 tspns sesame oil just before serving.

滷桶筍
Marinated Bamboo Shoots

INGREDIENTS (SERVES 6)

450 g/1 lb pickled bamboo
    shoots
2 star anises
2 red peppers, seeded
4 cloves garlic, finely
    chopped
4 tblspns corn oil
50-75 ml/2-3 fl oz water

SEASONING
1 tspn salt
2 tblspns light soy sauce
1½ tblspns rock sugar
    powder

METHOD

1   Tear the pickled bamboo shoots into long shreds. Wash them thoroughly, then squeeze out all the water.
2   Put the bamboo shreds into a saucepan and cover with water. Add the star anises, bring to the boil and boil for 5 minutes. Drain and rinse under running water. Squeeze out the water again.
3   Crush the peppers thoroughly with the back of the chopper then stir-fry with the garlic in the oil for 2 minutes. Add the bamboo shreds with the seasoning and the water. Stir for a few minutes, then simmer for about 20 minutes, stirring occasionally until the bamboo shoot is tender and most of the liquid has evaporated. Serve at once.

NOTE
A large quantity of this dish can be prepared at one time as it will keep for up to 3 days in the refrigerator. Reheat as you want to serve it. This is why it is called *Marinated* Bamboo Shoots.

Spiced Sour Cabbage

INGREDIENTS (SERVES 4)

450 g/1 lb sour cabbage
4 tblspns corn oil
450 ml/¾ pint water or clear
soup stock (see p. 261)

SEASONING
2 tblspns light soy sauce
1 tblspn rock sugar powder
1 tblspn brown sugar
½ tspn white pepper

METHOD

1 Wash the sour cabbage very thoroughly, discarding any old leaves. Squeeze out the liquid, then shred the cabbage and soak in cold water for 10 minutes. Drain.
2 Heat the oil in a wok. Mix the seasoning into the cabbage and stir-fry over a high heat for a few minutes. Add the water or soup stock, bring to the boil, then lower the heat, and simmer, covered, for 15 minutes, stirring occasionally. Drain off most of the liquid and serve at once.

NOTES
1 A large quantity of this dish can be prepared at one time as it will keep in the refrigerator for up to 5 days. Do not drain off the excess liquid until you heat it up to serve. The liquid helps to preserve the dish.
2 If you like a hot taste, add 2 finely chopped chillis to the seasoning ingredients.

Marinated Chives

INGREDIENTS (SERVES 4)

275 g/10 oz chives
1½ tblspns salt

SEASONING
white wine vinegar
sesame oil

METHOD

1 Discard any old leaves from the chives. Wash the remainder and dry in a clean cloth.
2 Sprinkle the salt over the chives, then rub them with your hands until they have softened. Rinse the chives and squeeze out the liquid. Chop the chives finely and put into a dish.
3 Serve spoonfuls at a time, passing the white vinegar and sesame oil for each person to help themselves.

NOTE
This dish comes from northern China, where garlic is usually added to it.

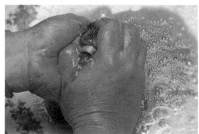

Soup of Five Blessings

INGREDIENTS (SERVES 4)

50 g/2 oz longan pulp
50 g/2 oz red dates
50 g/2 oz fresh lotus seeds
25-50 g/1-2 oz gingko fruits
25-50 g/1-2 oz fresh lily
1.2 litres/2 pints water
100 g/4 oz rock sugar,
    crushed

METHOD

1   Wash the longan pulp and the red dates. Soak the dates in cold water for 1-2 hours.
2   Wash the lotus seeds and the gingko fruits. Wash the lily and remove the outer membrane.
3   Put all the ingredients together with the water and crushed rock sugar into a saucepan. Bring to the boil, then lower the heat and simmer for 1 hour. Serve.

NOTE
If fresh lily and lotus seeds are not available, buy dried ones and soak them in cold water for 2-3 hours and overnight respectively.

Lotus Root with Red Dates

INGREDIENTS (SERVES 4)

2 sections of lotus root
1 tspn salt
50 g/2 oz red dates, soaked
    overnight in cold water
25-50 g/1-2 oz rock sugar
900 ml/1½ pints water

METHOD

1   Peel the lotus root and chop it into bite-sized pieces. Wash thoroughly, adding the salt to the water. Drain.
2   Wash the red dates under running water after their soaking.
3   Put the lotus root pieces into a large saucepan with the dates, rock sugar and water. Bring to the boil, then lower the heat and simmer for 1-1½ hours until the mixture smells sweet. Keep an eye on the pan and add more water if it evaporates too much.

如意帶玉

Stir-Fried Green Celery with Bean Sprouts

INGREDIENTS (SERVES 4)

450 g/1 lb bean sprouts
2 spiced bean curds
3 stalks Chinese celery
5 tblspns oil

SEASONING
1 tspn salt
1 tblspn light soy sauce
1 tblspn clear soup stock
(see p. 261)
1 tspn sugar

METHOD

1   Wash the bean sprouts and drain thoroughly.
Chop the spiced bean curds into shreds.
2   Cut off and discard the old stalks and leaves from
the celery. Wash and cut into 2.5-cm/1-inch sections.
3   Heat the oil in a wok and stir-fry the bean sprouts,
bean curds and celery together with the seasoning for
about 10 minutes. Cover and simmer for 2 minutes
more, then serve.

堆金積玉

Golden Glutens with Emerald Peppers

INGREDIENTS (SERVES 4)

225 g/8 oz gluten puff
2 tblspns dark soy sauce
6 green chillis
1 pan of corn oil for deep
frying plus 4 tblspns extra
oil

SEASONING
1 tspn salt
1 tblspn sugar
2 tblspns clear soup stock
(see p.261)

METHOD

1   Chop the gluten puff into diagonal slices and
marinate with the soy sauce for 20 minutes.
2   Crush the green chillis gently with the chopper,
then slice them into 2.5-cm/1-inch sections.
3   Heat the pan of oil for deep frying and fry the
gluten until browned. Remove with a slotted spoon
and drain on absorbent paper.
4   Heat the 4 tblspns oil in a wok and stir fry the
chillis, fried glutens and seasoning over a high heat
for 1 minute. Serve at once.

NOTE
If this dish is going to be too hot for you, substitute
green peppers for the chillis.

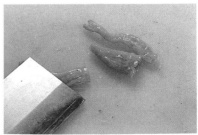

Green-Stemmed Flat Cabbage with Chinese Mushrooms

INGREDIENTS (SERVES 4)

8 large Chinese mushrooms
1 tsp salt
3 tblspns corn oil
450 g/1 lb green-stemmed
   flat cabbage
125 ml/4 fl oz clear soup
   stock (see p. 261)
1½ tblspns cornflour mixed
   with 1½ tblspns water

SEASONING
1 tspn salt
1 tspn sugar

METHOD

1   Soak the Chinese mushrooms in boiling water for 20 minutes. Drain. Cut off and discard the stalks and chop the caps in half.
2   Remove the outer withered leaves of the cabbage and wash the remainder. Chop into 6-cm/2½-inch pieces, then chop these in half lengthways. Blanch in boiling water mixed with the 1 tspn salt for 1-1½ minutes. Drain and soak in cold water until cold. Drain and squeeze out the water, then arrange the cabbage on a plate.
3   Heat the oil in a wok and stir-fry the mushrooms for 1-2 minutes. Add the stock and seasoning and cook for 5 minutes. Stir in the cornflour mixture and when the stock has thickened, spoon it and the mushrooms carefully over the cabbage. Serve at once.

Shredded Water-Bamboo Shoots

INGREDIENTS (SERVES 4)

275 g/10 oz water-bamboo
   shoots

SEASONING
1 tspn salt
½ tblspn light soy sauce
½ tspn white pepper
3 tspns sesame oil
1 tspn sugar
1 tspn white vinegar

METHOD

1   Cut away the outer skin of the water-bamboo shoots and chop off the end part. Slice each piece in half lengthways. Steam these pieces over boiling water for 12 minutes.
2   Remove from the steamer and shred the shoots finely. Mix with the seasoning and serve.

NOTES
1   You can keep this in the refrigerator for up to 3 days. It makes a refreshing summer dish.
2   Substitute 275 g/10 oz shredded Chinese cabbage for the water-bamboo shoots.

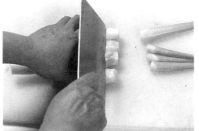

芝麻腐竹片

Bean Curd Sheets with Black Sesame Seed

INGREDIENTS

150 g/5 oz dried bean curd
   sheets
1 pan of corn oil for deep
   frying
1 tblspn black sesame seeds
1 tblspn corn oil
2 tblspns garlic soy sauce
   (see NOTES)

METHOD

1 Use scissors to cut the bean curd sheets into thin
strips and drop them, a few at a time, into the pan of
oil, heated until it is smoking. Fry until they turn
crispy. Remove and drain on absorbent paper while
you fry the remainder.
2 Pick out and discard any impurities in the black
sesame seeds, then stir-fry them with the 1 tblspn oil
for 1-2 minutes over a gentle heat. Remove.
3 Mix the garlic soy sauce with the fried bean curd
sheets and sprinkle the black sesame seeds over the
top.

NOTE

To make garlic soy sauce, mix together 3 tblspns light
soy sauce, 1 tblspn crushed garlic and ½ tspn white
pepper. Keep in a screw-top jar.

蒜豉苦瓜

Bitter Gourd with Fermented Beans

INGREDIENTS (SERVES 4)

1 bitter gourd
½ tblspn salt
1 tblspn fermented black
   beans
6 tblspns corn oil
½ tblspn crushed garlic
½ tblspn finely chopped
   chillis
3 tblspns water

SEASONING

1 tblspn soy sauce
½ tspn salt
1 tblspn sugar
½ tspn white pepper

METHOD

1 Chop the bitter gourd in half lengthways. Remove
the seeds and cut off the peel, the stalk and the end
part. Slice the flesh and sprinkle it with the salt. Leave
for 20 minutes, stirring the pieces with your hand
frequently, then squeeze out the juice. Blanch in
boiling water for 30 seconds and drain.
2 Crush the fermented beans with the back of the
chopper.
3 Heat the oil in a wok and stir-fry the beans, garlic
and chillis over a medium heat for 2-3 minutes. Add
the bitter gourd and stir everything together. Add the
seasoning and the water and simmer, covered, for 3-5
minutes. Serve.

核 桃 酪

Sweet Walnut Soup

INGREDIENTS (SERVES 4)

50 g/2 oz large red dates
100 g/4 oz walnut halves
100 g/4 oz rice flour
½ tblspn rock sugar powder
900 ml/1½ pints water

METHOD

1 Wash the red dates, then soak them in cold water for 4 hours. Cut open and remove the seeds. Wrap the pieces in a square of muslin and rub together by tapping with the back of a knife to loosen the skins. Soak in water for 10 minutes more to remove the skins, then mash the dates.
2 Grind the walnut halves to a powder. Mix together with the dates, rice flour and rock sugar powder. Tip into a pan and gradually stir in the water. Bring to the boil, stirring over a medium heat and serve.

NOTES
1 Walnuts are very nutritious and said to be particularly good for the elderly.
2 If you cannot get hold of rock sugar powder, use crystal rock sugar and crush it with the back of the chopper.

芝 麻 糊

Sesame Paste

INGREDIENTS (SERVES 2)

3 tblspns sesame powder
3 tblspns brown sugar
450 ml/¾ pint boiling water

METHOD

1 Blend the sesame powder with the sugar. Gradually add the boiling water, stirring to keep the mixture smooth. Serve at once.

NOTES
1 There are two kinds of sesame powder on the market. One is pure sesame powder, the other a mixture of sesame powder and rice powder or cornflour. If using the pure one, add 1 tblspn cornflour, stirring this in with the sugar.
2 This dish is traditionally served as a dessert.

脆皮豆腐

Crispy Bean Curds

INGREDIENTS (SERVES 4)

350 g/12 oz fresh bean curd
1 egg, beaten
175 g/6 oz plain flour
corn oil, for deep frying
1 spring onion, finely
chopped, to garnish

SEASONING

3 tblspns light soy sauce
1 garlic clove, crushed
½ tspn sugar
2 tspns sesame oil

METHOD

1 Cut the bean curd into 2.5 x 5 cm/1 x 2 inch pieces. Place in a bowl and scald with boiling water for 1 minute.
2 Dip each rectangle of bean curd first in the beaten egg and then in the flour, shaking off any excess flour.
3 Heat the oil in a deep-fat fryer and deep-fry the bean curd pieces for 3-4 minutes until golden. Remove with a slotted spoon and place on a serving plate.
4 Blend the seasoning ingredients together to make a dipping sauce and place in a small bowl.
5 Sprinkle the bean curd with a little chopped spring onion and serve with the dipping sauce.

炒皮笛

Stir-fried Bamboo Shoots

INGREDIENTS (SERVES 4)

4 spiced bean curds
100 g/4 oz bamboo shoots
4 Chinese black mushrooms,
   soaked (see NOTE)
3 tblspns sesame oil
2.5 cm/1 inch piece fresh
   root ginger, sliced
2 fresh red chillis, seeded and
   thinly sliced
3 tblspns clear soup stock
   (see p. 261)
1 tblspn cornflour

SEASONING

½ tspn salt
½ tblspn light soy sauce
½ tspn sugar

METHOD

1 Slice the bean curd, slice the bamboo shoots and cut the mushrooms into small pieces.
2 Heat the sesame oil in a wok or frying pan and stir in the ginger. Stir-fry for 30 seconds and then remove the ginger with a slotted spoon and discard.
3 Add the red chillis and fry for 15 seconds. Stir in the bamboo shoots, mushrooms, spiced bean curd and the soup stock. Cook for 1 minute and then reduce the heat and simmer for a further minute.
4 Blend the cornflour with a little water and stir into the mixture. Cook for about 1 minute until thickened and serve.

NOTE

Soak the Chinese mushrooms in warm water for 30 minutes before using and remove stalks.

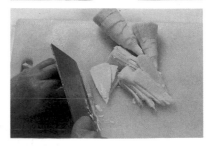

芝麻蘆筍

Asparagus with Black Sesame Seeds

INGREDIENTS (SERVES 4)

450 g/1 lb fresh asparagus
1 tspn salt
2 tblspns black sesame seeds
(see NOTE)
1 tblspn corn oil

SEASONING
½ tspn salt
1 tbspn light soy sauce
½ tspn white pepper

METHOD

1 Cut off the ends and peel away the tough skin from the ends of the asparagus. Cut into 2.5 cm/1 inch pieces.
2 Bring a large saucepan of water to the boil. Add the salt and throw in the asparagus. Cover and cook over a moderate heat for 5 minutes.
3 Drain the asparagus and soak in cold water for 5 minutes. Drain thoroughly.
4 Dry-fry the black sesame seeds in a wok or frying pan for 30 seconds. Remove and set aside.
5 Heat the oil in the wok or frying pan, add the asparagus and stir-fry for 10 seconds. Add the seasoning ingredients together with the black sesame seeds and stir well.
6 Turn onto a serving platter and serve at once.

NOTE
Black sesame seeds have the same flavour as white sesame seeds and these can be used if the black ones are not available.

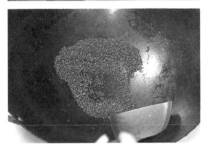

芋泥

Creamed Taro

INGREDIENTS (SERVES 4)

1 taro, about 275 g/10 oz in weight
1.2 litres/2 pints chicken stock (see p. 149)

SEASONING
1½ tspns salt
½ tspn white pepper
2 tspns sugar

METHOD

1 Peel the taro and cut into large pieces. Place in a colander or steamer and steam, covered, over a high heat for 30 minutes. Mash with a fork or potato masher.
2 Bring the chicken stock to the boil and stir in the mashed taro and the seasoning ingredients.
3 Simmer for 20 minutes and then turn into a serving dish.

枸杞渾元

Medlar with Egg

INGREDIENTS (SERVES 1)

4 tblspns fresh medlar leaves
300 ml/½ pint water or clear
   soup stock (see p. 261)
1 egg
⅓ tspn salt

METHOD

1 Pick the medlar leaves off the stems. Wash them and wipe dry on a clean cloth. Put into a soup bowl.
2 Put the water or soup into a small saucepan and bring it to the boil. Ladle out about 125 ml/4 fl oz and put this into a small bowl.
3 Break the egg into the small bowl and let it stand for about 30 seconds. Then stand the bowl in the saucepan of simmering liquid. Cook for 3-5 minutes until the white of the egg is setting. Pour the egg with the liquid over the medlar leaves. Add the salt and serve.

NOTE
Choose young tender medlar leaves for this dish; they will lose their bright green colour as soon as they come into contact with the boiling liquid.

Steamed Milk Egg

INGREDIENTS (SERVES 1)

1 egg, beaten
150-175 ml/5-6 fl oz milk
1 tblspn castor sugar

METHOD

1 Strain the beaten egg, then stir in the milk and sugar. Pour into a small bowl.
2 Place the bowl in a steamer and steam, covered, over gently boiling water for 5 minutes. Remove the lid and steam for 5 minutes more. Serve.

NOTE
Use 1 tblspn honey instead of castor sugar.

奶汁冬瓜帽

Winter Melon Pieces with Milk

INGREDIENTS (SERVES 4)

450 g/1 lb winter melon
8-10 Chinese mushrooms
3 spiced bean curds
6-8 button mushrooms
3 tblspns corn oil
125 ml/4 fl oz milk
1½ tblspns cornflour

SEASONING A

50-75 ml/2-3 fl oz clear soup
   stock (see p. 261)
1 slice fresh root ginger
½ tspn salt
½ tspn white pepper

SEASONING B

1 tspn salt
1 tspn sugar
½ tspn white pepper

METHOD

1 Cut away the skin from the winter melon and discard the seeds. Chop the flesh into rectangular pieces about 5 mm × 4 cm/¼ × 1½ inches. Place these in a large bowl and add seasoning **A**. Put the bowl in a steamer and steam for 20 minutes. Drain off the liquid and reserve it, but discard the ginger.

2 Soak the Chinese mushrooms in boiling water for 20 minutes. Wash the bean curds and button mushrooms. Cut off and discard the stalks from the Chinese mushrooms, then chop the caps very finely with the bean curds and button mushrooms. Sprinkle over seasoning **B** and mix everything together well.

3 Heat the oil in a wok and stir-fry the Chinese mushroom mixture for 2 minutes. Press this on top of the winter melon. Steam for 15 minutes more, then remove and turn the bowl upside-down on a plate.

4 Mix together the milk, the liquid drained from the melon and the cornflour. Pour into a small pan and bring to the boil slowly, stirring all the time. Let the mixture bubble for a minute or so until it thickens, then pour it over the winter melon and serve at once.

冰心玉潔

Crystal Beauty

INGREDIENTS (SERVES 4)

1 section lotus root
½ packet dried
   agar-agar powder
450 ml/¾ pint clear soup
   stock (see p. 261)
maraschino cherries, to serve

SEASONING

1½ tspns salt
½ tspn white pepper

METHOD

1 Peel the lotus root and chop into small pieces. Soak these in water for 30 minutes.

2 Put the agar-agar powder into a pan with the stock and the seasoning. Simmer gently for 30 minutes, then remove from the heat. Strain through a sieve lined with a piece of muslin.

3 Drain the lotus root and put it into the strained liquid. Tip back into the rinsed out pan and bring to the boil. Pour into a square loaf tin, cover with cling film, and when cool, put in the refrigerator.

4 When ready to serve, remove the tin from the refrigerator – it should have set into a firm jelly. Cut into strips and serve with ice cubes and maraschino cherries.

NOTE

This dish is a delightfully fresh one to serve on a hot summer's day.

Clear Soup Stock

INGREDIENTS

175 g/6 oz parsnips
175 g/6 oz turnips
2 onions
4 celery stalks
2 tblspns corn oil
4 tblspns chopped button
  mushroom stalks
1.5 litres/2½ pints water
2 tspns salt
bouquet garni (see NOTES)
3 black peppercorns

METHOD

1   Wash the parsnips and turnips but do not peel. Chop them into chunks. Peel the onions, wash the celery and chop these into chunks, too.
2   Heat the oil in a large saucepan and add all the chopped vegetables and the mushroom stalks. Cook, stirring occasionally, for 5-7 minutes over a medium heat.
3   Add the water, salt, bouquet garni and peppercorns to the pan. Bring to the boil, then lower the heat and simmer for 30 minutes.
4   Strain the liquid into a bowl, pressing the vegetables with the back of a wooden spoon to extract as much liquid as possible. Discard the vegetables left in the strainer.
5   Let the stock cool completely, then cover with cling wrap and put in the refrigerator.

NOTES
1   Make a bouquet garni by tying together 2 sprigs of parsley, 1 sprig of thyme and 1 bay leaf.
2   Keep the stock for 2-3 days in the refrigerator, or freeze it in small quantities (ice-cube trays or small yoghurt cartons make ideal containers) and use as required.

Rich Soup Stock

INGREDIENTS

100 g/4 oz carrots
100 g/4 oz turnips
100 g/4 oz button mushrooms
2 onions
4 celery stalks
100 g/4 oz tomatoes
2 tblspns corn oil
1.5 litres/2½ pints water
2 tspns salt
bouquet garni (see NOTES
  above)
3 black peppercorns

METHOD

1   Wash the carrots and turnips but do not peel. Wipe the mushrooms with damp absorbent paper. Peel the onions and wash the celery and the tomatoes. Chop all these vegetables into chunks.
2   Heat the oil in a large saucepan and add all the chopped vegetables. Cook, stirring occasionally, for 8-10 minutes, over a medium heat.
3   Add the water, salt, bouquet garni and peppercorns to the pan. Bring to the boil, then lower the heat and simmer for 30 minutes.
4   Finish off as outlined above in Clear Soup Stock.

RICE AND NOODLES

Except in the northern, wheat-producing regions, rice is undoubtedly the single most important food in China. The Chinese phrase implying "to eat a meal" literally translated means "to eat cooked rice" and all the meals of the day concern eating rice. For instance, the Chinese word for "breakfast" means "morning cooked rice" when literally translated.

Consequently, unless you plan to cook a typical northern-style dinner, no Chinese meal would be complete without rice. Somewhat surprisingly, the Chinese do not tend to serve their rice in very elaborate forms. *Fried Rice* is far more common in western restaurants than in China itself. Traditionally long-grain rice is boiled until tender and then served in individual bowls. While the accompanying dishes add flavour to the meal, rice is still considered the centrepiece of any meal and it is a common belief, that, if necessary, a man could survive on nothing else.

Noodles are frequently eaten in the north, where wheat is widely grown. Wheat noodles can be bought fresh or dried and are made with or without eggs. There are also several other types of noodle available, principally rice noodles, made from rice flour, and cellophane noodles or transparent vermicelli, made from ground mung beans.

Unlike rice, noodles tend to be cooked with other ingredients – they can be steamed, stir-fried or stirred into soups. Cellophane noodles, particularly, are eaten more as a vegetable or bean curd, since they absorb the tastes of other ingredients and add a slippery texture. Other grains, such as oatmeal, are also included in this chapter, since, like rice, they provide bulk and substance to a meal.

Fried Rice

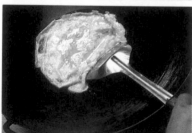

INGREDIENTS (SERVES 4)

600 g/1¼ lbs cooked long-
grain rice (see NOTE)
3 tblspns corn oil
6 eggs, beaten
4 tblspns finely chopped
spring onions
1 tspn salt
½ tspn rice wine or dry
sherry

METHOD

1 Break up the cooked rice with chopsticks or a fork.
2 Heat the oil in a wok, add the beaten eggs and fry
for 1 minute. Add the rice and stir thoroughly.
3 Stir in the chopped spring onions and salt and
stir-fry the mixture for 3 minutes until the eggs are
cooked and the rice is loose and dry.
4 Stir in the rice wine and cook for a further minute
and then serve.

NOTE

To produce 600 g/1¼ lbs cooked rice: place 225 g/8 oz
long-grained white rice in a bowl, cover with cold
water and stir to loosen the grains. Strain off the
cloudy water and repeat this two more times. Place
the rice in another bowl of cold water and stand for 5
minutes. Bring a large saucepan of salted water to the
boil, add the rice and the soaking water and cook over
a medium heat for 10-12 minutes or until the rice is
tender. Strain the rice through a sieve and leave to
drain. Place in a serving dish, cover with a lid and keep
warm in a gently heated oven.

肉燥麵

Noodles with Minced Pork Sauce

INGREDIENTS (SERVES 6)

150 g/5 oz bean sprouts
4 leeks, sliced
600 g/1¼ lbs fresh egg
   noodles
1½ tblspns sesame oil
725 ml/1¼ pints clear soup
   stock (see p. 261)
6 slices of cooked lean pork
12 cooked peeled prawns

PORK SAUCE

4-6 tblspns corn oil
6 spring onion bulbs,
   chopped (reserving the
   tops for a garnish)
1 tblspn ginger juice
   (see NOTE 3, p. 39)
5 tblspns soy sauce
225 g/8 oz lean minced pork
3 tblspns rice wine or dry
   sherry
½ tblspn salt
1 tblspn rock sugar
725 ml/1¼ pints water

METHOD

1 Make the pork sauce: heat the oil in a frying pan or
wok, then add the spring onions and fry for 2 minutes
until browned. Add the ginger juice and stir-fry for a
few seconds. Stir in the soy sauce and minced pork
and cook for 2-3 minutes, stirring constantly.
2 Add the rice wine, the salt and the rock sugar
together with the water. Bring to the boil and then
reduce the heat to low, cover and simmer for 40
minutes.
3 Bring a saucepan of water to the boil, and scald
the bean sprouts and leeks in it for 2 minutes. Drain
and place the vegetables in 6 soup bowls.
4 Cook the noodles in plenty of salted boiling water
for 3-5 minutes or until the noodles are just tender.
Drain. Stir in the sesame oil and toss.
5 Place the noodles in the soup bowls containing the
bean sprouts and leeks.
6 Bring the soup stock to the boil in a saucepan, and
pour over the noodle mixture in each soup bowl. Add
to each bowl 2 tblspns of the minced pork sauce, and
garnish with 1 slice of lean cooked pork, 2 cooked
peeled prawns and the chopped spring onion tops.
Serve at once.

腊腸飯糰

Rice Dumplings with Pork Sausage

INGREDIENTS (SERVES 4)

1 tspn corn oil
4 Chinese pork sausages (see NOTE)
450 g/1 lb cooked long-grain rice (see NOTE p. 264)
4 tspns Worcestershire or sweet and sour sauce

METHOD

1 Heat the oil in a wok or frying pan and fry the sausages for 5 minutes, turning occasionally. Cut in half lengthways.

2 Take four pieces of cellophane, about 20 × 25 cm/8 × 10 inches and lay one piece on top of a piece of damp cloth or muslin. Lay a quarter of the cooked rice in an oval shape on top of the cellophane.

3 Place two sausage halves in the centre of the rice (see small picture 2, right) and sprinkle with a little Worcestershire or sweet and sour sauce.

4 Slide your hands under the damp cloth. Bring them round to fully enclose the rice mixture, using your thumbs to push the cellophane over the rice. Mould the rice into a sausage shape and twist the ends of the cellophane to seal tightly.

5 Wrap the rice 'sausage' in foil and repeat to make four dumplings.

6 Place the rice packets in a colander or steamer, cover and steam over a high heat for 15 minutes. Tie a ribbon around the dumpling, if liked, and serve.

NOTE
Chinese sausages are dried and sold in pairs, linked by string. They need to be steamed for 30 minutes before using.

咖喱飯糰

Curry-Flavoured Rice Dumplings

INGREDIENTS (SERVES 4)

3 tblspns corn oil
1 baby onion or spring onion bulb, finely chopped
1 carrot, diced
2 garlic cloves, finely chopped
1-2 tblspns Chinese curry powder
50 g/2 oz cooked pork, diced
225 g/8 oz cooked long-grain rice (see NOTE, p. 264)

SEASONING
1½ tspns sugar
1 tspn white pepper
pinch of salt

METHOD

1 Heat the oil in a wok or frying pan and fry the onion for 1 minute. Add the diced carrot and fry for 30 seconds and then add the garlic, curry powder and pork and stir-fry for 1 minute.

2 Stir in the seasoning ingredients, stir-fry for 2 minutes and add the cooked rice, stirring thoroughly.

3 Take four large (20 × 25 cm/8 × 10 inch) or eight small (12.5 × 15 cm/5 × 6 inch) pieces of cellophane. Divide the rice among the pieces, bring the edges together and twist, and then wrap each cellophane ball in foil.

4 Place the rice balls in a colander or steamer and steam over a high heat for 15 minutes.

5 Unwrap the foil and tie the neck of the cellophane with ribbon. Serve hot or cold.

腊鴨飯

Rice with Duck and Ginger

INGREDIENTS (SERVES 4)

½ cooked duck
225 g/8 oz raw long-grain
rice
fresh parsley or majoram, to
garnish

SEASONING

1 tblspn ginger juice (see
NOTES)
1 tblspn rice wine or dry
sherry
½ tspn white pepper
1 tblspn lard

METHOD

1   Remove excess fat from the duck and cut into
bite-sized pieces.
2   Wash the rice and turn into a large saucepan. Add
the duck pieces and the seasoning ingredients and
sufficient water to come about 2.5 cm/1 inch above
the surface of the rice.
3   Bring to the boil and then cover and cook very
gently for 10-12 minutes or until all the water has been
incorporated and the rice is tender.
4   Garnish with fresh parsley or majoram and serve.

NOTES

1   To make ginger juice, finely grate a section of fresh
root ginger into a saucer. Squeeze the grated ginger
with the back of a spoon and the juice will run off.
Alternatively, place the ginger in a garlic press and
squeeze over a cup to catch the juice.
2   If you have a rice steamer, use this to cook the
rice. Follow the instructions on the box.

腊味飯

Rice with Assorted Meat

INGREDIENTS (SERVES 4)

50 g/2 oz ham, thickly cut
2 Chinese pork sausages (see
NOTE p. 267)
2 pieces of dried chicken or
duck
225 g/8 oz raw long-grain
rice
1 tblspn dried shrimps (see
NOTE)
50 g/2 oz garden peas
spring onion flowers, to
garnish (see NOTE p. 82)

SEASONING

½ tblspn finely chopped
fresh root ginger
1 tblspn rice wine or dry
sherry
1 tblspn lard
1 tspn salt
½ tspn white pepper

METHOD

1   Cut the ham, sausage and dried chicken or duck
into small cubes. Place in a small pan, cover with
boiling water and simmer for 5 minutes. Drain.
2   Rinse the rice and place in a large saucepan. Add
the diced meats, the shrimps, the peas and the
seasoning ingredients. Stir in enough water to come
2.5 cm/1 inch above the surface of the rice
3   Bring to the boil, cover and cook very gently for
10-15 minutes or until the water has been absorbed
and the rice is tender. Serve at once, garnished with a
spring onion flower.

NOTE
Soak the dried shrimps in warm water for 30 minutes
before using.

Pekinese Noodles in Special Sauce

INGREDIENTS (SERVES 4)

600 g/1¼ lbs fresh egg
   noodles
2 tblspns sesame oil
5 tblspns corn oil
2 spring onions, finely
   chopped
½ small cucumber, cut into
   thin shreds
225 g/8 oz cooked pork,
   diced
2 carrots, diced
50 g/2 oz bamboo shoots,
   diced

SEASONING

2 tblspns yellow bean sauce
2 tblspns sweet bean sauce
½ tblspn dark soy sauce
½ tblspn sugar

METHOD

1 Bring a large saucepan of water to the boil, add the noodles and cook for 2 minutes. Drain thoroughly and turn into a serving bowl. Stir in the sesame oil and mix thoroughly. Cover and keep warm while making the sauce.
2 Place the corn oil in a wok or frying pan. Add the spring onions and the seasoning ingredients and stir-fry for 1 minute.
3 Reserve a few cucumber shreds for garnishing and add the remainder with the pork, carrot and bamboo shoots to the wok. Mix thoroughly and cook for 3-4 minutes until hot and bubbly.
4 Pour the sauce over the noodles and garnish with the reserved cucumber shreds.

Shanghainese Thick Noodle Soup

INGREDIENTS (SERVES 4)

50 g/2 oz Chinese
   mushrooms
6 tblspns corn oil
2 spring onions, finely
   chopped
2 garlic cloves, crushed
75 g/3 oz Chinese leaves,
   sliced
225 g/8 oz cooked pork,
   thickly sliced
600 ml/1 pint clear soup
   stock (see p. 261)
2 tblspns cornflour
4 tblspns water
2 eggs, beaten
450 g/1 lb fresh egg noodles

SEASONING A
1½ tblspns light soy sauce
1 tspn salt

SEASONING B
3 tspns sesame oil
1 tspn white pepper

METHOD

1 Soak the Chinese mushrooms in warm water for 30 minutes. Discard stalks. Drain and cut into large pieces.
2 Place the oil in a large flameproof casserole and stir-fry the spring onions and garlic for 1 minute.
3 Add the Chinese leaves, the sliced pork, the mushrooms and seasoning **A** and cook, stirring for 2 minutes.
4 Add the soup stock and bring to the boil. Blend the cornflour with the water and stir into soup. Cook for a few minutes until it is slightly thickened and then remove from the heat and stir in the eggs using chopsticks or a fork.
5 Bring a large saucepan of water to the boil, add the noodles and cook for 5 minutes. Drain and place the noodles in a soup tureen. Pour the soup over the noodles and sprinkle with seasoning **B**. Serve immediately.

Chicken E-Mein Soup

INGREDIENTS (SERVES 4)

2 chicken legs
900 ml/1½ pints boiling water
1 tblspn ginger wine
1½ tspns salt
pinch of white pepper
275 g/10 oz fresh E-Mein
　noodles (see NOTE)
Chinese parsley, to garnish,
　optional

METHOD

1　Chop the chicken legs into large pieces. Place in boiling water for 1 minute to scald and then drain and place in a bowl.
2　Add the boiling water and the ginger wine. Place the bowl in a steamer, cover and steam over a medium-high heat for 40 minutes or until the chicken is cooked. Stir in the salt and pepper and set aside while cooking the noodles.
3　Place the noodles in a large bowl, cover with boiling water and scald for 30 seconds. Drain and stir into the soup. Garnish with parsley, if liked.

NOTE
E-Mein noodles are a type of egg noodle that are flat and twice as wide as normal egg noodles. They are mainly used for festivals, birthdays and banquets. If you have difficulty buying E-Mein noodles, the normal thin noodles can be used (pictured left, centre). If using dried egg noodles, soak in boiling water for 5 minutes.

Homemade Bean Threads

INGREDIENTS (SERVES 4)

150 g/5 oz green bean flour
450 g/1 lb rice flour
lard, for greasing
4 tblspns corn oil
2 spring onions, finely
　chopped
50 g/2 oz cooked pork, cut
　into thin strips
1 dried squid, soaked (see
　NOTES)
2 dried black mushrooms,
　soaked (see NOTES)
25 g/1 oz bamboo shoots, cut
　into thin strips
1 large carrot, grated
600 ml/1 pint clear soup
　stock (see p. 261)
carrot strips to garnish

SEASONING
1 tblspn light soy sauce
1 tspn rice wine or dry sherry
1½ tspns salt
½ tspn white pepper

METHOD

1　Mix the green bean flour with the rice flour and slowly add enough cold water to make a thick paste.
2　Grease a large skillet or frying pan with the lard. Smooth a thin layer of paste over the pan, spreading it out towards the edges to make a large pancake.
3　Place the pan over a low to medium heat and cook gently until the underside is lightly brown. Flip over and cook the other side until lightly brown. When cooked, turn the pancake onto a large plate and cut into long strips. Repeat until all the mixture is used. These are the green bean threads.
4　Heat the oil in a wok, add the spring onions and stir-fry for 1 minute. Add the pork, squid, mushrooms, bamboo shoots and carrot and fry for 2 minutes, stirring occasionally.
5　Add the soup stock and bring to the boil. Stir in the seasoning ingredients and the green bean threads and cook for 5 minutes. Garnish with carrot strips and serve at once.

NOTES
1　Soak the dried squid in cold water overnight before using. Then remove head and tentacles and cut into thin pieces.
2　Soak the black mushrooms for 30 minutes before using. Discard the stalks. Cut into thin strips.

江西辣味米粉

Spicy Rice Noodles

INGREDIENTS (SERVES 4)

300 g/11 oz packet thin rice vermicelli
100 g/4 oz pork fillet
25 g/1 oz small dried fish
2 or 3 red chillis
6 tblspns corn oil
150 ml/¼ pint clear soup stock (see p. 261)
100 g/4 oz Chinese leaves, shredded
salt and pepper

SEASONING

1 tblspn light soy sauce
large pinch of five-spice powder
½ tblspn rice wine or dry sherry
1 tspn cornflour

METHOD

1 Place the noodles in a bowl and cover with boiling water. Soak for 10 minutes, stirring occasionally with chopsticks or a fork to loosen and then drain. Rinse under cold water.
2 Cut the pork into thin strips. Blend the seasoning ingredients in a bowl, add the pork and marinate for 10 minutes.
3 Rinse the dried fish in cold water and shake off excess water. Cut the chillis thinly, discarding the seeds.
4 Heat the oil in a wok, add the dried fish and chillis and stir-fry for 5 seconds. Add the pork and stir-fry for another 2 minutes.
5 Stir in the soup stock and Chinese leaves, reduce the heat to medium and cook for 3 minutes or until the Chinese leaves are soft.
6 Add the rice noodles and salt and pepper. Cover and simmer for 3-4 minutes and then remove cover and stir-fry over a higher heat. Serve hot.

台式炒米粉

Stir-Fried Rice Noodles

INGREDIENTS (SERVES 4)

100 g/4 oz pork fillet
300 g/11 oz packet thin rice vermicelli
6 tblspns corn oil
2 red chillis, seeded and finely sliced
75 g/3 oz cooked peeled prawns
150 g/5 oz bean sprouts
125 ml/4 fl oz clear soup stock (see p. 261)
3 or 4 chives or spring onion tops, chopped

SEASONING A

½ tblspn light soy sauce
2 tspns cornflour
½ tblspn ginger wine

SEASONING B

3 tblspns light soy sauce
1 tspn salt
½ tspn white pepper
½ tspn sugar

METHOD

1 Cut the pork into thin strips and marinate in seasoning **A** for 20 minutes.
2 Soak the noodles in boiling water for 10 minutes. Drain thoroughly.
3 Heat the oil in a wok, add the chillis and stir-fry for 5 seconds. Stir in the pork and cook for 3 minutes, stirring all the time. Add the prawns, bean sprouts, soup stock, noodles and seasoning **B** and cook rapidly for 3-5 minutes or until almost dry.
4 Add the chopped chives or onion tops and stir. Serve at once.

Noodles of Dried Bean Curd Shreds

INGREDIENTS (SERVES 2)

3 Chinese mushrooms
150 g/5 oz dried bean curd
　shreds
1.2 litres/2 pints boiling
　water
1 tspn bicarbonate soda
2 tblspns corn oil
1 tblspn shredded bamboo
　shoot
1 tblspn shredded carrot
1 tblspn shredded celery
1 tblspn straw mushrooms
450 ml/15 fl oz clear soup
　stock (see p. 261)

SEASONING

⅔ tspn salt
2 tspns sesame oil

METHOD

1　Soak the Chinese mushrooms for 30 minutes in warm water. Drain. Cut off and discard the stalks and shred the caps.

2　Chop the dried bean curd shreds into sections and cook in the boiling water mixed with the bicarbonate of soda for 5 minutes. Drain and wash under cold running water.

3　Heat the oil in a wok and stir-fry the shredded Chinese mushrooms for 2 minutes. Add the bamboo shoot, carrot, celery and straw mushrooms and stir-fry for 3 minutes more. Add the seasoning and the soup. Bring to the boil, add the dried bean curd shreds, bring back to the boil and boil for 3 minutes. Serve at once.

NOTE

Substitute 175 g/6 oz white vermicelli for the dried bean curd shreds.

Chicken with Sweet Rice

INGREDIENTS
(SERVES 4–6)

1 tblspn oyster sauce (see
  NOTES)
1 chicken, about 1.4 kg/3 lbs
  in weight
350 g/12 oz glutinous rice
  (see NOTES)
10-12 tblspns corn oil
50 g/2 oz cooked ham,
  chopped
2 Chinese dried mushrooms,
  soaked and chopped (see
  NOTES)
1 tblspn light soy sauce
1 tspn sugar
1 tblspn rice wine or dry
  sherry
1.2 litres/2 pints water
2 eggs, beaten
3 tblspns cornflour
cherry tomatoes, to garnish

METHOD

1 Pour the oyster sauce over the chicken, and marinate for 30 minutes.
2 Wash the rice in cold water several times, until the water runs clear. Place the rice in a bowl and cover with boiling water. Stand for 1 minute, then drain.
3 Heat 2 tblspns of the oil in a wok or frying pan. Add the rice, and stir-fry for 1 minute. Add the ham, mushrooms, soy sauce, sugar and rice wine and continue stir-frying for a few more minutes.
4 Add the water to the rice mixture, bring to the boil, cover and simmer for 30 minutes or until the water is absorbed.
5 Stuff the rice mixture into the body cavity of the chicken, and place in a large steamer. Put 2.5 cm/1 inch boiling water in a large saucepan. Set the steamer over the saucepan, cover with a tight-fitting lid and steam for 2 hours.
6 Remove the stuffing from the chicken, and place on a serving dish.
7 Cut the chicken into bite-sized pieces and then coat with the beaten eggs. Dust thoroughly with the cornflour. Heat the remaining oil in a frying pan, add the chicken and fry for 5 minutes.
8 Arrange the chicken pieces around the rice on the serving dish, garnish with cherry tomatoes and serve.

NOTES

1 Oyster sauce is made from oysters cooked in soy sauce and brine, and is available from some supermarkets and from Chinese delicatessens.
2 Glutinous rice, which is also known as sweet rice, is available from Chinese delicatessens. Stickier and sweeter than ordinary rice, it should be washed and soaked before cooking.
3 Before using the Chinese dried mushrooms, soak them in warm water for 20-30 minutes or until they are soft. Remove the stalks, then chop.

牛肉湯刀削麵

Noodles in Beef Brisket Soup

INGREDIENTS (SERVES 6)

700 g/1½ lbs beef brisket
900 ml/1½ pints water
6 tblspns rice wine or dry
    sherry
2½ tspns salt
600 g/1¼ lbs plain flour
2 or 3 Chinese leaves, cut
    into 4 pieces
1 red chilli, to garnish,
    optional

SEASONING

12 mm/½ inch piece fresh
    root ginger
1 spring onion, sliced
½ tblspn aniseed or caraway
    seeds
½ tblspn cumin seeds
1 tspn salt

METHOD

1   Cut the beef into thin 2.5 cm/1 inch slices. Place in a flameproof casserole, cover with boiling water and simmer for 1 minute. Drain and return beef to the casserole.

2   Wrap all the seasoning ingredients in a piece of cloth or muslin, tie the end securely with string and add to the casserole together with the water, rice wine and 1 tspn salt.

3   Bring the pan to the boil. Reduce the heat and simmer for 1-1½ hours or until the beef is tender. Remove the spice pack.

4   Place the flour in a bowl and add sufficient water to make a dough. Knead slightly and then cover and set aside for 20 minutes. Knead again until smooth and shape into a fat sausage.

5   Bring a saucepan of water to the boil, add the remaining salt and throw in the Chinese leaves. Remove the leaves with a slotted spoon and add to the beef soup. Reserve the boiling water.

6   Hold the dough in one hand and, using a sharp knife, cut off the thin 'noodles' (see small picture, right). Bring the cabbage water back to the boil and drop the noodles into the water. Cook for 1 minute and then carefully remove and stir into the beef soup.

7   Cook for a further 2-3 minutes and serve, garnished with red chilli, if liked.

辣肉醬炒通心粉

Pasta in Pork Sauce

INGREDIENTS (SERVES 4)

225 g/8 oz pasta shells
4 tblspns corn oil
225 g/8 oz minced pork
2 spring onions, chopped
75 ml/3 fl oz clear soup stock
    (see p. 261)
onion rings, baby cucumbers
    and red chillis, sliced, to
    garnish

SEASONING

½ tblspn hot bean paste (see
    NOTE)
2 tspns cayenne pepper
½ tblspn ginger wine
1 tspn salt
1 tspn sugar
½ tspn white pepper

METHOD

1   Bring a large pan of salted water to the boil, add the pasta and cook for 8-10 minutes or until the pasta is tender. Drain and rinse in cold water.

2   Heat the oil in a frying pan, add the minced pork, spring onions and the seasoning ingredients. Stir thoroughly and pour in the soup stock. Cook for 2 minutes and stir in the pasta.

3   Stir-fry for a further 2 minutes until evenly mixed. Turn onto a serving plate and garnish with onion rings, sliced baby cucumbers and sliced chillis, if liked.

NOTE

Hot bean paste should be used carefully as it is very hot. It is made from crushed soya beans, chilli and sugar and is sold normally in jars from most Chinese supermarkets.

Pork Congee

INGREDIENTS (SERVES 4)

75 g/3 oz lean pork
600 ml/1 pint clear soup
   stock (see p. 261)
1 carrot, diced
50 g/2 oz garden peas
75 g/3 oz oatmeal
1 tspn salt

METHOD

1 Cut the pork into small pieces. Pour the soup stock into a saucepan and add the pork, carrot and peas. Bring to the boil and add the oatmeal.
2 Boil gently for 10-12 minutes and then remove from the heat, cover and stand for 5 minutes.
3 Serve with a sprinkling of salt.

Sweet Congee

INGREDIENTS (SERVES 4)

600 ml/1 pint milk
2 tblspns sugar
75 g/3 oz oatmeal

METHOD

1 Warm the milk in a saucepan and add the sugar. Heat, stirring, until the sugar dissolves and add the oatmeal.
2 Bring to the boil, stirring, and then reduce the heat and simmer gently for 4-5 minutes until the oatmeal is cooked. Serve.

茄汁飯糰

Rice Dumplings with Tomato Sauce

INGREDIENTS (SERVES 4)

3 tblspns corn oil
1 garlic clove, crushed
40 g/1½ oz garden peas
450 g/1 lb cooked long-grain rice (see NOTE p. 264)
75 g/3 oz cooked ham, diced
3 tblspns tomato sauce
1½ tspns salt
½ tspn white pepper

METHOD

1   Heat the oil in a wok and fry the garlic for 10 seconds. Add the peas, cook for 1 minute and then stir in the rice and diced ham.
2   Stir in the tomato sauce, salt and pepper and mix thoroughly.
3   Take 8 pieces of cellophane, measuring approximately 10 × 12.5 cm/4 × 5 inches and place a tblspn of the rice mixture in the centre of each. Gather up and twist the top securely and then wrap each in a piece of foil.
4   Place in a steamer, cover and steam for approximately 15 minutes over a high heat.
5   Unwrap the foil, tie the neck of the parcels with a ribbon and serve.

牛柳飯糰

Rice Dumplings with Beef

INGREDIENTS (SERVES 4)

350 g/12 oz rump steak
3 tblspns corn oil
450 g/1 lb cooked long-grain rice (see NOTE, p. 264)

SEASONING

1 tblspn light soy sauce
½ tblspn rice wine or dry sherry
½ tspn salt
½ tspn bicarbonate of soda
1 tblspn sugar
½ tspn white pepper
1½ tspns cornflour

METHOD

1   Slice the beef against the grain into long strips. Blend the seasoning ingredients in a bowl, add the steak and marinate for 30 minutes.
2   Heat the oil in a wok and stir-fry the beef for 3 minutes. Remove.
3   Take four pieces of cellophane, about 20 × 25 cm/8 × 10 inches, and lay one piece on top of a piece of damp cloth or muslin. Lay about a quarter of the cooked rice in an oval shape on top of the cellophane and place two or three strips of beef in the centre of the rice (see small picture p. 267).
4   Slide your hands under the damp cloth. Bring them round to fully enclose the rice mixture, using your thumbs to push the cellophane over the rice. Mould the rice into a sausage shape and twist the ends of the cellophane to seal tightly.
5   Wrap the rice 'sausage' in foil and repeat this process another three times until all the rice and beef has been used.
6   Place the rice packets in a colander or steamer, cover and steam over a high heat for 15 minutes. Tie a ribbon around the dumpling, if liked, and serve.

玉米筍湯

Baby Corn Shoot Soup

INGREDIENTS (SERVES 4)

6 Chinese mushrooms
12 baby corn shoots
3 salted bamboo shoots
4 tblspns green beans
600 ml/1 pint clear soup
    stock (see p. 261)
½ tspn salt
1 tspn sesame oil

METHOD

1   Soak the Chinese mushrooms in boiling water for 20 minutes. Drain. Cut off and discard the stalks and chop each cap in half.
2   Wash the baby corn shoots and chop them in half. Rinse the salted bamboo shoots under cold water and chop off the stalks and end parts. Wash again and chop into square sections. Wash the green beans.
3   Put all ingredients into a large bowl. Add the soup stock and salt and place the bowl in a steamer. Steam over boiling water for 20 minutes. Drizzle the sesame oil over the soup before serving.

NOTE
Salted bamboo shoots can be bought at Chinese supermarkets but you could substitute 50 g/2 oz of any salted vegetable for them.

韭菜干絲

Stir-Fried Dried Bean Curd Shreds with Chives

INGREDIENTS (SERVES 4)

50 g/2 oz chives
150 g/5 oz dried bean curd
    shreds or fresh egg noodles
4 tblspns corn oil
50-75 ml/2-3 fl oz clear soup
    stock (see p. 261)

SEASONING
1 tspn salt
1½ tspns sugar
½ tblspn light soy sauce
½ tspn white pepper

METHOD

1   Discard any old or withered leaves from the chives. Wash the remainder and chop into 4-cm/1½-inch sections. Chop the dried bean curd shreds into 2.5-cm/1-inch sections and wash in salted water.
2   Heat the oil in a wok. Add the soup stock with the dried bean curd shreds or noodles and the seasoning. Stir-fry over a gentle heat for 5-7 minutes, until the liquid has been absorbed. Add the chives and stir-fry for 30 seconds. Serve at once.

NOTE
A Chinese proverb runs "Chive is the chicken of the poor" and herbalists endorse that it is a very nutritious vegetable. It is easy to grow; do not neglect it.

麻油麵線

Egg Noodles with Sesame Oil

INGREDIENTS (SERVES 2)

1 packet (bundle) fresh egg
  noodles
3 tblspns sesame oil
2 eggs, beaten
1 tblspn finely chopped fresh
  ginger
1 slice fresh ginger
350 ml/12 fl oz clear soup
  stock (see p. 261)
1 tspn salt

METHOD

1 Wash the noodles very thoroughly.
2 Heat the oil in a wok and stir-fry the eggs over a
medium heat. When set, remove the eggs and stir-fry
the chopped ginger and the slice of ginger for 1
minute or so. Remove the slice of ginger and put on
one side. Pour the soup into the pan and add the salt.
Bring to the boil and add the noodles and fried egg.
Bring to the boil again and serve at once with the
slice of ginger to garnish.

NOTES
1 This is a famous dish from the Fuchow style of
cooking.
2 Fresh egg noodles are sold in bundles.

清湯銀耳

Soup of White Fungus

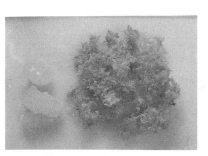

INGREDIENTS (SERVES 4)

25 g/1 oz white fungus
4½ tblspns rock sugar
900 ml/1½ pints clear soup
  stock (see p. 261)
4 maraschino cherries, for
  decoration

METHOD

1 Soak the white fungus in cold water for 4-6 hours.
Remove the root and any hard pieces and wash the
fungus until it is quite clean. Soak for a further 2 hours
in hot water to allow it to expand. Drain off the water.
2 Put the fungus and rock sugar into a bowl with
the clear soup. Place in a pan of hot water and simmer
very gently for 45 minutes to 1 hour until the soup
becomes glutinous. Check the pan from time to time
to make sure it does not burn dry. Serve the soup in
individual bowls with a cherry in each one.

NOTE
White fungus or silver ears is a dried fungi with little
flavour but a delicate texture. Normally available in
Chinese supermarkets

海鮮烏龍麺

Noodles in Seafood Soup

INGREDIENTS (SERVES 4)

4 crab claws
100 g/4 oz squid
8 clams
3 dried black mushrooms, soaked (see NOTES)
100 g/4 oz pork fillet
1.2 litres/2 pints clear soup stock (see p. 261)
3 tblspns fish stock or ½ fish stock cube
4 quail eggs, optional
275 g/10 oz u-dong noodles (see NOTES)
150 g/5 oz cooked prawns in their shells

SEASONING

1 tspn salt
1 tblspn ginger wine
½ tspn white pepper

METHOD

1 Crack the crab claws with a heavy rolling pin or hammer.
2 Pull away the head and entrails from the squid. Feel inside the body and remove the transparent cartilage. Peel off and discard the mottled skin from the body, and rinse the squid under running water. Cut into 2.5 cm/1 inch pieces.
3 Split the clams open with a knife, and rinse clean.
4 Remove the stems from the dried black mushrooms and discard. Slice the caps.
5 Cut the pork into slices.
6 Place the soup stock in a saucepan. Add the fish stock, sliced pork, black mushrooms and quail eggs if using. Bring to the boil.
7 Add the noodles and seasoning, and cook rapidly for 2 minutes.
8 Add the crab, squid and clams and cook for a further 3 minutes. Finally add the prawns and cook for 3 minutes. Skim the surface if necessary and then serve.

NOTES

1 Soak the black mushrooms in warm water for 20-30 minutes. Drain.
2 U-dong noodles are dried noodles made of wheat flour and water. They are straight, flat and quite thick. Soak in cold water for 10 minutes before using.

麻油鷄麺線

Thin Noodles in Chicken Soup

INGREDIENTS (SERVES 4-6)

4 chicken legs
2.5 cm/1 inch piece fresh root ginger, cut into 4 pieces
275 g/10 oz bundle mein-tsein noodles (see NOTE)
6 tblspns sesame oil
2 tblspns rice wine or dry sherry

METHOD

1 Using a cleaver or meat axe, cut the chicken legs into 4 pieces.
2 Using a meat hammer, pat the slices of root ginger flat.
3 Rinse the noodles and cut them into 10 cm/4 inch long sections. Lay on a piece of muslin or a clean tea towel and place on a heatproof plate. Place the plate in a steamer or large colander, cover and steam for 2 minutes.
4 Heat the oil in a wok or frying pan and fry the ginger for 10 seconds. Add the chicken and stir-fry for 8 minutes, until cooked and lightly browned.
5 Add the rice wine and 1.2 litres/2 pints water, and bring to the boil. Add the noodles, bring back to the boil and serve.

NOTE

Mein-tsein are thin dried egg noodles. They are sold either in bundles or coiled into packets.

Chow-Mein, Cantonese-Style

INGREDIENTS (SERVES 6)

250 ml/9 fl oz corn oil
2 chicken breasts cut into
   bite-sized pieces
450 g/1 lb fresh egg noodles
1½ tspns salt
½ tspn white pepper
275 g/10 oz spring greens,
   torn into thin shreds
4 black mushrooms soaked
   (see NOTE 1, p. 291) and
   sliced
40 g/1½ oz cooked peeled
   prawns
2 roasted duck breasts
10 slices cucumber
4 slices bamboo shoot
4 quail eggs, optional
1 tblspn sherry

SEASONING

½ tspn soy sauce
75 ml/3 fl oz water
2 tblspns cornflour

METHOD

1   Heat 3 tblspns of the oil in a pan and sauté the chicken for 8 minutes. Remove and set aside.
2   Cook the noodles in plenty of boiling salted water for 3-5 minutes or until just tender.
3   Heat 6 tblspns of the remaining oil in a wok. Add the noodles and stir to separate. Add the salt and pepper, and stir-fry for 4-5 minutes.
4   Arrange the noodles into a coil. Swirl 4 tblspns of the remaining oil slowly around the rim of the wok, just above the noodles. Cover and cook for about 4-6 minutes, or until the noodles are browned on one side.
5   When the noodles no longer stick to the bottom, turn them over. Splash the remaining oil around the rim, and fry till browned. Remove and place on a serving dish.
6   Re-heat the wok and stir-fry the spring greens, mushrooms, prawns, chicken, duck, cucumber, bamboo shoot and quail eggs, if using, adding a little more oil if necessary. Add the seasoning ingredients, stirring continually and bring to the boil. Cook for 1 minute. Sprinkle with the sherry, and remove from the heat. Pour over the noodles and serve.

Curried Beef Chow Mein

INGREDIENTS (SERVES 6)

275 g/10 oz rump steak
275 g/10 oz buckwheat
   noodles
6 tblspns corn oil
3 spring onions, chopped
1 tblspn grated fresh root
   ginger
3 garlic cloves, crushed
1 large onion, cut into
   wedges
350 ml/12 fl oz clear soup
   stock (see p. 261)
60 g/2½ oz mange-tout

SEASONING A

1 tblspn cornflour
1 egg white
1 tblspn ginger wine

SEASONING B

5 tblspns Chinese curry
   powder
125 ml/4 fl oz milk
½ tspn salt
1½ tblspns sugar

METHOD

1   Cut the steak into thin 2.5 cm/1 inch long slices. Blend seasoning **A** ingredients in a bowl, add the sliced beef and marinate for 20 minutes. Drain.
2   Bring a large saucepan of salted water to the boil and cook the noodles for 1½-3 minutes. Drain.
3   Heat the oil in a wok or frying pan and fry the spring onions, ginger and garlic for 1-2 minutes. Add the onion and seasoning **B** ingredients, fry for 2 minutes and then add the beef slices. Stir-fry for 2-3 minutes, or until the meat is evenly brown.
4   Add the noodles and the soup stock, and bring to the boil. Boil for 2 minutes, then add the mange-tout and stir-fry for 1 minute. Remove from the heat and serve.

Taiwanese-Style Noodles

INGREDIENTS (SERVES 6)

150 g/5 oz bean sprouts
450 g/1 lb fresh egg noodles
1 tblspn sesame oil
4 tblspns corn oil
2 spring onions, chopped
225 g/8 oz lean pork, sliced
100 g/4 oz Chinese leaves,
 shredded

SEASONING

1 tblspn ginger juice
¼ tspn five-spice powder
1½ tspns salt
1 tblspn soy sauce
½ tspn white pepper
½ tspn rice wine or dry
 sherry
125 ml/4 fl oz clear soup
 stock (see p. 261)

METHOD

1 Rinse the bean sprouts in cold water and drain.
2 Cook the noodles in a large saucepan of boiling salted water for 3-5 minutes. Drain, then toss in the sesame oil.
3 Heat the corn oil in a wok or frying pan, then add the spring onions and stir-fry for 20 seconds. Add the pork slices and stir fry for 3 minutes. Add the Chinese leaves, stir-fry for 2 minutes, until softened and then add the bean sprouts, noodles and seasoning ingredients.
4 Cook for 1 minute, uncovered, and then cover and simmer for 1 minute. Remove the lid and stir-fry for a further 2 minutes. Serve immediately.

Rice Noodles with Lettuce

INGREDIENTS
(SERVES 4-6)

450 g/1 lb fresh rice noodles
1 Cos or round lettuce
1.2 litres/2 pints chicken
 stock (see p. 149)
1 tspn salt
2 tblspns rice wine or dry
 sherry
1 tspn sesame oil

METHOD

1 Cook the noodles in a large saucepan of boiling, salted water for 1 minute, or until the noodles are just tender. Drain, and place in a serving dish.
2 Break the lettuce into individual leaves and rinse in cold water. Shred into even-sized pieces.
3 Heat the stock to boiling. Add the salt and rice wine and then throw in the lettuce leaves. Cook for 2 minutes and pour over the noodles. Sprinkle with sesame oil and serve.

DIM SUM

Dim Sum are the little snacks that are extremely popular in China. They are eaten in the morning and sometimes all afternoon as well! They frequently consist of little breads or pastries that have been stuffed with savoury or sweet fillings. They are normally steamed or deep-fried.

The wrappers that enclose these mouth-watering snacks are made from various types of dough. The dough is normally made of plain wheat flour, although occasionally recipes will call for rice flour when a specially light texture is required. The fillings themselves usually consist of meat – pork and beef are popular – which are then often flavoured with a sweet and sour seasoning, such as red bean paste. This strong, distinctive flavour contrasts particularly well with the slightly sweet flavour of the dough.

In Chinese restaurants, you can eat a complete meal made up of Dim Sum, but this may be unrealistic to attempt at home. However one, or possibly two, Dim Sum snacks, such as Steamed Pork Buns (p. 299) or Salted Vegetable Patties (p. 313) would be delicious to serve at the start of a meal or as a light lunch.

Steamed Pork Buns

INGREDIENTS (SERVES 4)

275 g/10 oz plain flour
125 ml/4 fl oz tepid water
1 tspn dried yeast
½ tspn sugar
1 tblspn lard

FILLING
600 g/1¼ lbs lean
    minced pork
1 tspn salt
1 tblspn ginger wine
4 tblspns water
½ tblspn sesame oil
pinch of white pepper

METHOD

1 Make up leavened dough with the flour, yeast, sugar and lard as instructed on p. 345
2 Make the filling: mix all ingredients together to make a smooth paste.
3 Break the dough into 20 small pieces, rolling each piece between floured hands to make a small ball.
4 Roll out the ball to make a circle, about 7.5 cm/3½ inches in diameter. Place 1 tblpsn of filling in the centre of each circle. Bring the edges together over the meat and press together firmly. Stand for 3-5 minutes.
5 Place a layer of muslin over bottom of a bamboo or metal steamer, place the buns on top and steam them, covered, for 10 minutes. Serve at once.

NOTE
Steamed buns can be served in a soup, if liked. Stir a little light soy sauce into chicken stock or rich soup stock, heat the soup and then float the steamed buns on top.

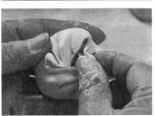

Steamed Pork and Vegetable Buns

INGREDIENTS (SERVES 4)

600 g/1¼ lbs plain flour
250 ml/8 fl oz tepid water
1½ tspns dried yeast
1 tblspn sugar

FILLING
350 g/12 oz lean
    minced pork
450 g/1 lb Chinese
    leaves, finely
    shredded
½ tblspn soy sauce
½ tblspn ginger wine
½ tblspn sesame oil
1 tspn salt
pinch of white pepper

METHOD

1 Prepare leavened dough with the flour, yeast and sugar, as instructed on p. 345. Place the filling ingredients in a large bowl and blend thoroughly.
2 Break the dough into 10 even-sized pieces and roll each piece into a ball to make a circle, about 12.5 cm/5 inches in diameter. Place 2 tblspns of filling in the centre of each and fold the edges over the filling, pressing together firmly to seal.
3 Cover the buns with a damp cloth and stand for 20 minutes.
4 Lay a piece of damp muslin over the bottom of a bamboo or metal steamer and place the buns on top. Steam, covered, over a high heat for 25 minutes and then serve at once.

NOTE
Both of these steamed buns are delicious served with a dipping sauce. Make a sauce by blending 3 tblspns finely grated fresh root ginger, 3 tblspns light soy sauce and 3 tblspns Chinese white (or cider) vinegar.

Cantonese-Style Congee

INGREDIENTS (SERVES 4)

275 g/10 oz minced pork
225 g/8 oz white glutinous
 rice
1.5 litres/2½ pints clear soup
 stock (see p. 261)
1-2 yiu-tiao (see NOTES)
3 parsley sprigs
1 tspn white pepper
salt

METHOD

1 Tie the minced pork in a piece of muslin.
2 Wash and drain the rice thoroughly. Put in a large saucepan with the soup stock and pork and bring to the boil.
3 Meanwhile, chop the yiu-tiao and put in a bowl. When the rice mixture – known as congee – is ready, discard the pork and pour the congee over the yiu-tiao. Finely chop the parsley and sprinkle on top. Season to taste with pepper and salt. Serve at once.

NOTES

1 Yiu-tiao is also known as twisted doughnut and is available in Chinese supermarkets. It is a long stick of deep-fried dough.
2 Beef, fish or pork liver can also be used to flavour the congee.

Taro Congee

INGREDIENTS (SERVES 4)

225 g/8 oz white glutinous
 rice
900 ml/1½ pints clear soup
 stock (see p. 261)
6 tblspns dried shrimps
½ large taro
3 tblspns corn oil
3 shallots, finely chopped
150 g/5 oz lean minced pork
2 tblspns spiced preserved
 vegetable root, finely
 chopped
3 tblspns water
1 spring onion, chopped, to
 garnish

SEASONING

2 tspns salt
1 tspn white pepper
2 spring onions, finely
 chopped

METHOD

1 Wash and drain the glutinous rice and simmer in the soup stock for about 1 hour.
2 While the rice is cooking, soak the dried shrimps in cold water for 10-15 minutes, then drain. Peel the taro and cut into large cubes.
3 Heat the oil in a wok or large frying pan and fry the chopped shallots for a few seconds. Add the soaked shrimps, pork and preserved vegetable and cook, stirring for 3-5 minutes. Add the taro cubes with the water. Cover and simmer for 5 minutes.
4 Add the rice mixture to the wok, stir well and bring to the boil. Lower the heat and simmer for 15 minutes. Add the seasoning ingredients, garnish with spring onions and serve straight away.

NOTE

Dried squid can be used instead of dried shrimps. Soak it in cold water overnight, then cut into small pieces. Dried squid is available at Chinese supermarkets and can be stored for some months in a dry place.

Pork and Onion Pancakes

INGREDIENTS (SERVES 4)

2 small onions
125 ml/4 fl oz corn oil
600 g/1¼ lbs plain flour
150 g/5 oz minced pork or
    beef
approx. 600 ml/1 pint boiling
    water
2 tblspns chopped parsley

SEASONING
2 tspns salt
½ tspn sugar
1 tspn white pepper

METHOD

1   Slice the onions very finely and fry them in 1 tblspn of the oil for about 2 minutes. Remove with a slotted spoon and mix with the flour, minced meat and seasoning ingredients. Stir in sufficient hot water to make a thick, smooth paste. Stir in the chopped parsley.
2   Heat 3-4 tblspns oil in a frying pan and heat gently. Add large spoonfuls of the mixture and fry on both sides until golden brown and crisp. Remove from the pan and keep warm while you cook the remainder of the pancakes in the same way, adding more oil to the pan as necessary.

Cabbage and Bean Curd Patties

INGREDIENTS (SERVES 4)

450 g/1 lb Chinese cabbage
    or Chinese leaves
2 tspns salt
1 fresh bean curd
225 g/8 oz minced pork
600 g/1¼ lbs plain flour
approx. 600 ml/1 pint boiling
    water
150 ml/¼ pint corn oil

SEASONING
½ tblspn light soy sauce
½ tblspn sugar
1 tspn white pepper
1 tblspn cornflour
½ tblspn sesame oil

METHOD

1   Remove old or withered leaves from the outside of the cabbage, then wash and drain the remainder. Rub the leaves with the salt and leave for 10 minutes. Wash off the salt, gently squeeze out excess water and chop cabbage finely.
2   Mash the bean curd, then mix with the chopped cabbage, pork and seasoning ingredients.
3   Prepare the scalded dough (see p. 344) using the flour and the boiling water. Knead the dough until smooth and shiny, then divide into 50 g/2 oz pieces. Roll these out to a circle about 10 cm/4 inches in diameter and place 1-2 tblspns of the bean curd mixture in the centre. Wrap the dough around the filling using your hands. Seal the edges firmly.
4   When the filling is enclosed in the dough, flatten the pancakes slightly with a rolling pin.
5   Heat the oil in a wok or frying pan and fry the pancakes for about 20 minutes, until lightly golden on both sides. Serve.

Steamed Dumplings

INGREDIENTS (SERVES 4)

400 g/14 oz minced pork
600 g/1¼ lbs plain flour
approx. 600 ml/1 pint boiling
   water

SEASONING

1 tblspn ginger wine
½ tspn white pepper
1½ tspns salt
2 tspns sesame oil
3 tblspns clear soup stock
   (see p. 261)

METHOD

1   Mix the minced pork with the seasoning
ingredients and keep stirring until the mixture is very
sticky and well-blended.
2   Prepare the scalded dough (see p. 344) using the
flour and boiling water. Knead well, then shape into a
long roll and cut into 15 g/½ oz sections. Roll each
section to a thin circle.
3   Place 1 tblspn of the filling in the centre of each
dough circle, then pinch the edges of the dough
around the filling (see small picture 2, right).
4   Put a piece of damp muslin or cheesecloth in the
bottom of the steamer and carefully place the
dumplings on top. Steam, covered, over rapidly
boiling water for 8-10 minutes and serve at once.

NOTE

Make sure the water is boiling hard before placing the
dumplings in the steamer.

Doubled Pancakes

INGREDIENTS (SERVES 4)

400 g/14 oz plain flour
175 g/6 oz self-raising flour
approx. 600 ml/1 pint boiling
   water
25 g/1 oz lard, melted

METHOD

1   Sift the flours together and mix with boiling water
to make scalded dough (see p. 344). Divide the dough
into 50 g/2 oz pieces, shape into balls and flatten each
one.
2   Brush one side of each piece of dough with melted
lard and place them together in pairs, greased side
inside. Roll out to a thin circle.
3   Dry-fry the pancakes in a heavy-based pan over
medium heat until beginning to brown. Turn the
pancake over and cook the other side, then remove
and keep warm while you cook the remainder in the
same way.
4   Separate the two pancakes for serving.

NOTE

Serve these pancakes with slices of crispy duck.

Glutinous Rice Dumplings

INGREDIENTS (SERVES 4)

275 g/10 oz pork
600 g/1¼ lbs white glutinous
   rice
large pinch of salt
bamboo leaves and straw
   (see NOTES)

SEASONING

125 ml/4 fl oz dark soy sauce
1 tblspn rice wine or dry
   sherry
1 tspn white pepper

METHOD

1 Cut the pork into 5 cm/2 inch wide strips. Mix the seasoning ingredients together and pour over the pork. Coat thoroughly, cover and leave in a cool place overnight. Drain the pork, reserving the marinade.
2 Wash and drain the rice and add to the reserved marinade with the salt. Mix well, leave for about 10 minutes, then mix again.
3 Place the wrong sides of two bamboo leaves together and fold down the top quarter tucking it inside the "cupped" shape. Put 2 tblspns of the rice into the second quarter of the leaves and place 2 meat strips on top. Cover with another 2 tblspns of rice, pressing it down well.
4 Fold the bottom half and the sides of the leaves over the rice, wrapping neatly and tightly. Tie with straws to secure parcels.
5 Put the parcels in a large saucepan and cover with cold water to come about 7.5 cm/3 inches above the parcels. Bring to the boil, then lower the heat and simmer very gently for about 4 hours.
6 Turn off the heat, but leave the parcels in the pan, covered, for 1 further hour before serving.

NOTES
1 Fresh and dried bamboo leaves are available in Chinese supermarkets, together with the straw for tying the tsung-tzu. You could tie the parcels with fine string if you prefer.
2 These rice dumplings are traditionally served around the time of the Dragon Boat Festival which occurs on May 5th each year.

Red Bean Dumplings

INGREDIENTS (SERVES 4)

200 g/7 oz minced pork
175 g/6 oz sugar
275 g/10 oz red bean paste
   (see NOTE p. 61)
50 g/2 oz lard, melted
600 g/1¼ lbs white glutinous
   rice
bamboo leaves and straw
   (see NOTE above)

METHOD

1 Mix the pork with the sugar and leave, covered, overnight.
2 Mix the red bean paste with the lard, then wrap 2 tblspns of this around the pork mixture. Press into an oval shape.
3 Wash and drain the rice, then assemble and cook the dumplings as outlined above, from Step 3.

Ho-Fun Soup

INGREDIENTS (SERVES 6)

275 g/10 oz sirloin steak or quick-frying steak
275 g/10 oz Chinese cabbage or Chinese leaves
4 spring onions
450 g/1 lb rice noodles or Ho-Fun
4 tblspns corn oil
1.2 litres/2 pints clear soup stock (see p. 261)

SEASONING A

½ tblspn ginger wine
½ tspn five-spice powder
1 tspn sesame oil
1 tblspn cornflour mixed with 5 tblspns water
½ tspn salt

SEASONING B

1½ tspns salt
½ tspn white pepper
½ tblspn light soy sauce
2 tspns corn oil

METHOD

1 Cut the beef thinly and mix thoroughly with seasoning **A**. Leave for 20 minutes.
2 Discard any old or withered leaves from the Chinese cabbage, wash and drain the remainder and chop roughly. Finely chop the spring onions and cut the rice noodles into short lengths.
3 Heat the oil in a wok or frying pan and stir-fry the spring onions for a few seconds. Add the shredded beef and stir-fry for 1-2 minutes, until the beef is browned.
4 Add the soup stock to the pan together with the cabbage, noodles and seasoning **B**. Bring to the boil, then simmer for 5 minutes. Serve at once.

Two Different Styles of Sushi

INGREDIENTS (SERVES 4)

50 g/2 oz glutinous rice
2 eggs
15 g/½ oz butter
4-6 pieces laver or 20 dried bean curd sheets
½ cucumber
50 g/2 oz chopped cooked pork

SEASONING A

3 tblspns white vinegar
4 tblspns sugar
1½ tblspns water

SEASONING B

½ tspn pepper
1½ tblspns light soy sauce
½ tspn five-spice powder

METHOD

1 Cook the rice in boiling water until just tender. Drain and put in a bowl.
2 Beat the eggs together; melt the butter in a small omelette pan and add the eggs. Cook over a medium heat until the egg is set. Cool and cut into shreds.
3 Place seasoning **A** ingredients in a small saucepan and heat gently until sugar has dissolved. Pour slowly over the cooked rice, stirring it in thoroughly.
4 If using laver, place it under a hot grill for 5 seconds, then spread thinly with the rice. Finely shred the cucumber and sprinkle over the rice together with the egg shreds and pork. Roll the laver around the filling to form a long roll. Cut into 2.5 cm/1 inch sections and serve.
5 If using dried bean curd, put the sheets in a saucepan with seasoning **B**. Bring to the boil and then simmer for 5 minutes. Drain and gently squeeze dry. Cut each one in half, open up and carefully remove the soft inside. Stuff with the rice filling and serve.

Pork-Stuffed Balls

INGREDIENTS (SERVES 6)

5 Chinese mushrooms
150 g/5 oz dried turnip
 shreds
275 g/10 oz lean pork
75 g/3 oz bamboo shoots
150 g/5 oz raw prawns
4 tblspns corn oil
900 g/2 lbs sweet potato flour
approx. 900 ml/1½ pints
 tepid water
vegetable oil, for deep frying

SEASONING

1½ tspns salt
1 tblspn cornflour mixed with
 a little water
½ tblspn ginger wine
½ tspn white pepper
½ tblspn light soy sauce

METHOD

1   Soak the Chinese mushrooms in warm water for 30 minutes. Drain. Cut off and discard the stalks and dice the caps.
2   Soak turnip shreds in hot water for 20 minutes. Drain and squeeze dry.
3   Dice the pork and the bamboo shoots.
4   Shell the prawns and remove the thin 'vein' or intestinal cord that runs down the spine.
5   Heat 3 tblspns of the oil in a wok or frying pan and stir-fry the mushrooms, turnip shreds, pork and bamboo shoots with the seasoning ingredients for 5 minutes.
6   Place the potato flour in a bowl and gradually add tepid water to make a thick paste.
7   Brush the insides of 4 rice bowls with the remaining oil and pour in about 2½ tblspns of the paste. Add 2-3 tblspns of the pork filling and sprinkle a few prawns on top. Cover with another spoonful of paste.
8   Place the bowls in a steamer and steam over rapidly boiling water for about 10 minutes. Remove and stand for 5 minutes.
9   Heat the oil in a deep-fat fryer to medium hot. Carefully remove the balls from the dishes and place them in the hot fat. Cook for a few seconds, so that the outside is very slightly crisp. Serve with a little soy sauce as a dip.

Oyster Omelette

INGREDIENTS (SERVES 4)

275 g/10 oz fresh oysters or
 clams
275 g/10 oz lettuce or
 Chinese spinach
100 g/4 oz cornflour
300 ml/½ pint water
75 ml/3 fl oz corn oil
4 eggs

SEASONING

4 tblspns tomato sauce
50 g/2 oz peanut powder

METHOD

1   Wash the oysters or clams and dry on absorbent paper. Wash and dry the lettuce or Chinese spinach and chop or tear roughly into pieces.
2   Blend the cornflour with the water to make a smooth paste.
3   Heat 1½ tblspns of the corn oil in a frying pan and add a quarter of the oysters or clams. Immediately spoon 6 tblspns of the cornflour mixture on top. Break an egg into the pan next to the oysters, and stir to break the yolk. Add some lettuce or spinach and 1 more tblspn oil.
4   Turn up the heat, add a little more of the cornflour mixture and cook for 5 minutes more. Turn the omelette over and cook for 2 more minutes. Remove and keep warm while you cook a further three omelettes in the same way.
5   Blend the seasoning ingredients and serve with the omelettes.

Salted Vegetable Patties

INGREDIENTS (SERVES 4)

600 g/1¼ lbs plain flour
approx. 225 ml/8 fl oz water
75 g/3 oz lean pork
100 g/4 oz salted vegetable
150 ml/¼ pint corn oil

SEASONING A
1 tblspn light soy sauce
large pinch salt
½ tspn sugar
2 tspns ginger wine
1½ tspns cornflour

SEASONING B
½ tspn white pepper
2 tblspns cornflour blended
    with 3 tblspns water

METHOD

1 Sift the flour into a large bowl and gradually stir in sufficient water to make a smooth, quite firm dough (see p. 343). Divide into 100 g/4 oz pieces.
2 Cut the pork and salted vegetable into fine shreds. Mix pork with seasoning **A**, stir well and leave for 20 minutes.
3 Heat 3 tblspns of the oil in a wok or frying pan and add pork. Stir-fry for 3 minutes, then remove with a slotted spoon. Put on one side.
4 Add the salted vegetable to the oil in the wok and cook for 2 minutes, stirring. Return the pork to the wok with seasoning **B**, and cook for 2 minutes, stirring all the time.
5 Roll the dough out into thin circles and place 1 tblspn filling in the centre of each. Pinch the edges together over the filling, then carefully flatten each patty slightly.
6 Heat the remaining oil in a frying pan and fry the patties over a medium heat, until they are golden brown and crispy on both sides. Drain on absorbent paper and serve at once.

Steamed Pork Dumplings

INGREDIENTS (SERVES 4)

600 g/1¼ lbs plain flour
approx. 225 ml/8 fl oz water
350 g/12 oz minced pork
24 raw prawns
4 cm/1½ inch piece fresh
    root ginger, thinly sliced
light soy sauce, to serve

SEASONING A
1 tspn salt
½ tblspn ginger wine
½ tspn white pepper

SEASONING B
1½ tspns ginger wine
2 tspns cornflour

METHOD

1 Make the dumpling wrappers with the flour and the water as outlined in the recipe above.
2 Mix the pork with seasoning **A** and leave for 20 minutes. Shell the prawns and remove the thin 'vein' or intestinal cord that runs down the spine. Mix them with seasoning **B** and leave for 20 minutes.
3 Roll the dough out into thin circles and place about 1½ tblspns filling in the centre of each. Pinch the edges to look like the top of a flower, leaving a small opening in the centre. Place a prawn in this.
4 Place the dumplings in a steamer lined with muslin or lettuce leaves, and steam for 25 minutes.
5 Finely shred the ginger lengthways and serve with the cooked dumplings. Serve some soy sauce as a dip.

NOTE
If you prefer you could buy wonton wrappers and use them instead of making the dumpling dough.

Pan Sticks Dumplings

INGREDIENTS (SERVES 4)

600 g/1¼ lbs plain flour
approx. 225 ml/8 fl oz water
275 g/10 oz minced pork
4 tblspns chopped chives
50 ml/2 fl oz corn oil

SEASONING A
½ tspn salt
½ tspn white pepper
1½ tspns ginger wine
1½ tspns sesame oil

SEASONING B
5 tblspns malt vinegar
½ tspn chilli oil

METHOD

1 Make a dough with the flour and water (see p. 343) and knead until smooth. Roll into a sausage shape, approximately 2.5 cm/1 inch in diameter and cut into 2.5 cm/1 inch lengths. Flatten these slightly, then roll each one out to a circle, slightly thicker in the centre than at the edges. Dust lightly with flour.
2 Mix the pork and chives together with seasoning **A**. Place about 2 tspns of this mixture in the centre of each dough circle and fold the edges together to form a long 'stick'. Press lightly to flatten the bottom.
3 Heat the oil in a frying pan and place all the dumplings in the pan. Cook for 1 minute over a medium heat, then raise the heat and add about 2 tblspns water to the pan. Cover and cook until the water has evaporated. Remove the lid and continue cooking until the dumplings are slightly scorched on the bottom.
4 Blend seasoning **B** together, sprinkle over the dumplings and serve.

Boiled Pork Dumplings

INGREDIENTS (SERVES 4)

600 g/1¼ lbs plain flour
approx. 225 ml/8 fl oz water
275 g/10 oz Chinese cabbage
350 g/12 oz minced pork
450 ml/¾ pint water

SEASONING
1 tspn salt
1 tspn sugar
½ tspn white pepper
1 tblspn ginger wine
½ tblspn sesame oil
25 ml/1 fl oz clear soup stock
  (see p. 261)

METHOD

1 Make a dough with the flour and water (see p. 343) then follow the instructions outlined in the recipe above to form dumpling wrappers.
2 Cut off and discard any old or withered leaves from the Chinese cabbage, then wash the remainder. Place in a saucepan of boiling water and simmer for 10 minutes, then drain thoroughly and chop finely. Mix with the minced pork and seasoning ingredients beating together thoroughly.
3 Place a small tblspn of the filling in the centre of each dumpling skin and pinch the edges together to make a boat shape.
4 Bring 300 ml/½ pint water to the boil in a saucepan. Add the dumplings one by one, stirring gently to ensure they do not stick to the bottom of the pan. Simmer for 5 minutes, then add the remainder of the cold water. Bring to the boil again, then simmer for 5 minutes. Serve at once.

Spring Onion Ho-Tsu

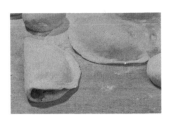

INGREDIENTS (SERVES 4)

450 g/1 lb spring onions
1 soft spiced bean curd
25 g/1 oz bamboo shoots
275 g/10 oz plain flour
approx. 300 ml/½ pint
   boiling water
50 ml/2 fl oz corn oil

SEASONING
2 tspns salt
½ tspn white pepper
1 tspn sesame oil

METHOD

1 Discard any withered leaves from the spring onions and wash and dry the remainder thoroughly. Chop finely. Mash the bean curd and chop the bamboo shoot. Place together in a bowl and mix with the seasoning ingredients.
2 Make scalded dough with the flour and boiling water (see p. 344). Divide into 4 pieces and roll each one into a 15-20 cm/6-8 inch diameter circle.
3 Divide the filling between the circles, then fold the dough over to make a semi-circle. Press edges together, and seal well.
4 Heat the oil in a frying pan and fry the ho-tsu slowly for about 15 minutes, until golden brown. Turn over and fry the other side until golden brown. Drain on absorbent paper. Serve at once.

Spring Onion Pancakes

INGREDIENTS (SERVES 4)

600 g/1¼ lbs plain flour
approx. 600 ml/1 pint boiling
   water
6 spring onions
125 ml/4 fl oz corn oil
2 tspns salt

METHOD

1 Make scalded dough with the flour and the boiling water (see p. 344) and divide into 150 g/5 oz pieces.
2 Finely chop the spring onions.
3 Roll out each piece of dough to a circle 3 mm/⅛ inch thick. Brush with a little oil, then sprinkle with spring onions and salt. Roll up the dough, bring the ends together and pinch them to seal. Roll into a rough ball, then roll this out with a rolling pin to a 15 cm/6 inch diameter circle.
4 Heat 1 tblspn of the remaining oil and fry each pancake over a medium heat until golden brown on both sides. Drain on absorbent paper and keep warm while frying the remainder. Add more oil to the pan as necessary. Serve at once.

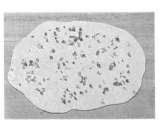

Steamed Dough Twists

INGREDIENTS (SERVES 6)

600 g/1¼ lbs plain flour
150 g/5 oz self-raising flour
approx. 300 ml/½ pint tepid
    water
2 tspns dried yeast
1½ tblspns sugar
2 tblspns melted lard
1½ tspns white vinegar

SEASONING
2 tblspns lard
green part of 2 spring onions,
    finely chopped
½ tblspn salt

METHOD

1   Make the leavened dough using all the ingredients
except the seasoning (see p. 345).
2   Roll out the dough into two large thin circles,
about 6 mm/¼ inch thick. Mix the seasoning
ingredients together and spread evenly over each
circle. Roll the two sides of the dough, into the middle
(see small picture 1 right).
3   Cut the roll in half, then fold the edges of each into
the centre and fold in half again (see small picture 2).
Place them side by side and press down in the centres
with a chopstick (see small picture right 3). Place the
squares on a plate, cover with a damp piece of muslin
or a tea-towel and leave for 20 minutes.
4   Place the twists in a steamer and steam over
rapidly boiling water for 20-30 minutes. Serve at once.

NOTE
Serve these dough twists hot with meat and fish
dishes, such as Salted Prawns (see p. 25).

Steamed Bread

INGREDIENTS (SERVES 6)

600 g/1¼ lbs plain flour
150 g/5 oz self-raising flour
2 tspns dried yeast
1½ tblspns sugar
2 tblspns melted lard
1½ tspns white vinegar
approx. 225 ml/8 fl oz tepid
    water

METHOD

1   Make a leavened dough following instructions on
p. 345. Knead well and shape into a roll about 7.5 cm/3
inches in diameter. Cut into 5 cm/2 inch pieces, cover
with a damp piece of muslin and leave for 20 minutes.
2   Place the flat cakes in a steamer and steam over
rapidly boiling water for 20-30 minutes. Serve at once.

NOTES
1   The Chinese name for these dumplings is man-
tou. It is similar to the Dough Twists (above) but
makes a better accompaniment to such dishes as
Spiced Brisket (see p. 125)
2   The secret of making good man-tou is to knead the
dough really well. It will take about 20 minutes to do
this properly.

火燒
Huo-Shao

INGREDIENTS (SERVES 6)

275 g/10 oz plain flour
275 g/10 oz elf-raising flour
approx. 225 ml/8 fl oz water

METHOD

1 Sift the flour together into a bowl and add sufficient water to make a firm dough. Knead, then cover and leave for about 25 minutes. Knead again to make a smooth dough – it should feel quite stiff.
2 Divide the dough into 6 pieces and shape each one into a circle, roughly 6-7.5 cm/2½-3 inches in diameter. Flute the edges by pinching the dough with your thumb and index finger.
3 Place the huo-shao on a baking sheet and cook at 230°C/450°F/Gas Mark 8 for 15-20 minutes until golden brown. Turn the buns once or twice to ensure they brown evenly.

NOTE
Hard and crispy, huo-shao is a very popular 'dry' bread in China. If you find it too hard, serve it dipped in a soup.

油煎包
Pork and Vegetable Buns

INGREDIENTS (SERVES 4)

600 g/1¼ lbs plain flour
1½ tspns dried yeast
1 tblspn sugar
approx. 225 ml/8 fl oz tepid
  water
600 g/1¼ lbs Chinese
  cabbage or spring greens
400 g/14 oz lean minced pork
25 g/1 oz black or white
  sesame seeds
3 tblspns corn oil
125 ml/4 fl oz water

SEASONING A
1½ tspns salt
1 tblspn ginger wine
1 tspn white pepper
½ tspn sesame oil
4 tblspns clear soup stock
  (see p. 261)

SEASONING B
2.5 cm/1 inch piece fresh
  root ginger, finely chopped
3 tblspns light soy sauce
3 tblspns malt vinegar

METHOD

1 Make a dough with the flour, yeast, sugar and water (see p. 345). Divide into 75 g/3 oz pieces.
2 Discard any old or withered leaves from the Chinese cabbage and wash the remainder. Drain thoroughly, then chop finely. Mix with the pork and seasoning **A**.
3 Roll the dough pieces into 7.5-10 cm/3-4 inch circles, slightly thicker in the middle than round the edges. Place 2 tblspns of the pork filling in the centre and bring the dough up around the filling. Pinch the tops to close.
4 Cover the buns with a damp piece of muslin or a tea-towel and leave for 30 minutes. Then put a wet piece of muslin in the bottom of a steamer, put the buns on top and steam over rapidly boiling water for 20 minutes.
5 While the buns are steaming, dry-fry the sesame seeds for 2 minutes to roast them. Remove the buns from the steamer and sprinkle with the sesame seeds.
6 Heat the oil in a large frying pan and fry the buns for 2 minutes. Add the water, cover the pan with a lid and cook for 10 minutes.
7 Serve the buns at once with seasoning **B** mixed together.

Moon Cakes

INGREDIENTS (SERVES 4)

1 quantity water and oiled
  dough with oiled dough
  filling (see p. 347)
2 tblspns peanut oil
corn oil, for deep frying

PORK FILLING
400 g/14 oz lean pork
4 tblspns preserved
  vegetable
½ tblspn ginger wine
½ tblspn cornflour
½ tspn salt
1 tspn white pepper
½ tblspn sesame oil

METHOD

1 Prepare the water and oiled dough and roll out into
circles as instructed on p. 349.
2 Finely chop or mince the pork and mix thoroughly
with the preserved vegetable, the ginger wine,
cornflour, salt and pepper and sesame oil.
3 Heat the peanut oil in a wok or frying pan. Add the
pork mixture ingredients, and fry, stirring, for a few
minutes, until the pork has lost all its pinkness.
4 Place 2 tblspns of the filling in the centre of each
wrapper and seal the dough around the filling. If you
like, make decorative cuts around the cakes.
5 Heat the oil in a deep-fat fryer and deep-fry the
cakes until they are golden brown all over. Drain on
absorbent paper and serve.

Red Bean Pastries

INGREDIENTS (SERVES 4)

450 g/1 lb red bean paste (see
  NOTE p. 61)
1 quantity oiled dough (see
  p. 346)
50-75 ml/2-3 fl oz corn oil

METHOD

1 Divide the red bean paste into 25 g/1 oz balls and
roll into oval shapes.
2 Make the dough as instructed on p. 346. Divide
into 16 pieces and roll each of these to an oval shape
large enough to encase the red bean paste.
3 Wrap the paste in the dough and place on a baking
sheet. Brush with a little oil and bake for about 30
minutes at 230°C/450°F/Gas Mark 8, brushing with
more oil from time to time. Serve hot.

E Kuo Pastries

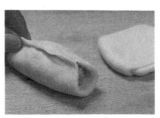

INGREDIENTS (SERVES 4)

1 quantity oiled dough (see
  p. 346)
1 quantity moon cake pork
  filling (see above)
corn oil, for deep frying

METHOD

1 Prepare the oiled dough as instructed on p. 346
and roll into several small oval shapes.
2 Place about 2 tblspns of the cooked filling onto
each dough shape and secure filling as shown in
pictures on the right.
3 Heat the oil in a deep-fat fryer and deep-fry the
cakes until they are golden brown all over. Drain on
absorbent paper and serve at once.

Chinese Breads

INGREDIENTS
(MAKES ABOUT 8)

400 g/14 oz plain flour
200 g/7 oz self-raising flour
¼ quantity oiled paste filling
    (see p. 348)
approx. 225 ml/8 fl oz water
50 g/2 oz black or white
    sesame seeds
3 tblspns corn oil

METHOD

1 Sift the flours together into a bowl and add 2 tblspns oiled paste. Mix together, then add sufficient water to make into a dough. Knead lightly, cover with a damp piece of muslin or a tea-towel and leave for 20 minutes. Knead again until smooth and shiny.
2 With your hands, roll the dough into a long roll about 4 cm/1½ inches in diameter. Cut into 75-100 g/ 3-4 oz pieces and roll each of these into a thin oval shape. Spread the oiled paste onto each oval and top with another oval piece of dough. Roll out lightly, then fold into three as shown in small picture 3 on the right.
3 Brush each parcel with a little water and sprinkle with sesame seeds. Place the parcels, sesame side down on the board or work surface and roll out to an oval shape measuring 15 × 10 cm/6 × 4 inches.
4 Heat the oil in a wok or frying pan and cook the breads over a low to medium heat for about 8-10 minutes until lightly browned. Turn over and cook the other side for the same time. Serve hot.

NOTE
Chinese Bread makes an excellent accompaniment to cold bean curd drinks or soup. Alternatively they are delicious served with crisp, deep-fried pastries.

Shao-Ping Sandwiches

INGREDIENTS
(MAKES ABOUT 15)

400 g/14 oz plain flour
200 g/7 oz self-raising flour
¼ quantity oiled paste filling
    (see p. 348)
approx. 225 ml/8 fl oz water
50 g/2 oz white sesame
    seeds
75 ml/3 fl oz corn oil
175-200 g/6-7 oz roast beef or
    pork, to serve

METHOD

1 Sift the flours together into a bowl and add about 3 tblspns of oiled paste filling. Mix together, then add sufficient water to make into a dough. Knead lightly, cover with a damp piece of muslin or a tea-towel and leave for 20 minutes. Knead again until smooth and shiny.
2 Roll out the dough to a large circle about 6 mm/¼ inch thick. Spread half the remaining oiled paste on top and roll up the dough into a long 'stick'. Roll this out again and spread the remaining filling on top.
3 Roll the dough into a long 'stick' once more and cut into 65 g/2½ oz pieces. Roll each of these into a small circle about 2 cm/¾ inch thick and brush with water. Sprinkle with the sesame seeds.
4 Heat the oil in a wok or frying pan and place in the shao-ping rolls, sesame seed side down. Cover the pan and cook over medium heat for about 5 minutes. Turn the cakes over and cook the other side for a further 5-10 minutes, until brown.
5 Remove the rolls from the oil. Quickly split them open and put a little roast beef or pork into each one. Serve hot.

Bamboo Wrapped Pork and Rice Dumplings

INGREDIENTS (SERVES 4)

100 g/4 oz unsalted peanuts
8-10 Chinese mushrooms
4 tblspns dried baby shrimps
275 g/10 oz pork
600 g/1¼ lbs white glutinous
 rice
4 shallots
4 tblspns melted lard or corn
 oil
150 ml/¼ pint clear soup
 stock (see p. 261)
bamboo leaves and straw

SEASONING

1½ tblspns light soy sauce
½ tspn black pepper
½ tspn salt

METHOD

1 Soak the peanuts in cold water overnight, then drain. Soak the Chinese mushrooms in warm water for 30 minutes. Drain, cut off and discard the stalks and dice the caps finely. Soak the shrimps in warm water for 30 minutes, then drain.

2 Cut the pork into 12 mm/½ inch cubes. Wash and drain the rice thoroughly and finely chop the shallots.

3 Heat the lard or corn oil in a wok or frying pan and stir-fry the shallots for 1 minute. Add the pork cubes and seasoning ingredients and stir-fry for 2 minutes more. Remove with a slotted spoon.

4 Stir the peanuts and rice into the oil left in the wok and stir-fry over medium heat for 2 minutes. Gradually stir in the stock, then simmer, covered, over a very low heat until the rice is cooked and all the liquid has been absorbed.

5 Return the pork to the pan with the mushrooms and shrimps and mix well. Remove from the heat and leave to cool.

6 Wrap about 3 tblspns of the rice mixture in each bamboo leaf as described in Glutinous Rice Dumplings, p. 307, but make these dumplings a little smaller. Tie securely.

7 Place dumplings in a steamer and steam for 1-1½ hours. Serve at once.

Oiled Rice

INGREDIENTS (SERVES 4)

4 Chinese mushrooms
4 tblspns dried baby shrimps
350 g/12 oz pork
600 g/1¼ lbs white glutinous
 rice
6 shallots
3 tblspns corn oil
75 ml/3 fl oz clear soup stock
 (see p. 261)
2 tspns rock sugar

SEASONING

½ tspn salt
½ tspn white pepper

METHOD

1 Soak the Chinese mushrooms in warm water for 30 minutes. Drain. Cut off and discard the stalks and shred the caps. Soak the shrimps in warm water for 30 minutes, then drain. Cut the pork into thin slices, about 2.5 cm/1 inch wide.

2 Wash and drain the rice, then cook in a large saucepan of boiling water for about 10 minutes. Drain.

3 Finely chop the shallots. Heat the oil in a wok or large frying pan and stir-fry the shallots for a few seconds. Add the mushrooms, shrimps and pork and the seasoning ingredients and fry for 5 minutes, stirring frequently. Remove from the wok using a slotted spoon.

4 Add the rice to the wok and stir-fry over a medium heat for a few seconds. Gradually stir in the stock and rock sugar, then cook over a low heat for about 15 minutes until the rice is very tender. Mix in the pork mixture and serve in small bowls.

Fried Nien-Kao

INGREDIENTS
(SERVES 4-6)

600 g/1¼ lbs nien-kao (see NOTE)
6 tblspns corn oil
2 tblspns water
4 sprigs parsley

SEASONING A

2 tblspns sweet and hot sauce
1 tblspn dark soy sauce
1 tblspn Hoisin sauce

SEASONING B

2 garlic cloves, crushed
3 tblspns light soy sauce
½ tblspn chilli sauce

METHOD

1 Cut the nien-kao into slices.
2 Heat 1 tblspn of the oil in a frying pan and add seasoning **A**. Stir well, then add seasoning **B** together with the water. Bring to the boil. Chop the parsley finely and add to the pan, stir for a few seconds, then remove the pan from the heat. Turn into a serving dish.
3 Heat the remaining oil in a clean frying pan and add the nien-kao in a single layer. Fry over a medium heat until both sides are golden brown.
4 Serve hot with the seasoning sauce.

NOTE
Ready-made nien-kao can be bought in Chinese supermarkets in the spring. It is one of the traditional dishes of the Chinese New Year.

Stir-Fried Nien-Kao with Vegetable

INGREDIENTS
(SERVES 4-6)

600 g/1¼ lbs nien-kao (see NOTE above)
20 dried Chinese mushrooms
275 g/10 oz green-stemmed flat cabbage (see NOTE)
4 tblspns corn oil
2 tspns sesame oil

SEASONING

3 tblspns light soy sauce
½ tblspn sugar
½ tspn salt
125 ml/4 fl oz clear soup stock (see p. 261)

METHOD

1 Cut the nien-kao into thin slices. Soak the Chinese mushrooms in warm water for 30 minutes. Drain. Cut off and discard the stalks and cut the caps in half. Wash the cabbage and chop into 2.5 cm/1 inch sections.
2 Heat the oil in a wok or frying pan, add the mushrooms and stir-fry for 2 minutes. Add the seasoning ingredients and cook, covered, for about 2 minutes.
3 Add the nien-kao and cabbage and cook, stirring frequently, for about 10 minutes, until the cabbage is tender.
4 Serve hot with the sesame oil sprinkled on top.

NOTE
If you are unable to buy Chinese flat cabbage, use kale or spring greens instead.

Po-Su Buns

INGREDIENTS

1 quantity leavened dough
  (see p. 345)
1 quantity scalded dough
  (see p. 344)
1 quantity oiled dough filling
  (see p. 347)
2 boneless chicken breasts
275 g/10 oz lean pork
6 tblspns canned, finely
  chopped bamboo shoot

SEASONING
1½ tspns salt
½ tspn white pepper
½ tspn sugar

METHOD

1 Make the leavened, scalded and oiled dough filling as instructed on p. 345, p. 344 and p. 347.
2 Knead the leavened and scalded doughs together, cover and leave to stand for 30 minutes. Roll out to a large circle. Roll out the oiled dough filling and place on top. With your hands, roll all the doughs together to make a long sausage. Cut this into 100-150 g/4-5 oz pieces.
3 Finely chop or mince the chicken and pork and mix with the chopped bamboo shoots and seasoning ingredients.
4 Roll out the pieces of dough to circles about 12.5 cm/5 inches in diameter, slightly thicker in the middle than at the edges. Place about 2 tblspns filling in the centre, then bring the dough up around the filling and pinch the edges to seal. Cover with a damp piece of muslin or a tea-towel and leave for 20 minutes.
5 Steam the buns over rapidly boiling water for 20 minutes and serve at once.

Easy-To-Make Bread Rolls

INGREDIENTS (SERVES 4)

2 tspns dried yeast
1 tspn sugar
50 ml/2 fl oz tepid water
1 tspn salt
65 g/2½ oz butter
125 ml/4 fl oz milk
2 eggs, plus 2 extra yolks
275 g/10 oz plain flour

METHOD

1 Blend the yeast with the sugar and water and leave for 10 minutes.
2 Put the salt into a saucepan with 40 g/1½ oz of the butter and the milk. Stir over a low heat until the butter has melted. Remove from the heat and beat in 1 whole egg and the 2 extra yolks. Pour into a large bowl.
3 Sift the flour twice onto a plate, then beat into the egg mixture. Beat in the yeast mixture. Turn the mixture out of the bowl and knead on a lightly floured surface for about 15 minutes, until the dough is shiny and smooth.
4 Place dough into a large oiled plastic bag. Tie the opening tightly and put into the refrigerator overnight.
5 Divide the dough into 100 g/4 oz pieces and form each one into a bun shape. Melt the remaining butter and brush the rolls with it. Place in the refrigerator for 10 minutes, then lightly dust with flour. Cover with greaseproof paper and leave in a cool place for 30-40 minutes.
6 Remove the greaseproof paper and place the rolls on a baking sheet. Sprinkle lightly with water, then bake at 220°C/425°F/Gas Mark 7 for 15-20 minutes.
7 Beat the remaining egg and brush over the top of the rolls. Return to the oven for 5 minutes more, until golden and shiny. Serve warm or cold.

Turnip Cakes

INGREDIENTS (SERVES 4)

4 tblspns dried baby shrimps
350 g/12 oz turnips
100 g/4 oz lean pork
2 garlic cloves
225 ml/8 fl oz corn oil
600 g/1¼ lbs plain flour
approx. 200 ml/7 fl oz water

SEASONING A
1½ tspns salt
1 tspn sugar

SEASONING B
1 tspn salt
½ tspn white pepper

METHOD

1 Soak the shrimps in warm water for 30 minutes. Drain and chop roughly.
2 Peel the turnips and grate into a bowl of water. Wash, then drain and squeeze dry. Mix with seasoning **A** and leave for 20 minutes.
3 Finely chop or mince the pork and slice the garlic thinly.
4 Heat 2 tblspns of the oil in a frying pan and fry the shrimps and pork for 2 minutes. Add the turnip, garlic and seasoning **B** and cook, stirring for a further 1-2 minutes.
5 Make a fairly soft dough with the flour and water (see p. 343) and divide into 8 pieces. Roll each one out to a thin circle.
6 Divide the filling between the pancakes and fold the dough up over the filling. Flatten with a heavy rolling pin into large patties.
7 Heat half the remaining oil in a frying pan and fry 4 of the patties over a medium to low heat. Cook for about 3 minutes, until golden brown. Turn over and cook the other side until golden brown. Drain on absorbent paper and keep warm while you fry the remainder of the patties in the same way, using the remaining oil.

Milk Pancakes

INGREDIENTS (SERVES 4)

300 ml/½ pint milk
50 g/2 oz sugar
275 g/10 oz plain whole
  wheat flour
butter, for frying
jam or cream and glacé
  cherries, to serve

METHOD

1 Place the milk and sugar in a saucepan and heat gently to dissolve the sugar. Still on the heat, gradually beat in the flour. Remove from the heat and beat until the mixture is really smooth. Leave to stand for 20 minutes, then beat again.
2 Heat a knob of butter in a frying pan and swirl to grease the bottom of the pan. Spoon 3-4 tblspns of the batter into the pan and tipping the pan to form a circle of batter. Cook until the batter is lightly set.
3 Turn the pancake over and cook the other side until lightly browned. Remove and keep warm while you cook the remainder of the batter in the same way.
4 Serve with jam or cream, decorated with glacé cherries.

Sweet Potatoes in Syrup

INGREDIENTS (SERVES 6)

900 g/2 lbs sweet potatoes
275 g/10 oz soft brown sugar
100 g/4 oz caster sugar
2-3 tblspns rock sugar
125 ml/4 fl oz water
3 tblspns corn oil
125 ml/4 fl oz golden syrup

METHOD

1 Peel the sweet potatoes and cut into 5 cm/2 inch sections.

2 Place all the brown sugar in a saucepan together with the caster and rock sugars, water and oil. Heat gently until the sugars have all dissolved, then bring to the boil.

3 Add the potatoes, bring back to the boil, then lower the heat and simmer gently for 30-35 minutes, until the potatoes are shiny and transparent-looking.

4 Heat the golden syrup until it is runny. Put the sweet potatoes in a serving dish and pour the golden syrup over the top. Serve at once.

Seafood Rolls

INGREDIENTS (SERVES 4)

400 g/14 oz fresh oysters or
   clams, shelled
225 g/8 oz fresh bean sprouts
100 g/4 oz lean pork
2 sticks celery
½ tspn salt
½ tspn chilli powder
8 pieces fresh bean curd
   sheet
2 tblspns plain flour
2 tblspns water
corn oil, for deep frying
3 garlic cloves

SEASONING

1 tblspn Hoisin sauce
2 tblspns sugar
2 tblspns vinegar
½ tspn white pepper
2 tspns cornflour mixed with
   4 tblspns water

METHOD

1 Wash the oysters or clams and dry on absorbent paper. Wash the bean sprouts and drain thoroughly. Cut pork into tiny cubes and chop the celery. Mix all these together with the salt and chilli powder.

2 Cut each bean curd sheet into 3 equal-sized pieces. Mix the flour and water to a paste and brush around the outside of the bean curd sheet pieces.

3 Place 2 tblspns of filling in the centre of each bean curd wrapper and roll up. The flour paste should seal the edges.

4 Heat the oil in a deep-fat fryer and fry the rolls until they are golden brown and crispy all over. Drain on absorbent paper and keep warm.

5 Chop the garlic roughly. Heat 2 tblspns of oil in a clean frying pan and fry the garlic for 1 minute. Add the seasoning ingredients and bring to the boil. Pour this over the seafood rolls and serve.

Rice Triangles

INGREDIENTS
(SERVES 4-6)

600 g/1¼ lbs white glutinous rice
7 g/¼ oz bicarbonate of soda
bamboo leaves and straw

METHOD

1 Wash and drain the rice thoroughly. Mix with the bicarbonate of soda and leave for 1-2 hours.
2 Pack the rice into the bamboo leaves as for Glutinous Rice Dumplings, see p. 307, but make these dumplings quite small and shape them into small triangles (see small pictures, right). Tie the parcels securely with straw or string.
3 Place the rice triangles in a large saucepan and cover with water. Bring to the boil and simmer very gently for about 4 hours. Keep the pan topped up with boiling water to cover the dumplings during this time. Turn off the heat, but leave the dumplings in the water for a further hour before serving.

NOTE
These dumplings can be served as a sweet or savoury dish. For a sweet dish, serve them with sugar; for a savoury one – with soy sauce or salt.

Spiral Dumplings

INGREDIENTS (SERVES 4)

175 g/6 oz dried red beans (see NOTES)
600 g/1¼ lbs white glutinous rice
½ tspn salt
bamboo leaves and straw

METHOD

1 Wash the beans and soak in cold water for 2 hours.
2 Wash and drain the rice thoroughly and mix with the salt in a bowl.
3 Drain the beans and stir into the rice.
4 Place the underside or rough side of 2 bamboo leaves together and fold into a cone shape. Push 2-3 tblspns rice and bean mixture into the case and then fold the leaves over the filling to make a triangular shape with a flat bottom. Tie securely and repeat with all the filling.
5 Bring a large pan of water to the boil and drop the dumplings into it – the water should cover them completely. Simmer very gently for 6 hours. Then turn off the heat and leave the dumplings in the pan for a further hour before serving.

NOTES
1 Dried red beans are available from some Chinese supermarkets. Red bean sauce can be used instead, if liked.
2 These dumplings can also be served as a sweet or savoury dish. Dip in sugar for a sweet dish, and into hot bean or soy sauce for savoury.
3 An alternative way of serving the dumplings, is to let them go cold, then unwrap them, coat lightly in flour and deep fry in hot oil until golden brown.

337

Smiling Muffins

INGREDIENTS (SERVES 4)

600 g/1¼ lbs self-raising
  flour
150 g/5 oz plain whole wheat
  flour
1 tspn bicarbonate of soda
½ tblspn baking powder
2 eggs
1½ tblspns melted lard
150 g/5 oz sugar
approx. 225 ml/8 fl oz water
75 g/3 oz white or black
  sesame seeds
corn oil, for deep frying

METHOD

1 Sift the flours, bicarbonate of soda and baking
powder into a large bowl. Make a well in the centre.
2 Beat eggs together. Pour into the well and add the
lard and sugar. Add sufficient water to make a firm
dough. Knead lightly, then cover with a damp piece of
muslin or a tea-towel and leave for 20 minutes.
3 Shape the dough into a long roll and cut into 2.5
cm/1 inch sections. Roll each of these into a ball, then
coat them with the sesame seeds.
4 Heat the oil in a deep-fat fryer and fry the balls,
turning them over in the oil, until they are slightly split
and golden brown in colour.
5 Remove from the oil and drain on absorbent paper.
Serve at once.

Sesame Snacks

INGREDIENTS (SERVES 4)

275 g/10 oz plain or whole
  wheat flour
2 tblspns melted lard
125 ml/4 fl oz tepid water
2 tblspns sugar
½ tspn salt
1½ tblspns black sesame
  seeds
corn oil, for frying

METHOD

1 Sift the flour and mix to a dough with the lard,
water, sugar and salt. Knead lightly, then cover with a
damp piece of muslin or a tea-towel and leave for 20
minutes.
2 Roll out the dough to a large circle, about 6 mm/¼
inch thick and sprinkle with the sesame seeds. Cut
into 2.5 cm/1 inch strips and cut these into diamond
shapes.
3 Make a lengthways slit in the centre of the
diamond shapes and push one end of the diamond
through the slit to give a plaited effect.
4 Heat the oil in a deep fat fryer and fry the twists, a
few at a time, until golden brown all over. Drain on
absorbent paper and serve.

NOTE
These crunchy twists are delicious served with drinks
before a meal.

糖年糕

Sweet Nien-Kao

INGREDIENTS
(SERVES 6-8)

275 g/10 oz soft brown sugar
900 ml/1½ pints water
450 g/1 lb glutinous rice flour
175 g/6 oz rice flour
3 tblspns melted lard
vegetable oil, for brushing
5 red dates or prunes, soaked
   (see NOTES)

METHOD

1 Place the sugar and water into a saucepan and place over a medium heat. When the sugar has dissolved, bring to the boil. Leave to cool.
2 Mix the flours together and gradually stir in the sugar syrup, keeping the mixture smooth all the time. Stir in the lard and mix well.
3 Place a large piece of cling film in the bottom of a steamer and brush with oil. Pour the flour paste into the steamer and place the dates or prunes on top.
4 Steam over rapidly boiling water for 2 hours. Test for doneness by inserting a knife or chopstick into the nien-kao; if it comes out clean, the cake is done.

NOTES
1 Soak the red dates for 4 hours before using. Soak the prunes overnight.
2 There are two types of nien-kao – brown and white, the difference being in the colour of the sugar used. Brown nien-kao is more popular.
3 Steam the nien-kao over a large pan of boiling water; it is better not to have to add any water to the pan during the steaming process.

廣式蘿蔔糕

Cantonese Turnip Cake

INGREDIENTS
(SERVES 6-8)

50 g/2 oz dried baby shrimps
1.8 kg/4 lbs white turnips
75 g/3 oz lard
2 tspns salt
75 g/3 oz smoked pork
2 Chinese sausages (see
   NOTE)
1½ tspns white pepper
1 tblspn sugar
600 g/1¼ lbs rice flour
225-300 ml/8-10 fl oz water
1 tblspn chopped parsley

METHOD

1 Soak the shrimps in warm water for 30 minutes, then drain. Peel the turnips and grate finely in a food processor.
2 Heat 50 g/2 oz of the lard in a wok or frying pan and fry the shrimps for 1 minute. Add the shredded turnip and salt and cook for a further 5 minutes stirring frequently.
3 Chop the smoked pork and sausage finely and add to the wok with the pepper and sugar. Stir well and cook for 5 minutes, then remove from the heat.
4 Mix the flour with water to make a thick, smooth paste. Stir this into the turnip mixture, blending together well.
5 Place a large piece of cling film in the bottom of a steamer. Melt the remaining lard and brush over the cling film. Spoon the turnip mixture on top, and steam over boiling water for 2 hours. Test for doneness by inserting a knife into the cake – it should come out clean. Leave to cool. Sprinkle with parsley and serve.

NOTE
Chinese sausages should be steamed for 30 minutes before using.

General instructions for making dough

1 Weigh out the ingredients carefully. Generally speaking, 100 g/4 oz flour is sufficient for one person. Sift flour into a bowl.

2 Make a well in the centre of the flour. Gradually pour in the water and mix it into the flour, adding sufficient water to bring the mixture together.

3 Use a knife or chopstick to blend the mixture. To make the dough shiny, add a little melted lard.

4 When you have added sufficient water to make the dough, flour your hands lightly and begin kneading.

5 Work the dough in the bowl, pressing it with the palm of your hand and turning it frequently. Continue until the dough is smooth.

6 Soak a piece of muslin, cheesecloth or a tea-towel in cold water, then squeeze it out very firmly.

7 Place the cloth over the bowl containing the dough and leave for 20-30 minutes. This allows the dough to rest.

8 If you want the pastry to be quite chewy and 'elastic', knead the dough vigorously for a short time by pulling and pushing it apart.

9 For a smoother pastry, knead the dough in the usual way. The longer you knead it, the smoother it will be.

10 If the dough feels sticky as you are kneading, flour the surface liberally and work a little into the dough.

11 If the dough feels too dry and is difficult to knead, cut it in pieces and sprinkle with water. Knead together again.

12 Knead the dough until it is quite smooth. If you do not want to use it straight away, cover it with a damp cloth.

How to make scalded dough

INGREDIENTS
275 g/10 oz plain flour
1 tblspn melted lard
approx. 300 ml/½ pint boiling
    water

This is the dough most commonly used for steamed dim sums.

1   Weigh the flour and sift into a large bowl. Stir in the melted lard.

2   Boil the water and measure out the required quantity.

3   Gradually pour the water into the flour, stirring all the time.

4   Keep stirring to mix thoroughly but do not bring the mixture together.

5   Cover the bowl with a damp cloth and leave to stand for about 10 minutes.

6   Knead the mixture to bring it together to a rough dough. Turn out of the bowl.

7   If necessary, add more flour or water – it should feel damp but not wet. Cover with a damp cloth and leave for 20 minutes.

8   Knead the dough vigorously by pulling and pushing it apart.

9   Finish off by kneading it with the palm of your hand until it is really smooth.

10   The kneading process will take 15-20 minutes. The dough is then ready for use.

11   If you do not want to use it immediately, put in a bowl and cover with a damp cloth.

How to make leavened dough

INGREDIENTS

275 g/10 oz plain flour
125 ml/4 fl oz tepid water
1 tspn sugar
1 tspn dried yeast

This dough can be used for baking as well as steaming and boiling. If it is to be used for cakes and biscuits, it is usual to add baking powder to the mixture. Vinegar and lard can also be added to the flour for some recipes, and occasionally milk is substituted for the water.

1 Ingredients used in making leavened dough. The yeast mixture is shown in the glasses and bowls (right).

2 Test the temperature of the water by pouring a little onto your wrist. It should be tepid. i.e. blood heat.

3 Pour the water into a small bowl and add the sugar.

4 Stir until the sugar has dissolved. The sugar is necessary to feed the yeast.

5 Sprinkle the dried yeast into the bowl but do not stir it in. Leave to stand for 7-10 minutes.

6 The yeast mixture is ready to use when small bubbles have appeared on the surface.

7 Sift the flour three times to make it as light as possible. Add the yeast mixture and stir, adding a little more warm water if necessary.

8 Mix the flour and liquid thoroughly, then knead into a rough dough.

9 Using a finger, make holes all over the dough. Sprinkle the surface with water.

10 Cover the bowl with a damp cloth and leave for 3 hours at room temperature.

11 The dough will expand and rise. This picture was taken after the dough had stood for 2 hours.

12 Knead the dough until completely smooth and shiny. Use immediately or leave to stand, covered, for another 20 minutes.

345

How to make oiled dough

INGREDIENTS

100 g/4 oz plain flour
250 g/9 oz self-raising flour
100 g/4 oz lard, melted

Oiled dough is most commonly used for deep-frying dim sums. It is easy to work and can be used to make various shapes and patterns, which look very pretty and decorative when cooked. Some patterns can be made by cutting into the dough, but care should be taken not to cut so deep that the filling is exposed during cooking. If you want the pastry to be shiny after cooking, brush it with some beaten egg. You can also add colour and flavour to the dough by adding soy sauce.

1 Sift the two types of flour together into a large bowl.

2 Add the melted lard, stirring it into the flour.

3 Add sufficient water to bring the flour together in small lumps.

4 Not enough water has been added here to form a smooth dough. A little more is needed.

5 Knead the dough until it is smooth and shiny. This will take about 15 minutes. Leave to stand for 20 minutes, then knead again before using.

How to make watered and oiled dough

WATERED AND OILED WRAPPING

INGREDIENTS

150 g/5 oz plain flour
150 g/5 oz self-raising flour
150 ml/¼ pint water
25 g/1 oz lard, melted
1 tblspn sugar, optional

This pastry is made by combining a watered and oiled dough wrapping with a dough or paste filling. It is used when a layered effect is required.

You can colour and flavour the pastry by adding curry powder to it. Replace ½ tblspn of the flour mixture with 2 tblspns curry powder.

1 Sift the two types of flour together into a bowl. Stir in the water and then the lard.

2 Add the sugar, if using, and mix the ingredients together with your hands.

3 Knead the dough thoroughly until smooth. Stand for 20 minutes, then knead again.

OILED DOUGH FILLING

INGREDIENTS

50 g/2 oz plain flour
200 g/7 oz self-raising flour
150 g/5 oz lard, melted
1 tspn sugar, optional

Sugar is added to the filling and wrapping dough to give the pastry a crisper, browner finish. Omit the sugar if you are intending to cut the dough into shapes.

1 Sift the two types of flour together. Stir in the lard and sugar, if using.

2 Mix together thoroughly. This is particularly important if sugar has been added as it has to dissolve into the other ingredients.

3 Knead the dough well, then leave to stand for 20 minutes. Knead again before using.

OILED PASTE FILLING

INGREDIENTS

225 g/8 oz lard
225 g/8 oz plain flour
1 tblspn pepper and salt,
  mixed
1 tblspn ground cinnamon

Oiled paste filling is used rather than the oiled dough filling when making cakes such as Chinese Breads (see p. 325).

1   Melt the lard in a wok or heavy-based saucepan, and stir in the flour, keeping the mixture smooth.

2   Cook the mixture over a high heat until it begins to turn brown and become slightly 'scorched'.

3   Add the pepper, salt and cinnamon. Stir for 1 minute more, then pour into a bowl to cool slightly.

HOW TO COMBINE WRAPPING AND FILLING

INGREDIENTS

1 quantity watered and oiled wrapping (see p. 347)
1 quantity oiled dough or paste filling (see p. 347 and 348)

There are two ways of combining the wrapping and filling to make the complete dough or pastry.

METHOD 1

The quickest way is to roll out the wrapping to a large piece about 6 mm/¼ inch thick. Place the filling on top and fold the wrapping around it. Roll out the dough again to a rectangle again about 6 mm/¼ inch thick. Fold the bottom third up over the dough and the top third down. Press the ends with the rolling pin to seal and roll out again. Repeat the folding process and roll out the dough again. Using your hands, roll up the dough to a long sausage shape, then cut into 2.5 cm/1 inch pieces and roll these out to thin circles to use as dumpling skins.

METHOD 2

1 Knead the wrapping and filling separately and roll each one into a long sausage shape using your hands. Cut into small sections.

2 Flatten the wrapping dough into a rough circle. Roll the filling into a small ball.

3 Place the filling ball on the wrapper and fold the wrapper around it to enclose filling completely.

4 Repeat with all the dough, then flatten the balls slightly in the palms of your hands.

5 Roll each piece out to an oval shape. Roll these up from one end then repeat the rolling out and folding up process once more.

6 Roll out the parcels to a thin circle if required for dumplings.

7 Alternatively, the pastry can be shaped into decorative patterns and shapes.

8 To make 'shell' shapes, roll up the thin circles and mould each roll into a 'shell' with a fluted edge.

9 Mould two 'shells' together to make a 'wheel' shape. The finished dough shapes are deep fried.

ENTERTAINING

One of the most notable and exciting features of a Chinese meal is that it contains so many different dishes.

For day-to-day eating in China, the general practice is to serve one savoury dish per person, in addition to a rice dish. Appetizers, soups and noodle dishes are also served, according to individual taste.

When planning a Chinese meal, choose dishes that will give a good balance of flavour, richness and colour. Harmony of taste and texture is an all important element of Chinese cuisine and a well-balanced menu will provide a gastronomic treat that few will forget! Any of the recipes from this chapter will make perfect dishes for a dinner party, but, to add variety you can also select one or two dishes from some of the other chapters in the book. To help you grasp the basic principles of planning a Chinese dinner party, try following any of the menu ideas featured on p. 384.

All the recipes in the book need to be served in conjunction with several other dishes, in order to make a reasonably complete meal. However, if time is short and authenticity is not strictly essential, simply double up the ingredients in selected recipes to create an instant Western compromise.

Cantonese Fried Chicken

INGREDIENTS (SERVES 4)

4 chicken pieces
25 ml/1 fl oz light soy sauce
2 egg whites, lightly beaten
100 g/4 oz plain flour
125 ml/4 fl oz corn oil
parsley, to garnish

SEASONING
2 tblspns rice wine or dry
   sherry
1 tblspn tomato sauce
2 tspns Worcestershire sauce
½ tspn sugar
pinch of salt

METHOD

1   Chop the chicken pieces into halves or quarters and pound with the back of a cleaver. Place the soy sauce in a bowl and add the chicken pieces. Set aside for 30 minutes.
2   Drain the chicken. Coat with the egg whites and then dust with the flour.
3   Heat the oil in a large wok and add the chicken. Fry for 6-7 minutes until the chicken is cooked and golden brown.
4   Drain the oil and add the seasoning ingredients. Stir thoroughly and serve, garnished with parsley.

Shredded Chicken and Pepper

INGREDIENTS (SERVES 4)

175 g/6 oz boned chicken
   breasts, skinned
1 egg white, lightly beaten
½ green pepper, seeded
½ red pepper, seeded
125 ml/4 fl oz corn oil
1 small onion, chopped
1 tblspn light soy sauce

SEASONING
1 tblspn rice wine or dry
   sherry
½ tspn cornflour
1 tspn salt
pinch of white pepper

METHOD

1   Cut the chicken into long thin shreds.
2   Beat the egg white with the seasoning ingredients and add the chicken shreds, stirring thoroughly. Cut the peppers into long, thin strips.
3   Heat the oil in a wok, add the chopped onion and fry for a few seconds. Add the chicken and stir-fry for 5 minutes.
4   Remove the chicken with a slotted spoon and drain all but 1 tspn of the oil. Add the peppers and stir-fry for 3 minutes.
5   Return the chicken to the wok and stir. Cook for 2 minutes, then sprinkle with the soy sauce and serve.

紫菜捲薄餅
Laver Pancake Rolls

INGREDIENTS
(SERVES 2-4)

75 g/3 oz plain flour
pinch of salt
1 egg
75 ml/3 fl oz water
corn oil, for shallow frying
4-6 pieces of laver

METHOD

1 Sift the flour and salt into a bowl, add the egg and the water. Beat thoroughly to make a smooth batter of dropping consistency, adding a little more water if necessary.
2 Heat a little oil in a large frying pan, add about a quarter of the batter, tilting the pan so that the pancake coats it evenly. Fry for a few minutes until golden and then flip over and fry the other side. Repeat this until all the mixture has been used up.
3 Grill the slices of laver for a few seconds. Place a pancake on top, roll up and serve.

咖哩通心粉
Chinese Curried Macaroni

INGREDIENTS (SERVES 4)

1 tspn salt
225 g/8 oz macaroni
150 g/5 oz boned chicken
   breast, skinned
1 carrot
50 g/2 oz green beans
2 tomatoes
50 g/2 oz button mushrooms
4 tblspns corn oil
3 garlic cloves, crushed
1 onion, finely chopped
2 tblspns Chinese curry
   powder
50 ml/2 fl oz clear soup stock
   (see p. 261)
1 tspn salt
½ tspn white pepper

METHOD

1 Bring a large pan of water to the boil, add the salt and throw in the macaroni. Cook for 8-10 minutes until the macaroni is tender and then drain and soak the pasta in cold water.
2 Cut the chicken into small cubes, finely chop the carrot and green beans, cut the tomatoes into wedges and slice the mushrooms.
3 Heat the oil in a wok or frying pan and add the garlic and onion. Stir-fry for 1 minute and then add the chicken, carrot, green beans, tomatoes, button mushrooms and curry powder.
4 Stir-fry for 2 minutes, then add the soup stock, salt and pepper. Bring to the boil.
5 Drain the macaroni and stir into the curry. Cook for 2-3 minutes until hot and serve at once.

銀耳甜湯

Sweet Fungus Dessert

INGREDIENTS (SERVES 4)

25 g/1 oz dried white fungus
   (see NOTE)
3 tblspns rock sugar
900 ml/1½ pints water
1 large can fruit cocktail

METHOD

1 Place the fungus in a bowl, cover with warm water and soak for about 1 hour until it expands slightly.
2 Place the white fungus, sugar and the water in a saucepan, bring to the boil and then simmer gently for 30 minutes.
3 Remove from the heat and cool slightly. Add the fruit cocktail. Serve either hot or cold.

NOTE
Dried white fungus or silver ear fungus is available in most Chinese supermarkets and can be kept for up to 6 months if kept in a cool place.

炸芋酥餅

Fried Potato Patties

INGREDIENTS (SERVES 4)

450 g/1 lb potatoes
knob of butter
1 tspn salt
50 g/2 oz smoked ham,
   chopped
1 tspn sugar
pinch of white pepper
1 egg, beaten
100 g/4 oz fresh white
   breadcrumbs
corn oil, for deep frying

METHOD

1 Cook the potatoes until tender and drain and mash them with the butter.
2 Stir in the salt, chopped ham, sugar and pepper and mix well.
3 Take large spoonfuls of mixture and mould them into balls in your hands. Dip in the beaten egg and then coat in the breadcrumbs, pressing down lightly between your hands to form patties.
4 Heat the oil in a deep-fat fryer and deep-fry the patties for 2-3 minutes or until golden brown, turning occasionally. Drain on absorbent paper and serve.

Sweet Lotus Roots

INGREDIENTS (SERVES 4)

2 sections of lotus roots (see
   NOTES)
8 black dates or prunes,
   soaked (see NOTE 1, p. 341)
50 g/2 oz rock sugar
600 ml/1 pint water

METHOD

1   Peel the lotus roots and cut diagonally into large
thick pieces (see small picture 1, right).
2   Place the lotus roots, the soaked dates and the
sugar in a saucepan with the water. Bring to the boil
and then simmer for 40 minutes over a low heat.
3   Pour the contents of the pan into a large bowl and
place in a steamer. Cover and steam over a low heat
for 1 hour.
4   Serve hot or cold.

NOTE

Fresh lotus roots are sometimes available during the
summer – look out for them in Chinese and Indian
supermarkets. When they are unobtainable, dried or
canned lotus roots can be used instead. The lotus root
will slightly discolour during cooking. If you prefer the
whiteness of the lotus, place it in a bowl with 25 ml/1
fl oz white vinegar and 225 ml/8 fl oz boiling water for
3 minutes.

Emerald Dumplings

INGREDIENTS (SERVES 4)

700 g/1½ lbs spinach
½ tspn salt
600 g/1¼ lbs plain flour
3 tblspns clear soup stock
   (see p. 261)
350 g/12 oz minced pork
1 small Chinese cabbage
4 tblspns malt vinegar
½ tspn chilli oil

SEASONING

1 tblspn ginger juice
1 tblspn sesame oil
1 tspn sugar
1 tspn salt
½ tspn white pepper

METHOD

1   Wash and trim the spinach. Chop into very fine
shreds and add the salt, pressing the salt into the
spinach with your fingertips to extract the green
spinach juice.
2   Stir in the flour and sufficient warm water to make
a soft dough (see p. 343). Knead slightly and then
place the dough in a basin. Cover with a damp cloth
and set aside for 20 minutes.
3   Blend the seasoning ingredients with the soup
stock in a large bowl. Stir in the minced pork and set
aside for 5 minutes.
4   Scald the cabbage in boiling water for 5 minutes.
Drain and soak in cold water until cold. Drain
thoroughly, and chop very finely. Mix with the pork
mixture to make a smooth, sticky paste.
5   Roll out the spinach dough on a floured surface to
make a long 2 cm/¾ inch-thick sausage. Cut the
'sausage' into 12 mm/½ inch sections and roll out
each piece thinly. Place a spoonful of the pork and
cabbage stuffing in the centre. Bring the edges round
and seal firmly, to make small dumplings.
6   Bring a pan of water to the boil and carefully add
the dumplings. Boil for 2 minutes, stirring occasionally
with a ladle. Add 25 ml/1 fl oz cold water. Cover, bring
to the boil and cook for a further 4-5 minutes. Remove
with a slotted spoon and serve with the vinegar and chilli oil.

Scalded Abalones

INGREDIENTS (SERVES 4)

450 g/1 lb abalones
  (see NOTE)
2 tblspns corn oil
1 spring onion, finely
  chopped
1 red chilli, seeded and finely
  sliced
2 tblspns water

SEASONING A
1 tblspn finely grated fresh
  root ginger
1 tblspn sesame oil

SEASONING B
1 tspn rice wine or dry sherry
1 tspn salt
1 tspn sugar

METHOD

1 Rinse the abalones and soak in cold water for 30 minutes. Drain and scald in boiling water for 10 minutes.
2 Heat the oil in a wok, add the spring onion and seasoning **A** and stir-fry for 1 minute. Add the abalones and cook for 1 minute.
3 Add the red chilli and seasoning **B**, together with the water. Cook for 1 minute and then remove the abalones with a slotted spoon and arrange on a serving plate. Spoon the sauce over the top and serve.

NOTE
If fresh abalones are not available, use canned ones, in which case, follow the recipe from Step 2, after draining them.

Spicy Clams

INGREDIENTS (SERVES 4)

450 g/1 lb fresh clams
4 tblspns corn oil
8 garlic cloves, crushed
2 fresh red chillis, seeded and
    thinly sliced
1 spring onion, sliced
1 tblspn rice wine or dry
    sherry
black pepper

SEASONING

1 tblspn light soy sauce
½ tspn salt
½ tspn white pepper
1 tspn sugar

METHOD

1   Rinse the clams in cold water, discarding any with broken shells. Soak in cold water for 25-30 minutes.
2   Heat the oil in a wok and add the garlic. Stir-fry for a few seconds and add the chillis and then immediately add the spring onion.
3   Drain the clams and tip into the wok. Cook over a high heat for 3 minutes, stirring and rearranging the clams with a metal spatula.
4   Add the seasoning ingredients and stir-fry vigorously for a further 2 minutes.
5   Spoon onto a serving plate and sprinkle with the rice wine and black pepper.

Stir-Fried Beef with Oyster Sauce

INGREDIENTS (SERVES 4)

350 g/12 oz lb rump steak
175 g/6 oz kale or Chinese
    cabbage
4 tblspns corn oil
2 cm/¾ inch piece fresh root
    ginger, sliced
2 tblspns water
½ tblspn rice wine or dry
    sherry
2 tspns sesame oil

SEASONING A

1 tblspn light soy sauce
½ tblspn rice wine or dry
    sherry
½ tspn white pepper
1 tspn cornflour
1 tspn sugar

SEASONING B

3 tblspns oyster sauce
½ tspn salt
½ tspn sugar

METHOD

1   Slice the beef against the grain into large thin pieces. Blend seasoning **A** in a bowl and stir in the beef slices. Set aside to marinate for 30 minutes.
2   Trim the roots from the kale or Chinese cabbage, place in a large bowl and cover with boiling water. Set aside for 5 minutes and then drain.
3   Heat the oil in a wok and when hot, stir-fry the ginger slices for a few seconds. Add the beef and fry over a high heat for 3 minutes. Discard the ginger.
4   Add seasoning **B** and the water and stir thoroughly. Stir in the greens and continue to cook, stirring, for 2 minutes until wilted.
5   Add the rice wine and sesame oil and stir to mix. Serve immediately.

Stewed Shark's Fin with Mushrooms

INGREDIENTS (SERVES 4)

6 Chinese dried mushrooms
600 g/1¼ lbs shark's fin,
   soaked (see NOTE)
2 tblspns finely grated fresh
   root ginger
4 tblspns corn oil
3 spring onions, sliced
125 ml/4 fl oz chicken stock
   (see p. 149)
1 tblspn cornflour
parsley, to garnish

SEASONING A

2 tblspns ginger wine
1 tspn white pepper

SEASONING B

2 tblspns dark soy sauce
1 tspn sugar
1 tspn salt
1 tspn white pepper

METHOD

1   Soak the Chinese mushrooms in warm water for 30 minutes. Drain and remove the stalks then slice thinly.
2   Place the shark's fin in a large saucepan with the ginger. Cover with boiling water and leave for 5 minutes.
3   Stir in seasoning **A** and bring to the boil. Simmer for 10 minutes and drain.
4   Heat the oil in a wok, add the spring onions and stir-fry for 5 seconds. Add the sliced mushrooms and stir-fry for a further minute.
5   Add the chicken stock and seasoning **B**. Blend the cornflour with a little cold water and stir into the wok. Bring to the boil, stirring, until mixture thickens and then reduce the heat and simmer for 15 minutes.
6   Pour the sauce into a deep serving dish and lay the shark's fin on top. Garnish with parsley and serve.

NOTE

Shark's fin is a great delicacy in China. It has little or no taste but adds a unique consistency to a dish. The best shark's fin is extremely expensive and takes four days to prepare. However a processed shark's fin which has been partially cooked and then redried is readily available from Chinese supermarkets.

五香煮花生

Five-Flavoured Peanuts

INGREDIENTS
(SERVES 6-8)

350 g/12 oz raw peanuts
2 star anise
2 tblspns light soy sauce
1 tblspn dark soy sauce
1 tspn rock sugar
½ tspn salt

METHOD

1 Rinse the peanuts, drain, then soak in water for 4 hours. Drain again.
2 Place the peanuts in a saucepan, and cover with water. Add the star anise, both soy sauces, rock sugar and the salt. Bring to the boil and cook for 10 minutes, until the peanuts are soft. Drain and serve when cool.

辣肉醬

Hot Pork Paste

INGREDIENTS (SERVES 6)

600 g/1¼ lbs lean minced
   pork
3 tblspns corn oil
lettuce, and chopped spring
   onions, to garnish

SEASONING
1 tblspn cayenne
1 tblspn hot bean sauce
2 tblspns sugar
3 tblspns soy sauce
1 tspn salt
1 tblspn ginger wine

METHOD

1 Mix the pork with the seasoning ingredients in a bowl.
2 Heat the oil in a wok or frying pan and then add the pork mixture. Stir-fry over a high heat for 5 minutes.
3 Arrange on a bed of lettuce on a serving dish, and garnish with chopped spring onions.

Two Kinds of Marinated Vegetable

INGREDIENTS (SERVES 4)

350 g/12 oz Chinese leaves,
    preferably the stalk end
½ cucumber
3 tspns salt

SEASONING A
1 tblspn light soy sauce
1 garlic clove, crushed

SEASONING B
1 red chilli, seeded and finely
    sliced
1 tblspn white vinegar
2 tspns sesame oil
½ tspn white pepper

METHOD

1   Slice off the stalk of the Chinese leaves and
separate the leaves. Cut the stalk end into thick
diagonal slices.
2   Peel the cucumber and cut into thin shreds.
3   Place the two vegetables in two separate bowls
and add 1½ tspns of salt to each. Marinate both for 20
minutes, stirring frequently.
4   Squeeze out any excess water, and then add
seasoning **A** to the Chinese leaves and seasoning **B** to
the cucumber. Serve at once.

Sour Baby Shrimps

INGREDIENTS (SERVES 4)

75 g/3 oz dried baby shrimps
6 tblspns white vinegar
½ tspn rice wine or dry
    sherry

METHOD

1   Rinse the baby shrimps in cold water and then
soak in warm water for 30 minutes. Drain and dry
thoroughly.
2   Dry-fry the shrimps in a wok over a medium flame
for 2 minutes. Turn onto a serving plate.
3   Mix the vinegar and rice wine and serve, as a
dipping sauce, with the baby shrimps.

油豆腐细粉

Pork Balls and Bean Thread Soup

INGREDIENTS (SERVES 6)

275 g/10 oz bean curd
  threads
1.2 litres/2 pints clear soup
  stock (see p. 261)
8 pork-stuffed meat balls (see
  NOTES)
6-8 fish balls (see NOTES)
2-3 tspns sesame oil

SEASONING

2 tblspns pickled cabbage,
  sliced (see NOTES)
2 tspns salt

METHOD

1 Soak the bean curd threads in cold water for 30
minutes. Drain and cut into 12.5 cm/5 inch pieces.
2 Place the soup stock in a large pan, add the pork
and fish balls and bring to the boil. Cook for 10
minutes and then add the bean threads.
3 Cook for a further minute and then add the
seasoning ingredients. Bring to the boil and serve,
sprinkled with a little sesame oil.

NOTES

1 Pork meat balls and fish balls are available from
most Chinese supermarkets and are normally sold in
sealed polythene packets.
2 Pickled cabbage is a red-root vegetable that has
been preserved in salt. It's available in cans. Rinse
before using.

炸龍鳳腿

Mock Chicken Drumsticks

INGREDIENTS (SERVES 4)

275 g/10 oz pork fillet
2 boned chicken breasts,
  skinned
75 g/3 oz water chestnuts
3 tblspns oil
1 celery stalk, thinly sliced
1 small carrot, coarsely
  grated
½ tblspn cornflour
1 large sheet of chu-wang-
  yiu (see NOTE)
4 tblspns plain flour
corn oil, for deep frying

SEASONING A

2 tspns salt
1 tblspn sugar
½ tspn five-spice powder

SEASONING B

3 tblspns chilli sauce
3 tblspns tomato ketchup

METHOD

1 Using a sharp knife, cut the pork into fine pieces.
Very thinly slice the chicken and chop the water
chestnuts.
2 Heat the oil in a frying pan and stir-fry the pork,
chicken, water chestnuts, celery and carrot for 1
minute. Add seasoning **A** and continue cooking until
the pork is lightly brown and the chicken no longer
pink. Blend the cornflour with a little water and stir
into the mixture. Bring to the boil and cook for about 1
minute until thick.
3 Cut the chu-wang-yiu into four 10 cm/4 inch
squares. Lay on a flat surface and place 2-3 tblspns of
the pork and chicken mixture in the centre of each.
Roll up, moulding the parcel into the shape of a
chicken drumstick.
4 Blend the flour with a little water to make a thick
paste and use a little of this to seal the parcels. Coat
each of the parcels in the remaining paste.
5 Heat the oil in a deep-fat fryer and fry the
'drumsticks' for about 7-8 minutes. Remove with a
slotted spoon and drain on absorbent paper.
6 Blend seasoning **B** and serve as a dipping sauce
with the 'drumsticks'.

NOTE

Chu-wang-yiu is a very thin dough, which when fried
has a deliciously crisp texture. It is available from
most Chinese supermarkets.

Spring Roll

INGREDIENTS (SERVES 4)

6 spring onions
3 tblspns corn oil
225 g/8 oz minced pork
40 g/1½ oz bamboo shoots,
 thinly sliced
3 dried black mushrooms,
 soaked (see NOTES)
2 tblspns cornflour
2 tblspns plain flour
2 tblspns water
about 15 spring roll wrappers
 (see NOTES)
corn oil, for deep frying

SEASONING

1 tblspn shrimp paste (see
 NOTES)
1½ tspns salt
2 tspns sugar
½ tblspn rice wine or dry
 sherry
pinch of black pepper

METHOD

1 Trim the spring onions, cut into quarters lengthways and then cut into 7.5 cm/3 inch sections.
2 Heat the oil in a wok. Add the pork, bamboo shoots, mushrooms and seasoning ingredients and stir-fry for 3-4 minutes over a high heat. Add the spring onions and cook for a further 3 minutes, stirring.
3 Blend the cornflour with a little water and stir into the pork and vegetable mixture. Cook over a moderately high heat until the mixture is thick and then remove from the heat and allow to cool a little.
4 Blend the plain flour with the water to make a smooth paste. Lay the spring roll wrappers out on a flat surface and place 2 tblspns of the filling in the centre. Roll the 'wrapper' up until semi-circular shaped and then brush the edges with the flour paste. Fold in the sides and continue rolling up.
5 Heat the oil in a deep-fat fryer and deep-fry the spring rolls for 4 minutes or until golden. Drain on absorbent paper and serve.

NOTES

1 Soak the black mushrooms for 20-30 minutes in warm water before using, then remove stalks and slice.
2 Spring roll wrappers are available in Chinese delicatessens, and many large supermarkets.
3 Shrimp paste is available from Chinese supermarkets.

Mixed Meat and Vegetable Broth

INGREDIENTS
(SERVES 4-6)

225 g/8 oz spareribs
75 g/3 oz black pudding
1 turnip
1 large carrot
1 large onion
12 mm/½ inch piece fresh
 root ginger
1 tblspn rice wine or dry
 sherry
1.5 litres/2½ pints fish stock,
 made with 2 fish stock
 cubes
6-10 fish balls (see NOTE
 p. 371)
300 ml/½ pint water

SEASONING
3 tblspns sweet chilli sauce
2 tblspns shrimp paste (see
 NOTE 3, above)
2 tblspns corn oil

METHOD

1 Roughly chop the spareribs into chunks and cut the black pudding into 2.5 cm/1 inch cubes. Peel the turnip and cut into 2.5 cm/1 inch cubes, thinly slice the carrot and cut the onion into wedges.
2 Place the spareribs in a large flameproof casserole with the ginger, rice wine and the fish stock. Bring to the boil and simmer for 30 minutes.
3 Add the black pudding, turnip, carrot, onion and fish balls, bring back to the boil and simmer for about 1 hour, covered, until the vegetables are very tender.
4 In a separate pan, heat the seasoning ingredients together with the water until boiling. When ready to serve the broth, swirl in the seasoning sauce.

Steamed Eggs with Whitebait

INGREDIENTS (SERVES 4)

50-75 g/2-3 oz whitebait
6 eggs
1 tblspn melted lard
5 tblspns clear soup stock
(see p. 261)

SEASONING
1 tblspn rice wine or dry
sherry
1 tspn salt
½ tspn white pepper

METHOD

1 Blend the seasoning ingredients and add the whitebait. Set aside for 5 minutes.
2 Beat the eggs thoroughly.
3 Mix the lard with the whitebait and place them in a deep bowl with the eggs and the soup stock.
4 Place the bowl in a steamer, cover and steam over a high heat for 10 minutes. Serve at once.

Bean Curd Sheet Rolls

INGREDIENTS (SERVES 4)

350 g/12 oz minced pork
4 water chestnuts
1 tblspn dried baby shrimps,
soaked (see NOTES)
5 Chinese dried mushrooms,
soaked (see NOTES)
16 bean curd sheets
4 tblspns corn oil
175 ml/6 fl oz clear soup
stock (see p. 261)
4 tblspns finely grated fresh
root ginger

SEASONING A
1 tblspn rice wine or dry
sherry
1 tspn salt
½ tspn white pepper

SEASONING B
½ tspn salt
1 tblspn soy sauce
½ tspn white pepper

METHOD

1 Mix the pork with seasoning **A** and set aside for 10 minutes.
2 Crush or finely chop the water chestnuts, chop the baby shrimps finely and chop the mushrooms into small cubes. Place together in a bowl, add the pork and work together to form a thick paste.
3 Soak the bean curd sheets in cold water until soft enough to handle. Dry on absorbent paper and lay on a flat surface.
4 Place 2-3 tblspns of the pork mixture onto one sheet. Roll up from one corner, tucking in the left and right hand corners as you go.
5 Heat the oil in a wok and carefully add the bean curd rolls. Fry for 3 minutes and then add the soup stock, seasoning **B** and ginger. Simmer for 15 minutes.
6 Remove the rolls with a slotted spoon and arrange on a serving plate. Spoon the sauce over the top and serve.

NOTES
1 Soak the baby shrimps in warm water for 30 minutes.
2 Soak the dried mushrooms in warm water for 20 minutes and then remove the stalks.

Savoury Congee

INGREDIENTS (SERVES 4)

1½ tblspns corn oil
1 spring onion, chopped
150 g/5 oz pork fillet, sliced
225 g/8 oz long-grain rice
25 g/1 oz dried baby shrimps
25 g/1 oz dried fish
5 Chinese mushrooms,
   soaked (see NOTE)
1.2 litres/2 pints water

METHOD

1 Heat the oil in a large flameproof casserole. Add the spring onion and fry for 30 seconds. Add the pork and the rice and fry for a further minute.

2 Rinse the baby shrimps and dried fish in cold water. Remove and discard the stalks from the mushrooms and cut into small cubes.

3 Add the water to the pork and rice mixture and then add the dried baby shrimps, dried fish and the mushrooms. Bring to the boil and simmer for 35-40 minutes or until the rice is tender. Serve with assorted nuts.

NOTE

Soak the shrimps, fish and mushrooms in warm water for 30 minutes before use.

髮菜四素

Dish of Five Vegetables

INGREDIENTS (SERVES 4)

25 g/1 oz black moss
   seaweed
1 carrot
100 g/4 oz button
   mushrooms
100 g/4 oz baby corn-on-the-
   cobs
100 g/4 oz mange touts
2 tablspns corn oil
½ tblspn cornflour
125 ml/4 fl oz clear soup
   stock (see p. 261)

SEASONING

1 tspn salt
1 tspn white pepper
2 tspns sugar
2 tspns sesame oil

METHOD

1   Soak the black moss seaweed in cold water for 20
minutes. Drain.
2   Cut the carrot into thin strips, cut the mushrooms
in halves or quarters, if large, and slice the baby corns
in half lengthways.
3   Place the carrots and baby corns in a bowl and
cover with boiling water. Blanch for 2 minutes, add
the button mushrooms and mange touts and blanch
for a further 3 minutes. Drain.
4   Heat the oil in a wok and add the carrot, baby
corns, mushrooms and mange touts. Blend the
cornflour with a little cold soup stock and stir with the
remaining stock into the vegetables. Cook for 5
minutes, stirring occasionally.
5   Add the black moss and seasoning ingredients and
simmer over a low heat for 1 minute. Arrange the four
vegetables on a plate and lay the black moss on top.
Pour over the sauce and serve.

Oyster and Vegetable Medley

INGREDIENTS (SERVES 4)

100 g/4 oz Chinese dried
oysters, soaked (see
NOTE)
1 tblspn salt
2 tblspns cornflour
175 ml/6 fl oz water
3 tblspns corn oil
1 egg, beaten
100 g/4 oz spinach
1 tblspn peanut powder or
ground peanuts

SEASONING A
¼ tspn salt
¼ tspn rice wine or dry
sherry
2 tspns ginger juice

SEASONING B
3 tblspns red bean sauce
1 tblspn sugar
1 tblspn soy sauce

METHOD

1   Place the dried oysters in cold water with the salt
and soak for 30 minutes. Drain. Rinse the oysters in
boiling water, and then soak again for 3 minutes.
Drain thoroughly and pat dry.
2   Blend the cornflour with the water, then mix with
seasoning **A**.
3   Blend seasoning **B** ingredients with a little water.
Heat 1 tblspn of the oil in a small saucepan, add
seasoning **B** and cook for 1 minute. Set aside.
4   Heat a further 1 tblspn of the oil in a pan, and pour
in seasoning **A**, tipping the pan to ensure it
completely covers the bottom of the pan. Place the
oysters on top, then pour in the beaten egg.
5   When the mixture has set, fold one half over the
other. Add the spinach and the remaining oil, and
cook for 2-3 minutes until the spinach is cooked.
Remove from the pan and arrange on a serving dish,
along with the peanut powder and seasoning **B**.

NOTE
Dried oysters are available from Chinese
delicatessens. However, they tend to be quite pricey.
If necessary use half quantities to those recommended
here.

Thin Noodles with Oysters

INGREDIENTS (SERVES 4)

275 g/10 oz dried oysters (see
NOTE above)
1½ tblspns salt
275 g/10 oz thin egg noodles
4 tblspns cornflour
1.2 litres/2 pints clear soup
stock (see p. 261)
50 g/2 oz bamboo shoots,
sliced
1 small carrot, sliced
3 Chinese mushrooms,
soaked
4 tblspns soy sauce
2 tspns salt
2 tblspns chopped parsley
125 ml/4 fl oz black vinegar
(see NOTE)
2 tspns white pepper
parsley sprigs, to garnish

METHOD

1   Place the oysters in cold water with the salt and
soak for 30 minutes. Drain. Rinse the oysters in boiling
water, and then soak again for 3 minutes. Drain
thoroughly and pat dry.
2   Separate the noodles and soak in cold water for 5
minutes. Drain.
3   Blend the cornflour with a little of the cold soup
stock. Place this and the rest of the soup stock in a
saucepan. Bring to the boil, stirring continually.
4   When the mixture has thickened, add the oysters,
bamboo shoots, carrot, sliced mushrooms, soy sauce
and salt. Bring back to the boil and boil for another 3-5
minutes.
5   Add the noodles, and boil for 3 minutes until they
are just tender.
6   Add the chopped parsley, vinegar and pepper.
Garnish with parsley sprigs and serve.

NOTE
Dark and rich, black vinegar is available from Chinese
delicatessens, but malt vinegar could be substituted if
necessary.

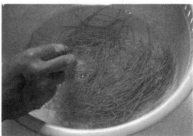

Steamed Pumpkin with Rice Flour

INGREDIENTS (SERVES 4)

1 small pumpkin or ½ large
   pumpkin
9 tblspns corn oil
1 tspn salt
½ tspn pepper
2 spring onions, chopped
8 tblspns rice flour
3 tblspns clear soup stock
   (see p. 261)

SEASONING
1 tblspn light soy sauce
1 tblspn oil
½ tspn salt

METHOD

1 Peel the pumpkin and cut into large pieces.
2 Heat 8 tblspns of the oil in a wok or frying pan and
stir-fry the pumpkin pieces for 5 minutes. Remove
from the wok with a slotted spoon and toss with the
salt and pepper. Set aside for 15 minutes.
3 Heat the remaining 1 tblspn of oil in the wok, add
the spring onions and stir-fry for 1 minute. Remove
and set aside for the garnish.
4 Mix the rice flour with the soup stock and the
seasoning ingredients and coat the pumpkin pieces in
this mixture.
5 Lay the pumpkin in a deep bowl and place in a
steamer. Cover and steam over a high heat for 30
minutes. Turn on to a plate, garnish with the fried
spring onions and serve.

Five-Flavoured Winter Melon

INGREDIENTS (SERVES 4)

900 g/2 lbs winter melon
3 Chinese dried mushrooms,
   soaked (see NOTES)
3 dried scallops, soaked
   (see NOTES)
2 small dried bamboo shoots,
   soaked (see NOTES)
3 tblspns corn oil
2 tspns finely grated fresh
   root ginger
50 g/2 oz dried shrimps
   (see NOTES)
50 g/2 oz smoked ham, diced
75 g/2 oz lean pork, diced
600 ml/1 pint clear soup
   stock (see p. 261)
2 tblspns cornflour

SEASONING
½ tspn salt
1 tspn sugar
½ tspn white pepper

METHOD

1 Peel the winter melon, remove the seeds and dice
into small cubes. Place in a large bowl, cover with
boiling water and set aside for 5 minutes. Drain.
2 Remove and discard the stalks from the
mushrooms and cut into small cubes; slice the
scallops thinly and finely dice the bamboo shoots.
3 Heat the oil in a wok or frying pan and stir-fry the
ginger for a few seconds. Add the mushrooms,
scallops, bamboo shoots, dried shrimps, ham, pork
and seasoning ingredients and stir-fry for 2 minutes.
4 Add the soup stock and stir to mix. Bring to the
boil. Add the winter melon, bring back to the boil and
simmer for 2 minutes.
5 Blend the cornflour with a little cold water and stir
into the soup. Simmer for 2 minutes until the soup has
thickened and serve.

NOTES
Since dried food keeps very well, it means all these
ingredients are available in this country too. In order
to use dried food, it needs to be soaked first:
dried mushrooms – soak in warm water for 30 minutes
dried scallops – soak in cold water for 1 hour
dried bamboo shoots – soak in cold water for 30
minutes
dried shrimps – soak in warm water for 30 minutes

Banana Jelly

INGREDIENTS (SERVES 4)

350 ml/12 fl oz water
25 g/1 oz gelatine
100 g/4 oz caster sugar
4 bananas
3 tblspns lemon juice
125 ml/4 fl oz orange juice

METHOD

1 Place 125 ml/4 fl oz of the water in a bowl and sprinkle the gelatine over the surface. Allow the gelatine to soak for 5 minutes. Bring the remaining water to the boil, add to the gelatine and stir until the gelatine has dissolved.

2 Add the sugar, stirring until it is completely dissolved. Set aside for 10 minutes.

3 Slice the bananas and sprinkle with 1 tblspn of the lemon juice to prevent them discolouring.

4 Mix the orange and remaining lemon juice in a bowl and stir in the gelatine mixture.

5 Arrange half of the banana slices in a jelly mould, pour one third of the gelatine mixture over the bananas and place in the refrigerator for 5 minutes.

6 Add half of the remaining jelly to the mould, place in the refrigerator for 5 minutes and then add the remaining jelly. Refrigerate for 30-60 minutes until set.

7 When the jelly is set, place the mould up to the rim in boiling water for 5-10 seconds, and then turn the jelly out onto a serving plate. Decorate the jelly with the remaining banana slices and serve.

Pineapple Jelly

INGREDIENTS (SERVES 4)

350 ml/12 fl oz water
25 g/1 oz gelatine
100 g/4 oz caster sugar
6-8 pineapple rings
2 tblspns lemon juice
125 ml/4 fl oz pineapple juice
6-8 pineapple rings

METHOD

1 Place 125 ml/4 fl oz of the water in a bowl and sprinkle the gelatine over the surface. Allow the gelatine to soak for 5 minutes. Bring the remaining water to the boil, add to the gelatine and stir until the gelatine has dissolved.

2 Add the sugar, stirring until it is completely dissolved. Set aside for 10 minutes.

3 Arrange the pineapple rings in a large jelly mould.

4 Mix the lemon and pineapple juice in a bowl and stir in the gelatine mixture. Pour over the pineapple rings and place in a refrigerator for 45-60 minutes or until set.

5 When the jelly is set, place the mould up to the rim in boiling water for 5-10 seconds, and then turn the jelly out onto a serving plate.

MENU IDEAS

MENU 1
(SERVES 8)

Soup of Assorted Shreds
page 221

Five-Spice Chicken Pieces
page 77

Marinated Pork
page 101

Fried Prawns with Black Sesame Seeds
page 57

Hot Beef
page 73

Paper-Wrapped Fish
page 41

Stuffed Green Peppers
page 126

Stir-Fried Spinach with Fresh Vegetables
page 189

Stir-Fried Rice Noodles
page 275

Crystal Beauty
page 259

MENU 2
(SERVES 6)

Chicken and Sweetcorn Chowder
page 81

Sautéed Prawns
page 13

Sweet and Sour Fish
page 27

Assorted Shreds
page 131

Beef Slices in Sauce
page 73

The Farmer's Joy
page 229

Chicken with Sweet Rice
page 279

Fresh Fruit

MENU 3
(SERVES 4)

Shanghainese Thick Noodle Soup
page 271

Baked Creamy Clams
page 15

Crystal Paper-Wrapped Chicken
page 95

Barbecued Beef
page 113

Home-Town Style Mange Tout
page 225

Fried or Plain Boiled Rice
page 264

Fresh Fruit

MENU

4

(SERVES 4)

Mixed Meat and Vegetable Broth
page 373

Spicy Clams
page 363

Cantonese Fried Chicken
page 353

Hot Pork Paste
page 367

Steamed Pumpkin with Rice Flour
page 381

Fried or Plain Boiled Rice
page 264

Fresh Fruit

MENU

5

(SERVES 4)

Stewed Shark's Fin with Mushrooms
page 365

Stir-Fried Beef with Oyster Sauce
page 363

Mock Chicken Drumsticks
page 371

Two Kinds of Marinated Vegetable
page 369

Chinese Curried Macaroni
page 355

Fried or Plain Boiled Rice
page 264

Sweet Lotus Roots
page 359

MENU

6

(SERVES 6)

Five-Flavoured Peanuts
page 367

Shredded Chicken and Pepper
page 353

Scalded Abalones
page 361

Spring Roll
page 373

Thin Noodles with Oysters
page 379

Dish of Five Vegetables
page 377

Fried or Plain Boiled Rice
page 264

Pineapple Jelly
page 383

Glossary

Abalone: a white-fleshed shellfish with a firm texture and a delicate scallop-like flavour.

Fresh abalones can sometimes be found in the larger and better Chinese delicatessens, imported not from the Far East but from the Channel Islands and Breton coast where they are occasionally caught.

Failing finding these, however, the canned variety are a good substitute and are widely available from Chinese stores. Once canned abalones are opened they should be used straight away.

Dried abalones are sometimes available, but bear in mind that they need to be soaked in water for 4 days before use.

Abalone Mushrooms: *see Chinese Mushrooms*

Agar-Agar: a gelatinous seaweed used for making sweet or savoury jellies. Since it sets without refrigeration, it is particularly suited to hot climates like south China and Hong Kong where it is used a great deal. However, it is virtually tasteless and gelatine, or aspic (for vegetarian dishes) are good substitutes.

Sold in most Chinese or Japanese supermarkets, it is normally only available in this country in dried form, either powdered or cut into strips. Keep in a covered container or wrapped in cellophane in a dry cool place, but not in the refrigerator, for up to 6 months.

Angled Luffas: sometimes known as Chinese okra or silk squash, this vegetable is a member of the gourd family. It is a long, thin vegetable with deep ridges running along its length. It has a sweet flavour and is used for soups as well as stir-fries.

Available from Chinese and Indian supermarkets, it tends to be mainly around in the summer months. If unavailable, use cucumber.

Aniseed: along with star anise, which has a similar flavour, aniseed is popular in Chinese cooking, adding a delicate liquorice taste to sweet and savoury dishes.

It is available whole, as tiny egg-shaped seeds, or in powdered form and can be bought in health food shops, Chinese delicatessens and some large supermarkets. If unavailable, use caraway seeds instead.

Bamboo Shoots: one of the most widely used vegetables in Chinese cooking, these fibrous, cream-coloured shoots have a pleasant, slightly acid flavour and a firm, crunchy texture.

Thanks to modern transport and greater demand, *fresh bamboo shoots* are now increasingly available from Chinese supermarkets. Peel away the outer skin until you reach the firm heart. This can then be boiled whole or sliced or cut into slivers according to the recipe.

Canned bamboo shoots are widely available from Chinese stores and most supermarkets too. They either come ready sliced or in large 7.5 × 10 cm/3 × 4 inch chunks. Drain and rinse in fresh water before using. Place any unused shoots in a dish, cover with fresh water and keep refrigerated for 3-4 days, changing the water daily.

Bean Curds: Made from puréed yellow soya beans, bean curd or tofu is used extensively in Chinese cooking. In many areas where meat is scarce or expensive, bean curd is an important source of protein and consequently there are many different varieties available.

Fresh Bean Curd: comes in cakes about 7.5 cm/3 inches square which can be cut to any shape. It has a fairly bland taste but when cooked with other ingredients, such as meat, fish or vegetables, acquires their flavours. It also adds extra protein and an interesting texture to a dish.

Fresh bean curd can be found in any health food store, Chinese delicatessen or large supermarket. Store in fresh water in a covered container until required.

Dried Bean Curd: this too is sold in cake form, which is sliced or cut into strips and then fried, braised or stewed according to the recipe. Available from Chinese supermarkets.

Dried Bean Curd Sheets/Skin: comes in thin, stiff sheets and must be soaked in warm water for about 10 minutes before use. It can be cut into strips and used in soups, or used as a wrapper for small meat balls.

Fermented Bean Curd/Bean Curd Cheese: made by fermenting small cubes of bean curd in brine, chillis and wine. It is very salty, with a strong, distinctive taste and while the Chinese often eat small quantities for breakfast with congee, it is mostly used for flavouring meat or vegetable dishes.

There are two types commonly available. The white fermented variety and the red Southern China one. Both are sold in jars or sealed packets and are available from Chinese supermarkets. They will keep for months in the refrigerator.

Pressed Bean Curd: a firmer form of bean curd often used in vegetarian cooking. There are various types available. *Spiced bean curd* is seasoned with spices and soy sauce. It is also known as *fragrant dry bean curd*. It can be shredded to make noodles and added to soups or stir-fries. Available from Chinese supermarkets.

Bean Sprouts: the young sprouts of mung beans, these are some 5 cm/2 inches long, have a fresh flavour and a delicious crunchy texture which makes them a popular addition to stir-fries. Stir them into a dish just before serving, otherwise they will lose their crispness.

Fresh bean sprouts are widely available from Chinese, Indian and Western supermarkets and from many greengrocers. They should be white stalked with pale yellow heads. Avoid any that appear to exude any brown juice since this means they are past their prime. They are best eaten on the day of purchase, but can be stored in a plastic bag in the refrigerator for up to a day. Canned bean sprouts are not quite as crisp as fresh ones, but are still quite acceptable. These too are widely available from most supermarkets. Drain and rinse canned bean sprouts in cold water before using.

Bitter Gourd/Bitter Melon: mostly light green to white in colour, this gourd has an unmistakable bumpy skin and when cut open, reveals rosy-red seeds. As the name suggests, it has a rather bitter taste which finely complements rich pork dishes. In China it is a common vegetable and is used frequently in Chinese cooking. It is available from some Chinese, Indian and West Indian supermarkets and can be kept, refrigerated, for up to 2 weeks. If not available use *chayoto* or marrow or courgette instead.

Black Bean Sauce/Black Bean Paste: also known as *brown-bean sauce*, this thick paste is made from black salted soya beans and is often used instead of soy sauce when a thicker sauce is required. It is very salty with a strong flavour and should be used sparingly. It is sold in cans or jars, either semi-whole or puréed. Buy from any Chinese store and keep unused sauce in a sealed container in the refrigerator for up to 2 weeks. *See also, Yellow Bean Sauce and Red Bean Sauce.*

Black Moss: *see Seaweed*

Black Mushrooms: *see Chinese Mushrooms*

Chayoto: a pear-shaped vegetable with a similar texture to the marrow. Like the marrow it varies widely in size and shape, with the larger specimens being rather insipid. Therefore, look out for the smaller varieties. They are commonly found in Chinese, Indian and West Indian stores and occasionally in Western supermarkets too. If not available, use marrow or courgette instead.

Chillis: these hot little green and red peppers are used frequently in Chinese cooking. There are many types, ranging from the hot to the unbearable; beware of recipes advocating the use of 6-10 chillis. For inexperienced palates it is safer to use just one or two until you feel acclimatised to such fiery eating experiences! As a general rule, the smaller the chillis, the hotter they'll be. Besides making a dish very hot, chillis also add a distinctive flavour. They are normally finely sliced before adding to a dish with the seeds removed and discarded.

Fresh chillis are available from all Chinese and many Western supermarkets and greengrocers. *Dried chillis* are lightly crumbled and used to flavour soups and stews. Available from health food shops and Chinese stores.

Chilli Oil: made from small red chillis which have been slowly fried in oil, this oil can be very hot indeed and should be used sparingly. It is reddish in colour and can be made at home. Fry finely sliced chilli gently in oil for 5 minutes until the oil has turned a dark colour – use 1 chilli to every 1 tblspn oil.

Chilli Sauce: made from small chilli peppers, this is a hot sauce used frequently in China as a condiment as well as in cooking. It is available from Chinese and Western supermarkets and is most commonly available in bottles. It will keep almost indefinitely. *Sweet chilli sauce* is not so hot and is a more popular condiment on Western tables. This too is widely available.

Chinese Cabbage/Chinese Leaves/Chinese Celery: a wide variety of cabbages are grown in China, where they are used in all sorts of dishes as well as in chutneys and pickles. The variety that is now commonly available in this country is, in China, known as the *pe-tsai*. A little like a large, pale Cos lettuce, it has a thick white stalk and pale yellow or green leaves. The leaves have a delicate savoury flavour, while the stalk is slightly sweet, similar to bean sprouts, with a crisp, celery-like texture.

Available from any greengrocers, it will keep up to 2 weeks in the salad drawer of a refrigerator.

Chinese Curry Powder: a sweet smelling curry powder, not to be confused with Indian curry powders, which would give a dish a completely different flavour. Chinese curry powders are normally composed of anise pepper, cassia (cinnamon), chilli, cloves, coriander seeds, fennel seeds, nutmeg, star anise and turmeric.

Available only from Chinese supermarkets; store in an airtight container in a dry place.

Chinese Mushrooms and Fungi: Mushrooms and fungi are widely used in Chinese cooking, both in fresh and dried forms. Although they don't tend to have a strong flavour, they are popular since they add a particular texture to a dish – a very important element in Chinese cuisine. Fresh Chinese mushrooms are not generally available in the West. However, there are a number of dried and canned varieties that can be bought.

These are normally only available from Chinese supermarkets. Dried mushrooms should be soaked in warm water for 20-30 minutes before use, rinsing before and after soaking. Once soaked, remove and discard the stalk which is very tough. Dried, the mushrooms and fungi will keep indefinitely, if stored in an airtight container. Once soaked, however, they should be used straight away.

Abalone Mushrooms/Oyster Mushrooms: large and flat ear-shaped mushrooms with grey/fawn caps and soft cream-coloured 'bellies'. They have an excellent flavour but need careful cooking as they can be tough.

Known in this country as oyster mushrooms, they are available fresh mainly from delicatessens and high class greengrocers.

Chinese Mushrooms/Dried Black Mushrooms/ Winter Mushrooms: one of the most common mushrooms in Chinese cookery, these dried dark brown or black mushrooms are used in a whole range of Chinese dishes and add a chewy texture. You will find they come in varying thicknesses, the thick-capped ones being considered the best. The name, Winter Mushrooms, refers to the time of their harvest.

Cloud Ears/Wood Ears: two common Chinese fungi which grow on the bark of trees. They are normally about 3 cm/1½ inches in diameter, dark-brown almost black in colour with crinkly skins. Although they have little flavour, they are popular since they add a slightly crunchy and firm texture to a dish and provide a contrast in colour.

Silver Ears: a dried white fungi with little or no flavour but a delicate texture. Used mainly in sweet dishes, it should be soaked for 50-60 minutes before using.

Straw Mushrooms: only available canned, these small conical mushrooms have a pleasant, delicate flavour a little similar to button mushrooms. Their texture is soft and slippery. Drain thoroughly and rinse before using. If unavailable, use button mushrooms.

Chinese Sausages: thin dried sausages made of pork, beef or pork liver and duck. Steam before using in a recipe.

Available from most Chinese delicatessens, they will keep for a few months, wrapped in a plastic bag and kept in the refrigerator.

Chinese Spareribs: not to be confused with American or English-style spareribs which are meaty and sold in slices, these spareribs are from the lower ends of the rib bones. They have very little meat on them but taste extremely good barbecued with Hoisin or barbecue sauce

Chinese Vinegar: a fermented rice vinegar, there are two principal types available, the *brown vinegar* and the *white vinegar*. Both are quite mild, with a slightly sweet taste. They can be found in Chinese supermarkets, however substitute cider vinegar and white wine vinegar respectively if preferred.

Cumin: a common Indian spice that is occasionally found in Chinese cooking. The dried seed is small and light brown in colour, while the ground seed is olive green. Cumin has a strong, heavy aroma, adding a distinctive, pungent flavour to savoury and sweet dishes.

Available from almost any supermarket.

Dates/Red, Black: dried dates that need soaking before use. The red dates are also known as *red jujubes*. Both should be soaked in cold water for 1-2 hours.

Available from some Chinese supermarkets, but when not, substitute prunes.

Dried Black Beans: *see Fermented Black Beans*

Dried Chestnuts: frequently used in Chinese cooking for their flavour and aroma, they are simply the fruit of the sweet chestnut. Dried they are hard and crinkly and should be soaked overnight in cold water before using in a recipe.

Available from health food shops, Chinese and Indian supermarkets and delicatessens.

Dried Duck/Dried Chicken: these are de-boned and pressed flat before being dried. They are used most frequently for flavouring stocks and soups and are available from most Chinese supermarkets.

Dried Fish: salted and dried in the sun, dried fish is used frequently both for flavouring other dishes or eating in its own right. Since dried fish will keep indefinitely, it is frequently imported to this country and is available from Chinese supermarkets.

Dried Orange Peel: *see Orange Peel, Dried*

Dried Scallops: white scallops that have been dried in the sun, they have a sweet, slightly musty flavour. Available from good oriental stores, they should be kept in a covered jar in a cool place.

Dried Shrimps: small and orange coloured, dried shrimps have been salted and dried in the sun and have a distinctive fishy smell and taste. They are available in several different qualities; in general, the larger they are the better. They should be soaked in lukewarm water for 30 minutes before using and then drained thoroughly.

Available only from Chinese shops, they will keep

indefinitely in an airtight container. Once soaked, however, use the same day.

Dried Squid: highly regarded by the Chinese as a delicacy, dried squid has a strong distinctive flavour, quite different from the rather fragrant mild taste of fresh squid. Soak overnight in cold water before using.

Available only from Chinese supermarkets.

Fermented Black Beans: small fermented soya beans commonly used in fish and seafood cookery. Since they are very salty, soak in cold water for 5-10 minutes. They are available in cans or jars and will keep 2-3 weeks if placed in an airtight jar in the refrigerator. *Dried black beans* can be used if canned beans are not available. They should be washed thoroughly and then marinated in brandy or rice wine for several hours.

Five-spice Powder: frequently used in all sorts of Chinese dishes, to many it summons up the taste and smell of China. As the name implies, it is made up of five ground spices – szechuan pepper, cinnamon, cloves, fennel seed and star anise.

Available from delicatessens, Chinese supermarkets and some health food shops, it should be kept in a sealed container in a dry place. Like most spices it will keep for several months, but will gradually loose its fragrance and flavour and therefore should not be kept for too long.

Flours: there are many different kinds of flour used in China, made from grains, pulses and tubers. They are used for making the many types of noodles, doughs and pancakes. They will normally be available from any Chinese and some Indian supermarkets. When not available, ordinary plain (wheat) flour can be used instead, or use the alternative listed below.

Cornflour: sometimes called cornstarch, this is a very common thickening agent in Chinese cooking. Arrowroot can be used as a substitute, but not ordinary wheat flour.

Potato Flour: often added to batters to give elasticity.

Rice Flour: made from finely ground white rice, this is used in various batters and sweet dishes.

Glutinous Rice Flour: made from glutinous rice this has more elasticity than ordinary rice flour, becoming clear and sticky when cooked. It is used for certain sweet dishes, batters and dough.

Green Bean Flour: sometimes known as *green pea flour*, this flour is made from ground mung beans. It is often light green in colour, although can be white or pale pink as well. It is used for various dim sum and noodle recipes. If not available, arrowroot can be substituted.

Fuzzy Melons/Summer Melons: looking a little like a cross between a cucumber and a courgette, when young, these fruit/vegetables are covered with a silky fuzz which comes away under running water. The flesh inside is soft and white with white spongy seeds.

Ginger, Fresh Root: a knobbly, pale-coloured root, this is probably the single most important spice in Chinese cooking. It is almost always used with fish and seafood cookery and with many meats as well, such as beef, venison and pork. It has a sweet, fragrant aroma and adds a distinct almost citrus flavour and slight piquancy to a dish. It should be peeled and then thinly sliced or grated. *Ginger juice* can be made by placing a few slices of fresh ginger in a garlic press and squeezing firmly.

Fresh root ginger is available from any large supermarket and will keep for 1-2 months if kept in a dry place. If it is not available, use ½ tspn ground ginger and 1 tblspn lemon juice for every 1 tblspn of fresh grated ginger.

Ginger Wine: an infusion of shredded ginger and Chinese rice wine, it is available commercially, although it is possible to make it at home. If Chinese rice wine is unavailable, dry sherry can be used instead. To make 150 ml/¼ pint, place 15 g/½ oz finely sliced fresh root ginger with the wine and leave for at least 1 hour before use. It will keep indefinitely in the refrigerator.

Ginkgo Nuts: small soft white nuts, a little larger than peanuts with a distinctive flavour. They should be blanched to remove the outer brown skin before use. Available from most oriental supermarkets, either canned or dried. Canned nuts should be drained and rinsed before using.

Gluten Puff: normally bought frozen from most Chinese supermarkets, it should be completely defrosted before using. Canned glutens are also sometimes available, but take care that the sauce they come in complements the recipe.

Gourds: *see Bitter Gourd*

Green Bean Flour: *see Flours*

Hoisin Sauce: made with garlic, chillis, spices and soya beans, this brownish-red sauce is frequently used as a dip with pork and beef dishes. It is also commonly used with soy sauce in stir-frying. It has a strong, sweet flavour and should be used sparingly, otherwise it tends to overpower the rest of the meal.

Available from any oriental and most large supermarkets, it is sometimes labelled Barbecue Sauce.

Jellyfish: dried shreds of jellyfish are quite frequently used in Chinese cooking, giving the favoured gelatinous texture to a dish.

Dried jellyfish can be bought from some Chinese stores. If not available, use shredded agar-agar or transparent vermicelli.

Laver: *see Seaweed*

Lily: *see Seaweed/Tiger Lily Buds*

Long Aubergines: exactly the same vegetable as the familiar short plump variety, long aubergines are, in fact, common in China and are now occasionally available from larger supermarkets and oriental stores.

Lotus Leaves: used only for wrapping food, lotus leaves impart a distinctive and delicate flavour to food during steaming. The food parcels are usually served in their leaves, which are then unwrapped at the table.

They are sold in most Chinese supermarkets, coming in cellophane packages or tied loosely with string. Soak for 20 minutes in warm water in order to soften them before using.

Lotus Root: a popular sweet in China, fresh lotus root is served simply chilled and sliced with a sweet apricot sauce. It is distinctive both in flavour and appearance, with a slightly musty taste and pale holey flesh that creates an attractive lacey pattern when sliced.

Dried and occasionally fresh lotus root can be bought from Chinese supermarkets. Canned lotus root is more commonly available from any oriental foodstore. Soak dried lotus root overnight in cold water before using.

Lotus Seeds/Nuts: used in a wide variety of dishes, both savoury and sweet, these seeds from the lotus flower are ivory-coloured and oval. They are available both dried and canned in syrup and if dried, should be soaked for 24 hours. They can be bought from most Chinese supermarkets.

Luffas: *see Angled Luffas*

Medlar Leaves: a green vegetable with long thin leafy stalks, resembling mint in appearance, but with a distinctive and unique flavour for which there is no real substitute. Available from Chinese and some Indian supermarkets.

Mustard Greens: a dark green vegetable with firm, pale green stalks. It has a faint mustardy taste. Though occasionally available from Chinese supermarkets, spring greens can be substituted when necessary.

Noodles: many different types of noodle are eaten in China. Prepared from all sorts of flour, they come in a variety of thicknesses and shapes and are tied into bundles or coiled into squares and rectangles. Today, more and more varieties are widely available, although for fresh noodles, it is necessary to visit a Chinese foodstore. Chinese dried noodles, however, can be bought from most large supermarkets.
Fresh Egg Noodles/E Mein: these large, yellow noodles are made of wheat and are either round or slightly flattened in shape. They should be rinsed and drained thoroughly before being fried and, like all fresh noodles, should not be kept for more than a day before using, otherwise they tend to become heavy.
Dried Egg Noodles/Mein Tsein: thin dried yellow noodles, which are either round or slightly flattened. Used in soups and fried noodle dishes, they are sold in bundles or coiled into square packets and should be soaked first to separate the strands.
Rice Noodles/Ho-Fun: made from rice flour, these are flat, opaque noodles, about 6 mm/¼ inch wide. They are available fresh or dried and can be boiled or fried. Dried noodles should be soaked for up to 30 minutes to soften.
Cellophane Noodles/Bean Threads/Transparent Vermicelli: glass-like opaque white threads made from mung bean flour. The noodles expand and become translucent upon soaking and are normally added to soups because they absorb large quantities of stock, giving them flavour and the soup substance. They should be soaked in hot water for 5 minutes before using. *Mung bean sheets* can be shredded according to the recipe. However, when not available, buy the packets of prepared noodles.
Buckwheat Noodles: these beige-coloured noodle strips are made of buckwheat flour. They are available dried.

Orange Peel/Tangerine Peel, Dried: this dried peel is often added to soups and casseroles to give a distinct and pleasant orange-flavour. The best skins come from large, brightly coloured fruit. The skin is threaded onto twine and dried in the sun for a week. It normally comes in packets and can be bought from most Chinese stores. Soak for 20 minutes before using. Dried, it will keep indefinitely, if stored in an airtight container.

Oyster Sauce: made from oysters and soya beans, this thick, salty sauce from South China is often used to flavour beef and occasionally vegetable dishes. Available from most Chinese supermarkets, once opened it should be kept in the refrigerator.

Peanut Oil/Groundnut Oil: although recipes in this book mostly call for corn oil, which is inexpensive and easily available, peanut oil is the type most favoured by the Chinese and for special occasions it is slightly preferable. It is available from most supermarkets.

Peppermint Leaves: a member of the mint family, peppermint has deep green, crinkled leaves which are occasionally tinged with reddish brown. It has a pleasant aromatic bouquet and a strong menthol taste, but unless home-grown it could be quite difficult to obtain. However, any kind of mint could be substituted if liked.

Plum Sauce: made from plums, sugar, garlic, salt and chilli, it adds a sweet, fruity flavour to various dishes and is often used when crisp-roasting meat and poultry. Sold in glass bottles or jars it is available from Chinese supermarkets.

Potato Flour: *see Flours*

Preserved Vegetable: a turnip-like vegetable, preserved in brine and spices and with a very strong, salty taste. It is usually cooked with meats and vegetables to add flavour and saltiness to a meal. Look out for it in Chinese supermarkets; it is normally sold in cans, although it can be occasionally bought by the weight. Rinse in cold water before use.

Red Bean Sauce/Paste: otherwise known as *sweet bean paste,* this thick sauce is mostly used as a dip or to brush on pancakes when serving Peking Duck. It is made from red beans, sugar and spices and is also used for sweet sauces or to accompany fish and seafood dishes. Keep covered in the refrigerator for up to 3 months.

Red Spinach: not really red, but with red-tipped leaves, this Chinese spinach will add a red tinge to soups and casseroles. It can sometimes be bought from Chinese supermarkets, otherwise just buy spinach.

Rice: a simple long-grained rice is probably the best choice for most Chinese dishes unless another type is called for. Unless it has been pre-rinsed, rice should always be washed in several changes of water. See p.264 for cooking long-grain rice.
Glutinous Rice: a round-grained rice used for puddings and certain savoury dishes and stuffings. It becomes very sticky when cooked. Use short-grained (pudding) rice when not available.

Rice Wine: a pale, rather sweet wine made from glutinous rice which is used frequently, both for marinades and in cooking. It is available from Chinese supermarkets, but dry sherry can be substituted if necessary.

Rock Sugar: amber-brown sugar crystals used for desserts and sweets and for glazing poultry. It is not as sweet as normal sugar and needs dissolving in warm water before use. It is sold in Chinese supermarkets and some delicatessens. It will keep indefinitely, stored in a covered container.

Salted Cabbage/Pickled Cabbage: thin brownish-green pieces of the stem of Chinese cabbage, that have been preserved in brine. It has a savoury, mildly salty flavour and a firm, crispy texture. Sold in jars, it can only be bought from Chinese supermarkets. Rinse thoroughly before use.

Salted Vegetable: *see Preserved Vegetable*

Seafood Sauce: *see Shrimp Paste*

Seaweed: several types of seaweed are used in Chinese cooking. Popular both for their flavours and textures, they are generally used in soups or stews and are normally only available from Chinese supermarkets.

Black Moss/Hair Seaweed: fine dried black seaweed that is used in several traditional Chinese dishes. It is very fine and is known as hair seaweed as it is supposed to resemble Chinese hair. It should be soaked for about 40 minutes before use.

Laver: sold in wafer-thin sheets, measuring about 20 cm/8 inches square this dark dehydrated seaweed is commonly used for wrapping rice and vegetables. It has a slightly fishy fragrant flavour. It can also be deep fried or shredded and added to soups and salads. Available from Chinese supermarkets or from Japanese stores, where it is called *nori*.

Tiger Lily Buds/Golden Needles: these have a musty, slightly mouldy flavour, which is very much an acquired taste. They are used to garnish various fish dishes and are occasionally used in pork and vegetable dishes. They should be soaked in cold water for 20 minutes before using.

Sesame Oil: a dark-brown, strong-tasting oil, used frequently in Chinese cooking as a seasoning. Made from sesame seeds, it gives food a distinct, slightly nutty flavour. Since it burns easily, it is never used by itself for frying but is sprinkled on stir-fried or deep fried dishes just before serving.

Widely available from large supermarkets and oriental stores, it comes in convenient small bottles. It will keep indefinitely.

Sesame Paste/Sauce: a thick, sticky paste made from ground seeds. It has a strong, dry flavour and is used in several north and west Chinese dishes. Two types are normally available, the dark paste, which has been ground with the husks of the seed, and the lighter paste.

Available from oriental stores and any health food shop, where it is known as *tahini paste*, it comes mostly in jars and should be vigorously stirred before using.

Sesame Seeds: white sesame seeds are used frequently for sweet and savoury dishes – often for coating food before deep frying. They have a pleasant, nutty flavour and are available from health food shops, Chinese delicatessens and large supermarkets. They will keep indefinitely in an airtight container. Black sesame seeds have exactly the same flavour as the white and are normally used in cooking when a contrast in colour is required. They are less widely available but can be bought from Chinese supermarkets.

Shrimp Paste: made from thousands of tiny shrimps, this strong-tasting sauce is used to add flavour to soups, noodles, vegetables and meat dishes. It is available either as a purée or as a more solid pâté. Both should be diluted in water before using. Surprisingly, it is not used in fish dishes. Available from Chinese supermarkets.

Soy Sauce: the most familiar ingredient in Chinese cooking, soy sauce is used in savoury dishes, almost without fail. Made from fermented soya beans, it is thin and dark brown in colour with a rich, salty taste. There are two principal types available: *dark soy sauce* is used with strong-flavoured dishes, like beef and pork while *light soy sauce* is used for more delicate food, such as seafood, poultry and vegetables. The lighter one is more generally served as a condiment at the table.

Spring Roll Wrappers: large paper-thin skins of rice flour dough, used for making spring rolls. They are sold in packets of 25 or 50 and if frozen, should be thoroughly defrosted before using. They are becoming increasingly widely available, not only from oriental stores, but from many western ones as well. Keep unused wrappers in cling film or covered with a damp cloth until ready to use.

Star Anise: a highly scented eight-pointed star-shaped spice used mainly in braised dishes. It is one of the spices that make up Five-Spice Powder. Available from Chinese and Indian stores and specialist herb and spice shops, it should be kept in an airtight container to preserve its aroma.

Straw Mushrooms: *see Chinese Mushrooms*

Szechuan Pepper: tiny round spice with a reddish brown colour, it goes into making Five-Spice Powder and is used, often with star anise, for red-meat dishes – especially those from the north and west of China. It has a very fragrant smell and can be used whole or ground. Available from most Chinese supermarkets.

Taro: a dark brownish-red root vegetable, shaped a little like a turnip with a thick hairy skin. Inside, the flesh is creamy to dark reddish-brown with a flavour similar to a sweet potato. Popular in Chinese vegetarian cooking, it can be cooked in as many ways as the potato – baked, puréed, braised, deep fried, boiled or mashed. Like the potato, it needs to be cooked until quite soft.

Vinegar: *see Chinese Vinegar*

Water Chestnuts: small round root plants, that can be halved or sliced and added to stir-fries and casseroles to give a crispy, crunchy texture and a fresh slightly sweet flavour. Fresh water chestnuts, occasionally found in Chinese supermarkets, are sold in their black-coloured skins. These should be rinsed and peeled. Canned water chestnuts are widely available on the other hand and simply need draining before use.

White Fungus: *see Chinese Mushrooms/Silver Ears*

Winter Melon: a large, torpedo-shaped melon, with a pale green to dark green skin and creamy white flesh. In cooking, the winter melon has more in common with the marrow than with the melon. It should be cooked gently until very tender and it is used in soups and casseroles. Available from oriental greengrocers and supermarkets, once cut it will last for about a week if kept in a cool place. It is also sold in cans, but if not available, use marrow or courgette instead.

Wonton Wrappers: ready-made squares of rice-flour skins used for wrapping 'wontons' – small Chinese ravioli. They can be bought in packets of 20 from Chinese supermarkets and some Western stores and any remaining wrappers should be rewrapped securely or covered with a damp cloth otherwise the wrappers will dry out and become useless. They can be frozen. Defrost before use.

Yellow Bean Sauce/Paste: often used instead of soy sauce when thicker consistency is required. It has a similar consistency to Black Bean Sauce, but has added sugar, so is sweeter. It is also lighter and not quite so salty. It is used for making dips, dressings and some marinades and is available in cans or jars from most Chinese supermarkets.

KEY TO VEGETABLES AND INGREDIENTS

Many of the vegetables illustrated here will be known to you; others are perhaps currently less identifiable. Not all of them appear in the recipes in this book, but you can use this guide to help you to identify the unknown vegetables you encounter during your forays into Chinese supermarkets.

1. Cabbage
2. Mustard Greens
3. White Chinese Cabbage
4. Fennel
5. Watercress
6. Chinese Spinach
7. Chives
8. Chinese Chives
9. Lettuce
10. Brussels Sprouts
11. White Wormwood
12. Chinese Flat Cabbage
13. Pea Shoots
14. Chinese Cress
15. Stem Lettuce
16. Red Leaves
17. Sweet Potato Leaves
18. Asparagus
19. Chou-Tu-Fu (Bean Curd)
20. Lotus Leaf
21. Chinese Cabbage
22. Fuzzy Melon
23. Pickled Bamboo Shoots
24. Angled Luffa
25. Pickled Melon
26. Pickled Cowpea
27. Cedar Shoots
28. Sour Cabbage
29. Salted Vegetable
30. Taro Stalk

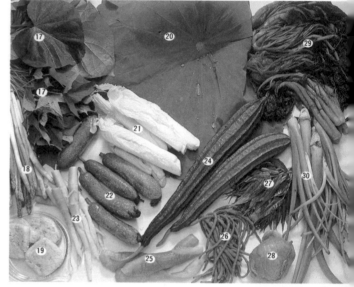

31. Mustard Flower
32. Kale
33. Celery
34. Rape Flower
35. Bitter Gourd
36. Green-stemmed Flat Cabbage
37. Spinach
38. Aubergines
39. Bottle Gourd
40. Large Cucumber
41. Turnip
42. Green Oriental Radish
43. Kale Flower
44. Red Radish
45. Red Peppers (Bell Peppers)
46. Cucumber
47. White Chinese Cabbage
48. Leek
49. Green Peppers
50. Carrot
51. Garlic Stem
52. Medlar
53. Corns
54. Winter Melon
55. Water Spinach
56. Mustard Stem
57. Chinese Greens
58. *Ma* Bamboo Shoots
59. Garlic Flower
60. Lotus Root
61. Uzura Beans
62. Sponge Gourd
63. Taro

64. Chinese Mallow
65. Water-Bamboo
66. Basil
67. *Kuei* Bamboo Shoots
68. Green Bamboo Shoots
69. Taro
70. Chinese Yam
71. Burdock
72. Tomato
73. Chinese Mushrooms
74. Pumpkin
75. White Yam
76. Bean Sprouts
77. Sweet Potatoes
78. Potatoes
79. Bur Clover
80. Rape (Field Mustard)
81. Broccoli
82. Cauliflower
83. Yam Bean
84. Mange Touts
85. Green Peas
86. Lima Beans
87. Green Beans
88. Baby Corn Shoots
89. Straw Mushrooms
90. Button Mushrooms
91. Jack Beans
92. Water Chestnuts
93. Kohlrabi
94. Bamboo Shoots
95. Abalone Mushrooms
96. Arrow Head
97. Long-stem Mushrooms
98. Fungus
99. Chayotes
100. Leaf Beet
101. Broad Beans
102. String Beans

INDEX

395

CHINESE STOCKISTS

Many of the ingredients featured in this book can be obtained from:

GREATER LONDON

Orchard Shop, 5 Wardour Street, W1. Tel: 01-439 9428

Chinatown Supermarket Ltd, 118–120 Shaftesbury Avenue, W1. Tel: 01-437 3352

Greatwall, 31–37 Wardour Street, W1. Tel: 01-437 6313

Loon Fung Supermarket, 42–44 Gerard Street, W1. Tel: 01-437 7332

Matahari Supermarket, 102 Westbourne Grove, W2. Tel: 01-221 7468

Cheong-Leen Supermarket, 4/10 Tower Street, Cambridge Circus, WC2. Tel: 01-836 5378

Golden Gate Hong, 14 Lisle Street, WC2. Tel: 01-437 0014

Sunki & Co, 25–27 Newport Court, WC2. Tel: 01-437 4448

Ken Lo's Kitchen, 14 Eccleston Street, SW1. Tel: 01-730 7734

Matahari Supermarket, 11 Hogarth Road, Earls Court, SW5. Tel: 01-370 1041

Chinese Food Centre Ltd, 156 Balham High Road, SW12. Tel: 01-675 3120

Nippon Food Centre, Mikado-Ya, 193 Upper Richmond Road, Putney, SW15. Tel: 01-788 3107

Matahari Supermarket, 328 Balham High Road, Tooting Bec, SW17. Tel: 01-767 3107

Lee Ho Fook Supermarket, 3 New College Parade, Finchley Road, NW3. Tel: 01-586 2204

Osaka Ltd, 17a Goldhurst Terrace, NW6. Tel: 01-624 4983

Maysun Markets, 869 Finchley Road, Golders Green, NW11. Tel: 01-455 4773

B & E Foods, Radiant House, Pegamoid Road, N18. Tel: 01-803 4271

SOUTHERN ENGLAND

S.W. Trading Ltd, 283 Water Road, Alperton, Middlesex HA0 1HX. Tel: 01-998 2248

The Delicatessen, 164 Old Christchurch Street, Bournemouth, Dorset. Tel: 0202 295979

Wai Yee Hong Supermarket, 4 Station Road, Bristol. Tel: 0272 428629

Jason's Oriental Shop, 16 Milton Road, Cambridge CB4 1JY. Tel: 0223 68735

Kam Cheung Chinese Supermarket, 28/30 Burleigh Street, Cambridge CB1 1DG. Tel: 0223 316429

C. R. Townsend, 24 Sun Street, Canterbury, Kent. Tel: 0227 65196

Kam Wah Chinese Supermarket, 37 Crouch Street, Colchester. Tel: 0206 561836

Gourmet Delicatessen, 32 Eld Lane, Colchester. Tel: 0206 67747

The Mecca, 5 Orford Hill, Norwich, Norfolk. Tel: 0603 614829

Rainbow Wholefoods, 16 Dove Street, Norwich, Norfolk. Tel: 0603 625560

Harvest Fare, 66 High Street, Watton, Norfolk. Tel: 0953 883488

MIDLANDS

Chum Nam Chinese Supermarket, 162–168 Bromsgrove Street, Birmingham 5. Tel: 021-622 4542

Janson Hong Chinese Supermarket, 17–18 St Martins House, Bull Ring, Birmingham. Tel: 021-643 4681

Wing Yip Supermarket, 96 Coventry Street, Birmingham B5 5NY. Tel: 021-643 8987

Alma Delicatessen, 89 Lower Precinct, Coventry CV1 1DS. Tel: 0203 28898

P.K.M. Chinese Co Ltd, 5 Melton Street, Leicester LE1 3NA. Tel: 0533 29656

Wah Yan Company, 77 Mansfield Road, Nottingham. Tel: 0602 474211

NORTHERN ENGLAND

Quality Goods Cash and Carry, Quality House, Edderthorpe Street, Bradford BD3 9JX. Tel: 0274 393328/663944

Tai Sun Chinese Supermarket, 49 College Road, Doncaster, South Yorkshire. Tel: 0302 4360

Chung Wah Trading Company, 31–32 Great George Square, Liverpool L1 5DZ. Tel: 051-709 2637

Hondo Trading Co Ltd, 149/153 Duke Street, Liverpool L1 4JR. Tel: 051-708 5409

Shun On Chinese Supermarket Ltd, 27–35 Berry Street, Liverpool. Tel: 051-708 0844/0474

Wing Yip Supermarket, 45 Faulkner Street, Manchester. Tel: 061-236 9288

Wing Yip Supermarket, 2 Cassidy Close, Manchester. Tel: 061-832 3215

Woo Sang Company Ltd, 19/21 George Street, Manchester. Tel: 061-236 4353

Wah Fung Hong Supermarket, 87 Percy Street, Newcastle upon Tyne. Tel: 0632 323125

Kung Heng & Company, 169 London Road, Sheffield. Tel: 0742 586652

SCOTLAND

Loon Fung Chinese Supermarket, 11 Howard Street, Canonmills, Edinburgh. Tel: 031-556 5535

Jim's Chinese Supermarket, 7a Bath Street, Glasgow G2. Tel: 041-332 4492

WALES

Eastern Supermarket, 26 Tudor Street, Riverside, Cardiff. Tel: 0222 397148

Nam Kiu Supermarket, 32–34 Tudor Street, Cardiff. Tel: 0222 45487

酥車輪蘇州月餅

夾肉小燒餅椰絲窩

菊花酥燒餅蝴蝶

夾肉小燒餅椰絲窩

燒餅咖哩餃鮮肉酥